THE SEXUAL DIMENSION IN LITERATURE

edited by
Alan Bold

VISION
and
BARNES & NOBLE

Vision Press Limited
11–14 Stanhope Mews West
London SW7 5RD

and

Barnes & Noble Books
81 Adams Drive
Totowa, NJ 07512

ISBN (UK) 0 85478 304 0
ISBN (US) 0 389 20314 9

Printed and bound in Great Britain by
Unwin Brothers Ltd.,
Old Woking, Surrey.
Phototypeset by Galleon Photosetting,
Ipswich, Suffolk.
MCMLXXXII

Contents

Introduction

by ALAN BOLD

To judge from the evidence available, few people willingly admit to an enjoyment of erotic literature. They claim to read it for scholarly, for historical, for critical reasons but rarely for fun though in other areas it is accepted that entertainment can be combined with enlightenment. Sexual inhibition is a complex affair and the residual shame that still attaches itself to erotic works has, no doubt, much to do with the connotations of what Lenny Bruce called 'stroke books'. Yet the general public and the critical community are united in being fascinated by erotica. Though few readers flaunt their purchases they avidly buy erotic books and magazines; the audience for erotica is so vast and dependable that publishers promote it with an enthusiasm they extend to hardly any other subject. But then publishers are only human and it is the human quality that makes erotic literature so diverse. Quite literally, it reaches from the gutters where ephemera is deposited to the ideal world promised by Plato and Plotinus. It is possible to be either cynical or philosophical about sex and the sexual dimension in literature encourages variety. So, come to that, do the contributors to this symposium.

The publicity given to the prosecutions, under the Obscene Publications Act 1959, of items as dissimilar as Lawrence's *Lady Chatterley's Lover* and the pornographic periodical *Ladies Directory*, led liberal sections of the public to assume that the law merely existed to make an egregious ass of itself. Somewhat facetiously Philip Larkin responded to the bizarre business of literary litigation by canonising Lawrence as the saint of permissiveness and hailing the trial of his Lady as a turning-point in history. As he expressed it in the opening quatrain of 'Annus Mirabilis':

> Sexual intercourse began
> In nineteen sixty-three
> (Which was rather late for me)—
> Between the end of the *Chatterley* ban
> And the Beatles' first LP.

Those interested in the history of the literary show trials of the 1960s can consult the facts in Harry Street's *Freedom, the Individual and the Law* (1963, 5th edn., 1982). However it is not true that the law was being asinine alone. Then, as now, it simply formalized a social assumption that too much of a good thing is necessarily bad. It is that pernicious notion that is under attack in the following pages.

If we examine the attitude of public libraries to literature we quickly realize there has been a quiet conspiracy, a tacit agreement to keep the general reader at a safe distance from material that might not only deprive and corrupt but actually excite. Few people would, for example, readily connect the British (Museum) Library with titles like *Bizarre Desires, Bandit in High Heels, Lace me Tighter, Trained in Leather, The French Maid* and *Males in Bondage*. However they are all to be found in the library's Private Case. Now that the bibliographer Patrick Kearney has made a complete record of the contents, in a handsome book called *The Private Case* (1981), all the so-called 'dirty' books can be consulted with a clean conscience. Yet such is the moral confusion caused by literary 'filth' that only scholars are likely to risk the obloquy of a full frontal approach to the material. To students of erotica and the psychology of censorship, Kearney's catalogue means they know exactly what salacious material the B.L. possesses and how to get their hands on it. What they will do with it is another matter. The censorious war is (almost) over, the qualitative battle continues.

In 1966 Peter Fryer's *Private Case—Public Scandal* focused attention on the existence of the B.L.'s clandestine collection and the fact that B.L. policy was to deny readers instant access to bawdy books. Now that the authorities have decided there is a place for an annotated display of the forbidden fruit preserved in the B.L.'s Arch Room, it is possible to look back on a quintessentially moral tale. The Private Case was created around 1866 when the library acquired the collection of George Witt. It expanded to something like its present proportions of more than two thousand titles thanks to the receipt of three individual collections. In 1900 the B.L. received the Henry Spencer Ashbee Bequest and in 1964 benefited from the erotic enthusiasm of two later collectors: Charles Reginald Dawes and Beecher Moore. When these were supplemented by smaller collections the result was only rivalled by the *Énfer* of the Bibliotheque Nationale in Paris (completely catalogued since 1913) and the library of sexual science of the Kinsey Institute for Sex Research at the University of Indiana. As Patrick Kearney observes of the material he has so carefully listed: 'today the collection can justifiably be regarded as one of the finest extant, displaying a unique range of titles and subject matter and including specimens that range from beautifully bound copies of eighteenth-century classics down to modern works of the most trashy sort written, apparently, by a computer.'

Henry Spencer Ashbee, the businessman who may have taken his pleasure as the Walter of *My Secret Life* fame, was a pioneer of erotic bibliography who (under the pseudonym Pisanus Fraxi) compiled three annotated catalogues of prohibited books. In the first of these, *Index Librorum Prohibitorum* (1877), he denied any personal interest in titillation and claimed a purely clinical approach: 'As little, it is my belief, will my book excite the passions of my readers, as would the naked body of a woman, extended on the dissecting table, produce concupiscence in the minds of the students assembled to witness an operation performed upon her.' Ashbee's blushingly virtuous attitude to his collection has become the norm for erotic bibliographers who never seem to take any pleasure whatsoever in the books they evidently take so seriously. Rolfe S. Reade (the anagrammatized pseudonym of Alfred Rose) who listed in his *Registrum Librorum Eroticorum* (1936)—the contents of the B.L.'s Private Case up to the mid-1930s— presented himself as a man motivated by a passion for order.

9

Patrick Kearney comes over as a crusader intent on righting a bibliographical wrong. The self-righteous purity of the erotic bibliographers is overwhelming; it is as if they had no knowledge of the books beyond the title pages. Yet the content is what counts.

Kearney's catalogue contains 1,920 entries, the majority of which relate to publications that could be classified as cheap and nasty. Revealingly *The Private Case* is introduced by a long essay in which no less a figure than Gershon Legman, the world authority on bawdy folklore, dissociates himself entirely from the nature of much of the material kept in the B.L.'s Private Case. He supports the censorship of violent material, condemns sexual perversion, and encourages the B.L. to keep a watchful eye on its Private Case. 'It should be emphasized again,' writes Legman, 'that the presumable goal of total desuppression of all the works in the Private Case is neither possible nor desirable. This would merely be playing the game for the psychotic book-mutilators and the professional thieves of rare books. All great libraries suffer a great deal from these dishonest cranks and criminals.' On the subject of sexual perversion Legman is even more explicit: 'Sexual perversion is not funny, not rare, and not to be taken lightly, as anyone who has ever been married to a homosexual or sadist or other pervert knows. It is hard for normals even to bear to look at the pitiful lineaments of sexual perversion.'

Yet Legman has spent a lifetime studying what he must consider to be literary recreations of perversion and would argue that he has done so in the interests of sociological research. This, eventually, is how most writers and readers justify their familiarity with erotica; they disclaim any interest in the emotive power of erotic literature and set the central subject aside in order to concentrate on marginal issues. What is needed is a collective discussion of erotic literature by writers who understand its appeal; hence the zeal of the writers gathered together in this book. Personally I cannot accept that the only function of erotic literature is to serve as a record of the pathological condition of a given society. I feel Legman, and other bibliographical scholars, are being irresponsible in refusing to establish a meaningful line of demarcation between positively erotic literature and mercifully

10

ephemeral productions. An assessment of literary quality is essential.

In my introduction to *The Bawdy Beautiful: The Sphere Book of Improper Verse* (1979) I suggested that we begin to discriminate by keeping the word *pornography*, since it simply denotes the portrayal of prostitutes; and by using the word *carnography* to describe nastily impure work since the neologism carries the sense of a desire to masticate flesh (an activity even self-righteous amoralists might admit is ethically inadvisable). The division between good erotica (including pornography) and vicious carnography is a line each reader must draw for himself or herself. It is not a barrier erected by society; it is a projection on the part of the individual.

In their respective essays Angeline Goreau and Peter Webb stress the brutal, or carnographic, nature of many male fantasies. At the root of this impulse is the desire to deny any element of mystery to sex and to degrade and insult women. Paradoxically the male chauvinist writer has much in common with the strident women's libber whose most dogmatic (and therefore suspect) desire is to deprive women of any sexual allure. By simultaneously denying that women are sex objects and insisting on their obligation to make love indiscriminately, the hardline women's libbers reduce sex to a purely mechanical matter. Which is exactly what the carnographers do. Little wonder that some women, like Janet Radcliffe Richards in *The Sceptical Feminist* (1980), have come to feel that womanly sex appeal is not a biological betrayal but a creative contribution to society: 'We can keep some beauty of dress. . . . We may find we can keep some cultural sex differences. . . . Much of the present unattractiveness is quite unnecessary.'

To be or not to be carnographic: that is the question any discussion of erotic literature must ask. The answer involves the status of women since heterosexual sex is the crucial factor on which the survival of the species depends. It is important, I feel (and I realize this belief is not shared by all the contributors to this book), to grant some eternally feminine mystery to life. The alternative approach to women, whether embodied in chauvinistic males or cynical females, can be as hideously destructive as a strange book by Linda Lovelace suggests. *Ordeal* (1980) takes an awful lot of believing. First,

11

you have to believe that it is the work of *the* Linda Lovelace of skinflick fame even though the first sentence proclaims 'My name is not Linda Lovelace' and the confession has only materialized thanks to ghost-writer Mike McGrady. Second, you have to believe that the contentious text has been authenticated by legal and literary experts: this involves a considerable act of faith for, though *Ordeal* has the American imprint of Citadel Press and the prestigious British one of W. H. Allen, it is disfigured by so many misprints that it seems untouched by the human hand of a competent proof-reader. Third, you have to believe that the public *persona* of Linda Lovelace is not only misleading but hideously misguided. The porno queen is dead; long live the domestic doll whose greatest pleasure lies in keeping a tidy house.

The general public knows about Linda Lovelace as the star of *Deep Throat* (a movie that grossed more than fifty million dollars) and the reputation that launched the bestselling ghost-written autobiography *Inside Linda Lovelace*. Linda was, in the words of *Playboy* magnate Hugh Hefner, the 'sex goddess of the seventies'. She was attractive, available, young and apparently game for anything—especially if it could be filmed and marketed. She projected herself as an uninhibited swinger, a liberated chick whose philosophy was simple: 'I live for sex, will never get enough of it, and will continue to try every day to tune my physical mechanism to finer and finer perfection.' It turns out that Linda didn't write these words, didn't subscribe to the swinging philosophy, didn't want to perform. Everything connected with Linda Lovelace was false, including her silicone-boosted breasts.

As featured in *Ordeal*, the heroine is cast in the role of an innocent about to be corrupted—which she rapidly is and with a vengeance. Linda Boreman was the daughter of a policeman; she was raised in Yonkers, New York, and attended Catholic schools with a pure devotion. 'During grade school,' Linda says, 'my ambition was to be a nun. In ninth grade I was elected vice-president of my class and I enjoyed playing basketball more than anything else.' She was known, she says, as Miss Holy-Holy because she wouldn't neck like the other girls. Linda explains 'I was the kind of girl who liked to go down by the ocean and hold hands. I still am.' She regards herself as 'more of a prude than anyone I know' and asserts that 'Nothing makes me happier than cleaning a house.' It all has a familiar ring to it.

Then how, I hear the reader ask, did this sweet young Linda Boreman become the infamously indecent Linda Lovelace? The answer is given in two words: Chuck Traynor. This former Marine owned a bar in North Miami and was deeply committed to the sexploitation of women. His credo was succinct: 'A woman has a product and she should use it.' Traynor came into Linda's life and impressed her with his decisive personality. As amateur hypnotist and professional pimp, Traynor was also a Svengali devoted to perversion. In fact, if we believe all Linda says about him, he should have been behind bars instead of owning one. Traynor was a violent man, a 'sadistic madman', with a police record to prove it. He smuggled drugs into the U.S.A., lived off the immoral earnings of prostitutes, boasted of killing people. This supremely nasty piece of work was, moreover, a misogynist whose greatest pleasure was to abuse women physically. He first tormented and finally tortured Linda: he attacked her, threatened to cut up her face, promised to shoot her with one of his guns (and he had been a top marksman in the Marines). 'Every day,' Linda recalls, 'I either got raped, beaten, kicked, punched, smacked, choked, degraded, or yelled at. Sometimes, I got all of the above.' That was a normal day. On other days he would kill her. The pattern emerges: Traynor is a carnographer, Linda has subscribed to the liberated belief that women deserve no special treatment.

Aware of Linda's sexually experimental nature, Traynor wanted to cash in on her attributes. She had to learn the *Deep Throat* technique of oral sex, participate in group sex, do the hundred-and-one things she was told to do. That was only the beginning. Traynor subsequently introduced Linda to carnographic movies and involved her in bestial scenes. She claims her worst experience occurred when, at gunpoint, she was forced to make a movie with a dog: 'I've been raped by men who were no better than animals, but this was an actual animal. . . . There were no greater humiliations left for me. The memory of that day and that dog does not fade the way other memories do. The overwhelming sadness that I felt on

13

that day is with me at this moment, stronger than ever.' And yet here is Linda, apparently no wiser, serving up the experience as a piece of carnography. Nothing, apparently, is sacred in the world of Linda Lovelace which is what makes her career an allegory for the fall of the purely physical woman. Whether her memoir is trustworthy or not it has an irresistible shape.

Anticipating the obvious question forming in the astonished mind of the reader, Linda says 'Often I'm asked why I didn't escape' and provides the answer 'Because it's kind of hard to get away when there's a gun pointed at your head.' She did attempt to escape several times (she says) and each time she was caught and either beaten unconscious by Traynor or made the centrepiece of a sadistic scenario devised by Traynor. Linda's saga reads like a first-personal version of the *Story of O* (which, incidentally, Patrick Kearney firmly attributes to Dominique Aury, a secretary). She was the property of the man in her life and had to do everything he ordered or pay the brutal consequences. When Linda's film *Deep Throat* became a commercial and critical sensation—appealing to the self-consciously intellectual members of a supposedly liberated public—then Traynor saw that his property could also become his passport to privileged places. By a terrible irony, Linda was a symbol of permissiveness and yet was trapped in the reality of commercial exploitation. Sex cannot be treated as a squalid means to a remunerative end but has to be accepted as a creative end in itself. Or so the story told in *Ordeal* implies.

Strengthened by her fame, Linda attempted to escape from Traynor. Without friends or money she tried to find work but the only offers were for carnographic films and Linda 'never made another dirty movie and I never will.' She did, though, find a husband and become a devoted mother on her way to a happy ending. If her story is true (and the reader is encouraged to suspend disbelief for the persuasive reason that she names names and thus risks legal and physical retaliation), then it is an explicit account of the world of carnography. It describes an underworld where only profit counts, where sensitivity is a dirty joke, where men get their kicks by brutalizing women. In these circumstances, women need to be regarded as a protected species and the cynicism that says otherwise is liberated in fashion rather than in fact. At any rate

14

we need more, not fewer, value judgements; the study of literature promotes debate and decision.

It has always been argued by censorious groups that all porn corrupts and absolute porn corrupts absolutely. I doubt that if only because the great erotic bibliographers and others seem psychologically cleansed by constant immersion in forbidden literature and can see it in a general cultural context. Surely if we are in favour of an open society, we are also in favour of an open literature, since it is certain that, in competition with work of real quality, carnography would not be able to exist. It depends on being sold in plain brown wrappers or under the counter; such subversion gives it a gloss of excitement, enables it to promise more than it can deliver. Interestingly, the sexual liberation of publishing has made it possible for women to reject carnography in all its life-denying aspects. Their response has been positively creative and we have to live, as a result, with a newly emergent woman; not really a new woman but the eternal one clearly speaking for herself. She speaks with an urgency as if making up for lost time. She does not reduce sex to a mechanical process of spasmodic gratification but lifts it to a supremely artistic level.

The troubadours were right, in principle, when they thought of courtly love, since the mental effort involved enhances sensuality. Unfortunately they got one detail wrong. Carried away with rigid formal conventions they succumbed to masochism and assumed that women wanted to be put on a pedestal and worshipped from below. Actually the pedestal is fine, as a symbol of an urge upwards into an imaginative realm, but the sexes have to co-exist on it. They are doing so, increasingly, encouraged by a new style of writing produced by women. Erica Jong in the U.S.A. and Wendy Perriam in Britain (to cite two examples) are women whose frank sexuality and literary skill offer an affirmative antidote to carnography. They represent women who know what they are doing in a sexual sense and why they are doing it. Erica Jong has even shown that the study of erotic literature can lead to a creative act. In *Fanny* (1980) she recreates the mood of the eighteenth-century novel and comments perceptively that 'Fanny is not a typical eighteenth-century woman [because] I do believe that in every age there are people whose consciousness transcends their own time and that these people, whether fictional or historical, are those with whom we most closely identify and those about whom we most enjoy reading. I have tried to write an interesting and entertaining novel, not an historical treatise.' The result may be a fiction but then, as the following essays show, the essence of literature is to make a significant advance on the bare facts of life.

Part One:
TEXTS

1

Sex and Classical Literature

by PETER GREEN

1

The operative word, of course, is *literature*: signpost, definition, and, to the wary, warning. We are not primarily concerned with sex, as such, in antiquity, a topic for which the evidence— partly by the nature of the activities involved, partly on account of natural attrition over the centuries—is both mini- mal and ambiguous. Sex in literature (and, for that matter, in the visual arts) may, at times, be roughly congruent with the actual sexual habits of the society in which the writers or painters or sculptors lived and worked, but the equation remains at best intermittent. What we are dealing with here— and the rule is not restricted to Greek and Roman civilization— is not so much sex *per se* as sexual fantasy and propaganda: sex in the head, sex as the creative spirit may idealize or demean it, sex as society would like to believe it is or ought to be, private taboo-breaking orgies, surrealistic mythological sex (showers of sub-Freudian gold, cycnic or taurine miscegena- tions), sex as political camouflage or rhetorical *topos*, as lyrical comforter, as marital advertisement, as creative revision of personal inadequacy. For sheer compulsive ingenuity *l'esprit de l'escalier* runs a very poor second to *l'esprit du boudoir*, and the raw meat of a poet's or novelist's love-affair tends to get

19

cooked in ways that might surprise Claude Lévi-Strauss by the time it is served up for public consumption. To discuss sex in classical literature, then, is to analyse, tentatively, what, at various periods, segments of Greek and Roman society thought about themselves, the image a minority—often a minority of one—aimed to project. Any resemblance between that image and practical reality is not only coincidental, but in most cases quite impossible to detect.

If this sounds like a bad case of nit-picking academic particularism, blame the methodological inanities which, till very recently, characterized almost all investigations of sexual phenomena in the ancient world. Since the subject was sensitive, indeed largely taboo,[1] those who dabbled in it—unless they went anonymous, like Paul Brandt, the Ovidian scholar, who as 'Hans Licht' was responsible for *Sexual Life in Ancient Greece* (Eng. trans., 1932), or, like A. E. Housman, wrote in Latin—tended to be amateur *littérateurs*, often with a sizeable obsession of their own to work off. If there is still a vague belief among Western progressives that the ancient world was an indiscriminate paradise for homosexuals and orgiasts, the myths disseminated by these purveyors of *haute* (or, in many cases, *basse*) *vulgarisation* are largely responsible. Sex, like death, does not tend to bring out either logic or a sense of history in those who write about it. Above all, what got lost was the changing, evolutionary quality of sexual beliefs and fashions. Evidence to make a point would be culled indiscriminately from Greek or Roman authors over a thousand years and more, from Homer to Lucian, as though the civilization under review were one and indivisible: this would be rather akin to juxtaposing *The Miller's Tale* and *The Waste Land* as generic evidence for the sexual proclivities of middle-class Englishmen. The result—until collapsing taboos brought some first-class scholars into the field[2]—was a dubious mass of romanticized, and profoundly unhistorical, generalizations. Diachronic rather than topological treatment is called for as a corrective.

It might be tempting to follow the rhapsode's example and 'begin with Zeus', but this route bristles with more pitfalls than usual for the unwary. Nowhere do we find a more chaotic situation than in the field of religion and mythology, which

20

both tend, by the nature of the case, to be treated *sub specie aeternitatis*, a practice unconducive to good social history: worse, the subject's current trendiness, in universities and elsewhere, has further contaminated it with a foggy blanket of modern theorizing, structural or Freudian.[3] Since the gods were un-shackled by human restrictions, and in many ways clearly embodied projections of the psyche's unfulfillable aspirations, the degree to which erotic motifs proliferate in Greek and Roman myth should come as no surprise. Yet the nature of these fantasies, and their impact on social awareness, varied considerably with the progress of time. The emergence of a middle class, for instance, endowed—as always—with that genteel morality which forms its most characteristic feature, produced great embarrassment over traditional archaic-tribal tales of the gods' insatiable, and indiscriminate, sexual adven-tures. Yet we continue to treat evolving myths as timeless *contes drôlatiques*, cobbling together our evidence, virtually at random, from a range of witnesses that begins with Homer and Hesiod in the eighth century B.C. and progresses, by way of the Greek tragedians, Ovid's *Metamorphoses*, and various late mythographers, both Greek and Roman (Apollodorus, Hyginus, Antoninus Liberalis), to the browsings of that anti-quarian Byzantine archbishop Eustathius, who died only just before the Fourth Crusade of A.D. 1204.

Myth and literature, then, both insist that we should begin at the beginning: that is, with the *Iliad* and *Odyssey*. The evidential layer-cake *can* be made to yield much intriguing information—but not if all its layers are lumped together indiscriminately across cultures and centuries, nor if fiction, drama, lyric poetry, court-room speeches, letters, inscriptions and biography are treated *in pari materia* as direct, factual sources of sexual information, and that information is then assumed to represent actual practice, rather than literary artifice which may or may not approximate to real life. What I propose, then, is to follow significant *changes* of literary emphasis and fashion in the sphere of sexual *mores*, from Homer's day (eighth century B.C.) to that of Juvenal (second century A.D.), and, where possible, to suggest explanations for them. The human sexual instinct is powerful but, as such, both simple and uniform the world over. What makes it so

21

complex—in Greece, Rome, or anywhere else, during the Dark Age or under the Empire—is that wide spectrum of moral sanctions, social programming, and religious taboos employed to direct, encourage, or repress it, and reflected—whether in opposition or conformity—by the literature and art of each period.

2

Homer is a tricky witness on whom to start, because of course the *Iliad* and the *Odyssey* are themselves layer-cakes, preserving much from Bronze Age Greece, but recombining this material with assumptions that more properly belong to eighth-century B.C. Ionia—when Homer himself, and other oral poets like him, made a living by recalling the 'great deeds of heroes' at the courts of petty princelings who took pride in their supposed descent from Agamemnon or Nestor. Presumably Homer reflects the social outlook of his patrons. His attitude to sex is familial, civilized, domestic, and in many ways more modern than anything which succeeded it until Plutarch's day. Despite the electric charms of that *femme fatale* Helen it is the wives—Penelope, Andromache, Arete—who stick in the mind. Even flirtatious Nausicäa has her mind as solidly set on marriage as any deb. As Murray long ago saw, the poems show evidence of having quietly expurgated such traditional barbarisms as human sacrifice, mutilation of corpses, incest, and—in the case of Achilles' relation to Patroclus—homosexuality.[4] Bourgeois values were stirring in Ionia. A clear measure of how far, and fast, these developed is the famous attack upon Homer made, less than two centuries later, by Xenophanes of Colophon, who objected that the poet 'attributed to the gods everything that is a shame and reproach among men, stealing and committing adultery and deceiving each other' (fr. 169 Kirk-Raven). The charge was fair enough. What Homer in fact still preserved—on Olympus if not among more self-conscious mortals—was that old, basically aristocratic attitude to sex, which believed in the *droit de seigneur*, found intercourse pleasurable but not emotionally significant (Zeus's enthusiastic bout with Hera on a mist-clad mountain-top demonstrates this to perfection), and was prepared to treat adultery as a great joke provided—as in the case of Ares and Aphrodite—it was a social inferior, here lame Hephaestus, who wore the horns.

Mortals, as Heracleitus said, are immortal, immortals mortal; the contrast between Homer's sexually irresponsible gods and his human protagonists—whose ideal (however often they may fail it along the way) is that fine old bourgeois institution, a stable marriage—has more than casual significance. The conservatism of religious traditional beliefs was counterpointed, in the Greek psyche, against a quite unusually rapid social evolution from tribal to civic standards of behaviour. Thus not only in Homer's day, but throughout the Archaic and Classical eras, reason tended to get in advance of instinct, heart and head worked against each other. This dialectical tension lay behind many themes predominant in Attic drama (e.g. the head-on clash between familial and socio-political beliefs in Sophocles' *Antigone*), and it certainly explains why, as early as the *Iliad*, the old patriarchal ethic, still valid on Olympus, was slowly being replaced on earth—despite the heroic tradition—by a middle-class social code based on the nuclear family and a system of largely co-operative or defensive values. Hector dies for Troy, but also for his wife Andromache, his child, his home: he is the most uxorious of heroes. Odysseus may spend much of his homeward wanderings from Troy bedding nymphs and goddesses, who are fair game in every sense,[5] but his mind, ultimately, is set upon Penelope and Ithaca, upon that symbolically immovable marriage-bed, with its still-living olivewood post (*Od.* 23, 183ff.). Nor has there ever been a more moving tribute to the marital condition than that which Odysseus, again, pronounces—quite gratuitously—to the Phaeacian princess Nausicäa, a *jeune fille en fleur* buzzing with delightful dreams of marriage, who could be relied on to appreciate it at its true worth: 'For nothing is greater and better than when a man and a woman keep house with one mind together: much grief to their enemies, great joy to their friends, but they themselves know it best of all' (*Od.* 6, 182–85). This is, among other things, a testament to *equal partnership*, something we will not meet again for a very long time; and indeed one striking feature of Homer's women is their dignity, their independence, their freedom of action. This exists quite independently of those matrilinear hints that anthropologists have picked up among the Phaeacians and on Ithaca (e.g., why were suitors courting *Penelope*, clearly with an eye to the kingdom, while Laertes and Telemachus were both still very much around?). Victorian scholars were shocked to find Homeric kings' daughters not only doing the laundry, but unconcernedly bathing and rubbing down male guests, with no hint of impropriety, but rather that asexual casualness sometimes found today in a sauna. Wives, moreover, got Homeric consideration in that area often declared a product only of modern romanticism (understandably, when we look at some of the later evidence)—the lordly importation of concubines into the home. When Laertes first bought Eurycleia as a young maid, he 'treated her with as much respect as if they had been married, but never slept with her, to avoid offending his dear wife' (*Od.* 1, 432–33). Agamemnon was not so sensitive, and paid for it with his life; but the principle, even if later generations chose to forget it, had been established.

And sex? Homer's men and women both get great satisfaction from it, as do his gods; its power, sometimes personified in the moving force of Aphrodite, is recognized, but not over-venerated when it comes into conflict with more fundamental social values. Helen, after all, is the symbol and embodiment of what blindly ruinous passion, the pure gonadic urge, can do to a man.[6] Paris abused the laws of hospitality, stole his host's wife, and started a ruinous war in consequence; after nearly ten years of indecisive fighting (as Homer stresses) he can still be dragged from the battlefield, *coram publico*, and into Helen's bed, by his ungovernable urge to fuck her, an urge even more violent than at the time of their first incendiary coupling on Kranae (*Il.* 3, 380–448). It is remarkable, and seldom stressed, that the only other *grande passion* in the *Iliad*— with nice symmetry, it belongs on the Achaean side—is that between Achilles and Patroclus. Though this relationship is not delineated in crudely sexual terms, the mythic tradition was well aware of its motivation,[7] and Homer himself abundantly and repeatedly stresses the intensity and closeness of the two heroes' feeling for one another: if not homosexual in presentation, it is most certainly homoerotic. Aeschines was right to interpret this reticence, not as an indication that

24

Homer shrank from conceiving the relationship in erotic terms, much less that he disapproved of it, but rather as a pointer to his cultivated sensitivity. There is a nice blending here of aristocratic tolerance and middle-class restraint.[8]

3

Those who use the cultures of Greece and Rome as arguments against the Puritan ethic (whether Christian or secular), praising their alleged encouragement of guilt-free sexual pleasure, whatever form it may take—old myths, alas, die hard—never, I feel, give enough weight to the highly significant Greek and Roman terms for the sexual organs. *Aidoia* and *pudenda* both are to be construed as those parts concerning which one should feel shame or modesty (not always quite the same thing). There can be a considerable slide here in semantic emphasis, ranging between 'respect' at one end of the scale and 'disgust' at the other; the position of the indicator, so to speak, is often a very useful guide to a culture's social and psychological health. One reason why I have placed such emphasis on the Homeric poems is because the social and sexual tenets they uphold are, by modern standards, quite exceptionally adult, sane, and well-integrated. This fact should be kept in mind when examining the sexual conventions described by Greek city-state writers during the next two centuries, the so-called Archaic Age, since *polis* society is commonly held to be progressive, whereas Homer's world often gets written off as a backward-looking and feudally ossified hangover from the Bronze Age. Comparison, however, as we shall see, would appear in many cases to indicate regression rather than enlightenment. One of the more piquant paradoxes (as a modern student sees it) about the ancient world is that Greek and Roman intellectuals—thinkers, playwrights, poets, historians, pamphleteers—were associated neither with political nor with sexual radicalism, both of which, indeed, they more often than not actively opposed, being generally lined up, as good *rentiers*, with the ruling class, the forces of law and order. Those who attack governments, from Hesiod to Juvenal, tend to have purely personal reasons for doing so; and I cannot think of any ancient author—Aristophanes included—who argued a case for greater sexual freedom.[9]

Though Homer continued to command respect throughout antiquity, Homeric *mores* are largely conspicuous by their absence from subsequent Greek literature. The characteristics of the period between 750 and 450 B.C., the pre-classical or Archaic Age, are radically different. These centuries saw the spread of alphabetic writing, and the consequent establishment of law-codes; a great colonizing movement from Spain to the Black Sea; pioneering scientific and philosophical exploration in Ionia and South Italy; and the evolution of the city-state (*polis*), with which democratic institutions were so closely associated. It was an age of ferment, of intellectual discovery and organization, culminating, appropriately enough, in the Persian Wars, which found Greeks standing off an authoritarian regime in the name of freedom. Socially, it was remarkable for the skill with which a tenacious aristocracy managed to adapt itself to new democratic political rules, while at the same time preserving intact its own code of manners, not least as regards sexual relations. The Athenian upper classes never entirely capitulated to *polis* respectability. Various apparent anomalies in our evidence all spring from this persistent conflict. We find, to begin with, a sudden upsurge of individualism in our literary sources: poets are now talking about themselves and their emotional affairs, cracking the old shell of bardic anonymity. They analyse the psychology of the heart, they cultivate unruly passions, they anatomize private sex in a way quite alien to Homer. The swing is away from heroics or familiality to non-socialized, and very often homosexual, relationships. At the same time, our sources also suggest a widespread, and oddly intolerant, depreciation of women, which persists into the classical period. Misogynistic contempt and fear flourish in a new, non-Homeric world peopled by faceless kitchen drudges or cheap whores. Taboo words are on occasion employed, taboo activities described. At the same time, as we have noted, genteel middle-class objections begin to be raised against the behaviour, in particular the sexual behaviour, sanctioned by Homer. (This is not such a paradox as might be thought; pornography always flourishes best in strict Bible-belt areas.) It is clear that what the Greeks—or, more specifically, the Athenians—went through now was a lengthy conflict, largely class-based, over sexual values, between the old aristocratic code and those new bourgeois conventions which the *polis* made peculiarly its own. In the end, the *polis* might be thought to have won; by the time Aristophanes wrote *The Clouds* (423 B.C.) many aristocratic conventions recognizable from Archaic art and literature had become mere historical curiosities. Yet the legacy they left was both persistent and pervasive, surviving not only in the works of Plato and Aristotle, but also being taken over by Rome.

All this, of course, very clearly demonstrates the perils of generalizing from inadequate or partial evidence. When we turn from Homer to his immediate literary successors, it looks, on the face of things, as though a rapid social revolution has taken place; and though such a possibility can't be entirely discounted, it is far more probable, first, that the *mores* we meet in Homer are, as it were, preserved only in epic aspic, and had been largely obsolete for centuries—during the whole of the Greek Dark Ages, in fact (*c*. 1100–*c*. 850 B.C.)—when Homer himself came to compose the *Iliad* and the *Odyssey*; second, that the aristocratic-homosexual tradition, as we meet it, variously, in writers as diverse as Sappho, Theognis, Pindar, or Plato, represented only a tiny élitist minority at any time, deceptive through its intellectual force and articulate creativity; and third, that the surly misogynistic chauvinism which crops up in Hesiod and Semonides of Amorgos was a far more deeply-rooted, and perennial, element in the Greek social structure than it has hitherto been fashionable to admit. We often forget that Greece was, and to a remarkable extent still remains, an agrarian peasant culture.[10] Hesiod's basic farm equipment is a homestead, a plough-ox—and a woman to do the ploughing (*Works and Days* [WD], 405–6). He assumes that if a woman shows interest in a man, what she's after is his barn (WD, 373–75). A wife is simply a chattel, to be worked like a slave; yet her sex also makes her an object of unease and alarm.[11] Despite refrigeration, T.V., and the transistor radio, things have not changed all that much in the Greek countryside to this day; as Walcot rightly says (pp. 66–7), 'Hesiod is only a misogynist in the sense that all Greek males, whether ancient or modern, are misogynists when measured by the standards

27

of sophisticated Western Europe and North America. . . . . His mistrust of women is an expression of the prevalent attitude towards women in Greek society.' This attitude is distilled in the famous poem by Semonides (7–6 century B.C.), comparing various types of women to animals: the sluttish sow, the wicked vixen, the yapping bitch (who won't shut up even if a man 'knocks out her teeth with a stone'), the greedy, promiscuous ass, the sex-mad ferret, the lazy, extravagant mare, the ugly monkey ('oh the poor man who gets an armful of *that* disaster'). Only the hard-working, sexually aseptic bee wins a clean bill of health. *'Women!'* Semonides snorts, 'the biggest evil Zeus ever made!'[12] The Pandora legend should be read with these strictures in mind. Even today, when the Olympian religion is no longer in favour, a woman who bears a daughter tends to receive sympathy rather than congratulations; and only a male child can be taken behind the *eikonostasis* (roodscreen) and there blessed by the Orthodox priest.

A society that depreciates its legitimate wives almost invariably compensates by creating a special niche for courtesans, and Greece was no exception to the rule.[13] From now on we hear a good deal about the *hetaira* (a nice euphemism: its literal meaning is 'female companion') who became a standard fixture—well illustrated by Attic vase-painters—at Greek drinking-parties, prostitute in essence but, as time went on, acquiring, geisha-like, various ancillary social graces, from dancing and musicianship to the art of good conversation. The rough uncertainties of a colonist's life, as we know from Archilochus, encouraged the usual camp-followers and campaign whores. Archilochus himself (?715–?650 B.C.), who spent his life, as he tells us in numerous surviving fragments, fighting, drinking, and fornicating,[14] mostly in Thrace or on the newly-settled island of Thasos, was just as ready to seduce respectable ladies as tarts: a recently discovered fragment describes his conquest of his ex-fiancée's sister in strikingly graphic terms ('and let the white strength of me come/ while stroking her yellow hair'). While the tradition that both girls hanged themselves for shame because of his attacks is probably untrue, to have such kiss-and-tell ballads hawked round a smallish island must have been, in that tight-knit village society, something worse than embarrassing.

Some erotic activities, however, were not to Archilochus's taste. In particular, he exhibits the kind of guffawing revulsion from homosexuality that marks the *macho* male in any age; if he were alive today he would be laying down the law about fruits and pantywaists like any locker-room pundit. There are two interesting points to notice here: first, that in that rough colonists' world the phenomenon not only existed, but was visible enough to attract notice; and second, that what it aroused in Archilochus was derision and contempt. Significantly, those he accuses of it seem to have been aristocrats, cavalry officers, members of an élite. This should not surprise us. Throughout the whole period during which homosexuality was most openly and approvingly represented, both in literature and art—that is, during the last two centuries immediately prior to the Persian Wars (490–479 B.C.)—we always find it closely bound up with notions of inherited excellence, pedigree, and privilege, with the politics and responsibilities of blood. It stands in direct opposition to that progressive political democratization which distinguishes sixth-century Athens; and this is an important clue to understanding its later manifestations.

For example, Theognis of Megara (fl. *c.* 540 B.C.), who preached Spartan-style moral uplift to his beloved Kyrnos— and whose vigorous, not to say earthy, erotic verse employed much imagery drawn from that perennial élitist occupation, the breeding and training of horses—was a passionate reactionary, exiled for his anti-populist politicking.[15] Sappho and her contemporary Alcaeus of Lesbos were both similarly exiled, again because of involvement in, or sympathy with, aristocratic *coups* of some sort; Sappho may have ranked affairs of the heart above naval or military glory (fr. 16. 1–4 Lobel-Page), but socially she too aligned herself with the Best People, while Alcaeus, a more activist poet, like Theognis cultivated a paederastic image (Cic. *Tusc. Disp.* 4.71; Horace, *Odes* 1.32, 9–11). Solon (fr. 25) not only acknowledged the pleasures of paederasty, but also (Plut. *Sol.* 1) passed a law forbidding slaves 'to have a boy-lover, so that his intention was evidently to class this as an honourable and dignified practice and thus, in a sense, to recommend it to reputable men by the act of forbidding it to the unworthy.' The class-emphasis is un-

29

mistakable. Pindar (who died in the arms of his lover Theoxenos) reveals an identical atmosphere, which numerous more or less explicit representations on high-quality black-figure vases[16] only serve to confirm. The sixth-century cult of homosexuality, at least as revealed in our surviving evidence, was indissolubly associated with aristocratic values and politics. (This is not, of course, to suggest that homosexual practices were in fact restricted to an élite: Eros is no respecter of parties. What it *does* mean is that paederasty, in its more public aspects, did carry élitist connotations for the Athenian man-in-the-street.) The subsequent triumph of democracy through Salaminian sea-power—nothing élitist about the 'naval rabble' that rowed the triremes—together with the establishment of a middle class based on wealth rather than blood, forced the traditional peasant and élitist values of Attica's old two-class society into a fresh confrontation, and compromise, during the so-called Periclean Age.

4

It is worth noting that neither Theognis nor Sappho regarded their homosexual proclivities as in any way incompatible with marriage. They were both married themselves, and Theognis tells Kyrnos (*Theog.* 1225–256) that 'nothing is more delectable than a good wife'. He can testify to this from personal experience, he says, and advises Kyrnos to follow his example. This attitude highlights one fundamental difference between ancient and modern homosexual *mores*: with certain special exceptions (Plato, as we shall see, is atypical in the extreme), neither Greeks nor Romans professed to find any kind of psychological or moral barrier between heterosexual and homosexual experience. Some practices earned their contempt (e.g. an adult male who cultivated the passive, feminine role), and various formal restrictions (see below, p. 34) were imposed on the type of homosexual relationship sanctioned by society; but it was taken for granted, by Greeks and Romans alike, that any person was liable to be erotically aroused by members of either sex, and that susceptibility of one sort did not preclude the other. Kritoboulos, who in Xenophon's *Symposium* (4.12–16) so enthusiastically praises the charms of his boy-lover

Kleinias, is represented as being newly married at the time (ibid., 2.3). Generalizations about sexual patterns in antiquity are dangerous, but the assumption of bisexual excitability does seem to have been virtually universal, at all periods, and this is something to bear in mind, since our own moral conditioning on the subject tends to be so very different.

On the other hand, though bisexualism may have been an unquestioned fact of life, its mere existence does not in any way imply universal sexual permissiveness. *Tout comprendre* was by no means *tout pardonner* in the ancient world, and nothing could be further from the truth than to treat, say, Plato's Athens (which was not most people's Athens), or even the Rome of Petronius (which, equally, was not most people's Rome), as a beautiful playground for highminded or socially endorsed *amitiés particulières*. The period from the Persian Wars to the death of Alexander (479–323 B.C.), including the Periclean Age, marks the zenith and initial decline of the city-state: we can understand neither the social evolution of sexual *mores* during this period, nor the way in which these *mores* were reflected in art and literature, if we assume that their general underlying attitude was a kind of indiscriminate anti-Christian sensualism. Sexual abstinence was a prominent feature of religious ritual long before thinkers such as Plato made a moral or philosophical virtue out of it. To copulate in a temple was unthinkable; no one could enter any shrine after inter-course until he had undergone ritual purification.[17] Such provisions, like the names of the private parts (above, p. 25), hardly suggest a total absence of shame or guilt.

It is also significant that only one or two specific literary *genres*—e.g. iambic raillery in the tradition of Archilochus and Hipponax, or Attic Old Comedy, typified for us by Aristophanes—were permitted overt sexual or scatological allusions, much less the use of 'four-letter words'. Tragedy, even the work of an 'advanced' playwright like Euripides, remained circumspect almost to prudishness in its language and subject-matter, though euphemistic metaphor (then as always) was a great standby: a serious Greek poet was not allowed to call a cunt a cunt, but he could, and did, talk about 'the split meadow of Aphrodite'. Euripides had to rewrite the original version of his *Hippolytus* because Athenians found a play

31

that showed Phaedra directly propositioning her stepson on-stage shocking to their sense of decorum.[18] If sex was taboo, so was violence: Clytemnestra could not murder Agamemnon, nor Medea her children, in full view of the audience. It is not hard to deduce, from Aristophanes's ceaseless taunting of Euripides over his 'shocking' characters—and indeed, by contrast, from the violent obscenities that came cascading out on occasions of licensed buffoonery: compare Carnival in the Mediterranean and Latin America today—just how rigid a standard of sexual restraint was normally imposed. Decorum, indeed, was a major factor in all public art.

Yet at the same time there can be no doubt that the actual range of sexual or excretory topics to which explicit reference could be made in literature or art shrank very considerably between the mid-sixth and the late fourth centuries B.C. This may have been in part an egalitarian reaction against aristo-cratic *mores*: the disappearance of homosexual vase-paintings and poetry certainly could be interpreted this way. But the artists, with Rabelaisian enthusiasm, had portrayed other activities it would take some ingenuity to define as élitist: intercourse *a tergo* (the most frequently represented position), group orgies, parties where everyone seems to be either masturbating, defecating, or throwing up, for the most part in full public view. What was the market for these cups and jolly jugs, and just why, about the mid-fifth century, did the bottom (so to speak) fall out of it? Whether the activities themselves went on or not (and there is some evidence that they did), there was clearly a new social unwillingness to publicize or describe them. Why? The answer would seem to be an up-surge of middle-class urban *pudeur*, a familiar phenomenon in any rapidly developing bourgeois society, and one for which Periclean Athens could provide all the necessary ingredients.

As we have seen (above, p. 22), intellectual criticism of sexual laxity in the traditional myths concerning the gods began as early as the sixth century, and was closely bound up with the new secular, rational morality of the *polis*. This not only laid the foundations for a progressive movement away from archaic tribal values, but by its very nature emphasized civic (i.e. in a modified sense, urban) centralization at the expense of the rural outback, with its local cults, its patriarchal landed gentry, and its outspoken, earthy, old-fashioned ways. Now urban intellectuals of any age, being brought up in the relatively artificial circumstances of the big city, away from midden, byre and barnyard, very soon lose that intimate acquaintance with, and respect for, the raw facts of life that mark the country squire or stockbreeder. Inexperience is the mother of distaste. The capacity for abstraction not only induces a sense of moral superiority over lesser breeds still rooted—and, pig-like, rooting—in the concrete vulgarity of brute facts, but also generates a self-protective cocoon of genteel euphemism to insulate thinkers from reality's more unpleasant edges. This at once suggests an explanation, not only for the increasing inhibition in sexual matters that marks the later fifth century, but also for that special intellectual enskyment of paederasty most familiar to us from Plato's *Symposium* and *Phaedrus*. Heterosexual eros, for such thinkers, lacked uplift because of its inevitable association with the mindless coupling of the farmyard: it was animal, sub-rational, a matter of mere instinct, creative only in the physical sense, and to be transcended (as Diotima revealingly observes) by those who are 'fertile in soul'. It is no accident that Plato reveals so profound an ignorance of animals. He personifies the aristocrat, not as working landowner, but as a relatively new phenomenon, the urban intellectual living *in absentia* off inherited wealth or the profits of his estates, and whose pre-occupation with (theoretical) eros has, in Plato's case, to be offset against a marked, and characteristic, distaste for actual sex.[19]

The older aristocratic tradition of stylish and luxurious hedonism is exemplified to perfection by that elegant ana-chronism Alcibiades (?451–404 B.C.), a man, if ever there was one, born out of his time, with his chariot victories and racing debts, his high living, good looks, and indiscriminate sexual conquests, his intellectual brilliance, his casual indifference to the social disapproval of inferiors and equals alike. (His parties were notorious, suitable material for the world of the black-figure vase-painters.) *Polis* loyalty was only one of the middle-class civic virtues that he discarded whenever it suited him. He moved in the Socratic circle, which he seems to have held spell-bound with his eternally adolescent charms: the perpetual *eromenos*, or teenage love-object, flirting with an older lover (*erastes*), in that formal sexual quadrille of pursuit and elusiveness that constituted the sexually acceptable homosexual relationship at Athens.[20] Even Plato was clearly fascinated by him, though their attitudes were about as diametrically opposed as they could be, since Alcibiades saw no virtue in sexual self-denial, and indeed, if we are to trust Plato (*Symp.* 218c–219d), made at least one spirited attempt to seduce Socrates himself. Alcibiades and Plato shared a common aristocratic background (including a marked distaste for democratic institutions), and indeed a common intellectual heritage, that of the philosophers and Sophists: where they differed, fundamentally, was in their social and moral assumptions. Plato's abiding concern was with the eternal verities behind the flux of appearances. But from the time when, as a precocious boy, he ran dialectical rings round his guardian Pericles (Xenophon, *Memorabilia* 1.2, 40–6), Alcibiades' only concern with the truth—as with a political situation—was to manipulate it to his own best advantage. If we treat him as a latterday throwback to the sixth-century Attic or Ionian aristocrat, we will not go far wrong.[21]

Equally symptomatic of the old ways, but at a quite different level, is the cheerful, lowbrow countryman who plays such a prominent role in several of Aristophanes' early plays: e.g. Dicaeopolis in *The Acharnians* (425) and Strepsiades in *The Clouds* (423). Both are foul-mouthed, coarse, pragmatic, sensual, stridently anti-urban and anti-intellectual, moving in a world of simple appetites and grossly physical pleasures, attributing all their troubles to city bureaucrats and politicians, whom they describe, generically, as a bunch of dish-cocking bum-boys, *euryproktoi* (literally 'stretched anuses'), the equivalent of such inferior creatures as women or foreigners (cf. Dover, op. cit., pp. 103ff.),[22] and, by implication, wholly alien to the procreative life of the countryside. When Strepsiades tries to shore up his tottering finances by learning sharp practice at the Socratic 'Think-Tank', he finds himself totally out of his depth in a world of (often bogus) abstractions.[23] Dicaeopolis, dismissing the war with Sparta as a profitable racket cooked up by demagogues and militarists, contracts out and makes his own private peace. Both are drawn as victims of that steady centralization of government in Attica that had been going on since Solon's day, strengthening Athens' power at the expense of the rural demes, replacing local cults and squirearchies by the Panathenaic Festival and more controllable voting claques in the Assembly.

This concentration of administrative powers, coupled with the intellectual revolution pioneered by the Sophists, did more than anything else to undermine the old rural-aristocratic *mores*, sexual and social alike. Thus farmers and big landowners became natural allies against the new order: no accident that Strepsiades marries an aristocratic lady. There I was, he reminisces of his wedding, smelling of wine-lees, sheepskins, and *profits*; and there *she* was, smelling of perfume, deep-throat kisses, and *extravagance* (*Clouds*, 49–52). He wants her class, she needs his cash; what they produce between them is a spendthrift son uncommonly like Alcibiades. These two deserve each other no less than the president's widow and the shipping millionaire. Yet both of them, though poles apart socially, subscribe to the values of the rural *ancien régime*. It is hard to imagine Coesyra, any more than her husband, embracing urban rule, abstract principles, middle-class values, or, worst of all, egalitarian demagoguery.

It should be stressed that there is nothing exotic or out of the ordinary about Dicaeopolis and Strepsiades: the characters who inhabit the Platonic dialogues are far rarer birds. Such countrymen remain, now as then, a major social factor in what has always been a predominantly agricultural economy. (Andreas Papandreou is no more typical of Greece outside Athens than was Cleon or Hyperbolus.) The interesting thing is that in the late fifth century, when rural conservatives were fighting a losing battle against City Hall, they happened to find, in Aristophanes, a passionate advocate who immortalized them in some of the finest political comedies ever written. This is one of the comparatively few occasions on which the urban intellectuals did *not* have it all their own way when establishing the literary and historical record for posterity. Yet even so, most of us, trying to visualize Athens' social, and in particular her sexual, *mores*, find Plato's dramatic special pleading obstinately uppermost in our minds. As Dover says (op. cit., p. 13): 'Modern readers of *Phaedrus* and *Symposium*, which they may

35

well have seen in the pornography section of a bookshop, are apt to believe that what they find therein is the quintessential doctrine of the Greeks on the whole topic of homosexuality, expressed in definite terms by their acknowledged spokesman.' As should by now be clear, this is a complete illusion. Plato, far from speaking for all Greeks, spoke for no more than a tiny (and unpopular) minority of Athenians. By making adult homosexual eros the foundation of his ethic, rather than a transitional phase of prolonged adolescence between puberty and marriage, he alienated a large majority of his fellow-citizens. By formulating a non-sexual (rather than a socially controlled, but sexually active) ideal, he not only emphasized his urban, non-agricultural position, but provided Aristophanic man—a far more typical representative of Athens than Plato and his circle—with a standing joke. Even today the phrase 'Platonic love', with its overtones of unreality and hypocrisy, is always good for a laugh and a flip definition (e.g. 'shooting yourself with a gun that isn't loaded'). Even as a philosopher Plato was challenged by other followers of Socrates.[24]

A less exalted, and for that reason probably more accurate, picture of the Socratic circle's quotidian activities is provided by another rural conservative, Xenophon (?430–?350 B.C.), a decent, unpretentious, and (fortunately for us) on the whole unimaginative writer, who in his youth cultivated Socrates, and had a retentive memory for what he heard. Xenophon also furnished a great deal of invaluable evidence concerning the kind of life led by an average Athenian-born country gentleman, well-read, but less intellectually and morally committed than Plato. We see him as a student of philosophy; as a cavalry commander and general; patiently and affectionately training a young wife in the intricacies of household management ('Ischomachus' is clearly a transparent mask for the author); hunting on his estate in the Peloponnese; writing treatises on horsemanship and elementary economics. As a testamentary counterbalance to the intellectual and social scene drawn by Plato his work is of immense value. He is altogether more relaxed about sexual relationships; though he too takes *paiderastia* in his stride, he is also capable—literally in the same breath—of portraying a husband and wife as passionately in love with one another (*Symp.* 8.3, cf. 4.8), which must have been a more common occurrence than we nowadays tend to assume. Marriage for Greeks—then as now—was not *solely* 'a mechanism for the inheritance of property'.[25]

The evidence of Xenophon and Aristophanes, then, together with the material to be gleaned from the fourth-century Attic orators (Dover PGM *passim*), comes as a welcome—and an unusual—offset to the more influential, more 'literary' picture projected by Plato's early dialogues. What these writers remind us of—and at times the reminder is very necessary—is how ordinary, how familiar to any European, ancient or modern, much of the classical Greek's day-to-day sexual conduct must appear. It reveals a pattern common to all Western cultures, a stockpot of social clichés as unremarkable then as now. No surprise to learn that stepmothers harboured designs (murderous or erotic) on their stepsons, that some husbands had it off with the maid, while others, more flamboyant, imported mistresses into their home; that some wives, like Deianeira, were jealous ninnies, while others hit the bottle, or sneaked out at night for assignations with lovers; that incest was at least well enough known to be employed as a regular smear-charge (like buggery against a mediaeval Pope); that adultery was a commonplace, masturbation a standing joke, and all the sexual variants, from cunnilingus to fellatio, in regular use,[26] despite the strict conventions governing their public discussion. In any society the range of sexual options is limited (marriage and fucking being universal constants), and most of the options will get taken up.

It is, of course, the atypical or socially significant case that attracts most attention. Plato is not the only example, though he remains the best-known. Why, for instance, does Herodotus have such a weakness for mildly kinky anecdotes, involving variously voyeurism, necrophilia, anal intercourse (with a woman), and sexual mutilation?[27] Surely not just because of his cosmopolitan East Greek background? And what should we make of the evidence, largely drawn from Attic drama, that suggests, if not an Athenian feminist movement, at least an increasingly forceful, and vocal, pressure applied by strong-minded women in social, moral, even political affairs—and which contrasts so strikingly with Pericles' briefly patronizing advice, in his Funeral Oration (Thuc. 2.45.2), that a woman's goal should be to have men talk about her as little as possible, whether in praise or reproof? (By a nice paradox Plato, in the *Menexenus*, 236B, suggests that this speech was actually the work of Aspasia!) Aeschylus's Clytemnestra is sexually as well as politically aggressive, a strong-willed, dominating, intelligent woman, a natural leader. Sophocles's Antigone—in her own way an aristocratic traditionalist—takes on the representative of a patriarchal *polis* bureaucracy with equal energy, brilliance, and arrogant contempt. Aristophanes's Lysistrata organizes a sexual strike by wives against war; both she and Praxagora (the heroine of the *Ecclesiazusae*) aim to take over the Assembly and run Athens' politics. All these plays—which span a period between 458 and 393 B.C.—likewise reveal deep anxiety, in their male characters, at such reversals of traditional sex-roles.[28] Euripides's heroines—even when, like Alcestis, they are given to self-sacrifice in the traditional and approved manner—still force us to take a very cool look at the (equally traditional, equally approved) Greek chauvinistic male, who remains with us to this day, in all his self-assertive, mother-fixated glory. As Pomeroy says (p. 110), Euripides 'shows us women victimized by patriarchy in almost every possible way'. Whatever the truth about women's status in Periclean Athens (a topic still hotly debated by scholars, not always on exclusively rational grounds), it is hard not to see, behind this dramatic obsession, a genuine—and unpopular—movement, encouraged by progressive opinion and the effects of a long and debilitating war, in favour of greater independence for women. It is the burning debates of the day that fill any theatre: if the dominant woman was not a problem, why does she so constantly reappear, in tragedy and comedy alike, taking her curtain-call, as it were, at the close of the Peloponnesian War, as Agave in the *Bacchae*, with her son Pentheus's severed head stuck on a thyrsus? Euripides, like Ibsen, only achieved real popularity after his death, when the causes he had fought for were won; and who, today, would argue that Ibsen was tilting at mere literary windmills?

5

Soon after the end of the fifth century B.C. some fundamental changes in Greek—which here, for all practical purposes, means Athenian—social attitudes become apparent: changes that foreshadowed the more cosmopolitan outlook of the Hellenistic world, and the mixed Graeco-Roman culture that succeeded it. We here reach more familiar ground, since what Rome took from Greece was, in essence, not Athens' classical heritage, but the later internationalized culture of Alexandria and Pergamon; and what modern Europe rediscovered at the Renaissance was, similarly, an amalgam of imperial Rome and post-Alexandrian Greece as refracted through Roman eyes. This, if any, is the phase of ancient culture that a contemporary reader can explore with some sense of shared values and continuity: the landscape, though pre-industrial, is at least one that we recognize. To take a simple but striking instance, it is in the fourth century that we first come across the (to us) obvious notion of romantic individualism, the idea that erotic passion and psychological self-awareness are there to be cultivated for their own sakes. Yet up to that point the archaic and classical writers had, with some unanimity, presented the onset of passionate love as something worse than infatuation, as a dangerous lapse from reason, a temporary madness that one prayed to all the gods to be relieved from as quickly as possible.[29]

There are other significant pointers. In sculpture the ubiquitous male nude becomes less aggressive, its musculature appreciably softer (as we can see at once from the Praxitelean Hermes), and, even more significant, there now appear equally soft and sensuous female nudes—in competition, as it were—rather than those sexless, decorously draped figures previously in vogue. (The subsequent striking obsession with hermaphrodites looks like a compromise solution designed to give everyone the best of both worlds.) Ironically, while Plato was promoting homoerotic Eros and arguing for less physical sex all round, his fellow-citizens seem to have been moving in precisely the oppsite direction on both counts: they were certainly looking at women with new eyes. Plato's 'Heavenly Aphrodite' never really stood a chance against the 'Common

Aphrodite' he so despised.[30] About the only thing the two Aphrodites had in common—in contrast to the old rural-aristocratic ethic—was a new genteel passion for euphemism: but then by now they were both very much urban ladies. No accident that at the same time the demand for Old Comedy's licensed ithyphallic horseplay dwindled and died, so that by Aristotle's day uninhibited sexual plain speaking was condemned as 'dirty talk' *(aischrologia)*, while a slave in Menander's *Ghost* (*Phasma*, vv. 39–43) apologizes, with prissy circumlocution, for using the word 'shit'—something it is hard to imagine Aristophanes doing. By the Hellenistic period commentators on Homer are tut-tutting about how 'unseemly' or 'inappropriate' it is for Thetis to tell her son Achilles (*Il.* 24, 129ff.) that going without sex and food is bad for him, in a context that makes the Homeric attitude crystal-clear: a good fuck and a square meal have the same therapeutic effect. Truism it may be, but the scholiast blushes regardless.[2] The new morality—middle-class, mealy-mouthed, romantic—has triumphed over peasant earthiness and aristocratic insouciance alike. In essence it is what has survived, with Roman accretions and Christian modifications, to the present day.

There is a striking—and, for some, alarming—sense of *déjà vu* about the Hellenistic era for a modern reader. The *polis*—already under centrifugal pressure from growing individualism and commercial interests—was dealt a fatal blow by Philip of Macedon at Chaeronea (338 B.C.), and finally succumbed, as an institution, to the vast bureaucratic kingdoms established by Alexander's successors and then absorbed piecemeal in the Roman empire. The teeming, polyglot cities of the third and second centuries B.C.—the Alexandria of Theocritus's affluent, concert-going, vapid suburban housewives (*Idyll* 15)—generated a new social pattern, characteristic and enduring, what Lewis Mumford has stigmatized as Megalopolis in decline: Rome itself offers the most aggravated example of it. The main features of this pattern[32] are large-scale capitalism and free enterprise, authoritarian government, the standardization of culture, the encyclopedic tabulation of science and scholarship, an obsession with mere size and number—the tallest buildings, the vastest food-supply—and, for the individual, an increasing sense of alienation, the determined pursuit of affluence, the retreat from political involvement to the private world of social and domestic trivia, a growing preoccupation with chance (Tyche), magic, astrology, exotic foreign cults, and, above all, sex. Hellenistic literature emphasized technique and artifice, obscure mythology, arcane scholarship, the psychopathology of character, books made out of books. In poetry and art alike, idealism was out, and realism in—or, more often, the seductive (and at times grotesque) pseudo-realism of kitsch, pastoral, and pornography. The romantic picaresque novel made its appearance, and proved vastly popular (it took the upper-crust Roman genius of Petronius to put a satirical pill inside the sugar). Small wonder, then, that the past few years have witnessed an unprecedented upsurge of interest in Hellenistic culture: for this troubled age of ours it offers, even more than the fourteenth century A.D., that 'distant mirror' so brilliantly formulated by Barbara Tuchman. It shows us our own flawed humanity.

The most immediately striking phenomenon is the enormous increase of heterosexual passion—whether with marriage as its prime object or not—as a motif in our surviving literature, and the regular assumption that its natural and desirable end is physical fulfilment: on both counts a flat reversal of Plato's attitude. Sweeter than ice-water in summer, wrote Asclepiades (*Anth. Pal.* 5.169), it is when one cloak covers two lovers. Characteristically, there is no indication of the lovers' sex in this epigram, and in fact Asclepiades, like many other ancient poets, wrote love-poems, with fine impartiality, to girls and boys alike. We should not assume a swing of opinion against *paiderastia*: there is ample evidence (including Book 12 of the Greek Anthology, exclusively devoted to homosexual themes) which suggests that boys were not only as popular as ever, but co-operated with their pursuers a good deal less coyly than they had done in the fifth century. Heterosexual activities did not supplant *paiderastia*, but simply supplemented it: variety, now, was the name of the game.

Antimachus and Philetas established the convention of writing volumes of love-poetry to one's mistress, a formula later taken over by Roman elegists from Catullus to Ovid, who exploited the idea of servitude in love to a dominant, capricious mistress with masochistic (and decidedly un-Greek) fervour.

The concept of the *grande passion* was popularized, with incalculable effects on subsequent European literature: the Medea drawn by Apollonius Rhodius (fl. third cent. B.C.) in his *Argonautica*—heart a-quiver for Jason like the flicker of sunlight on water, speechless, rapt, the original *jeune fille en fleur*—is the ancestor of too many star-crossed heroines, not least Virgil's Dido. It is also here that the cliché of Cupid's arrows, the fiery darts of love (*Ap. Rhod.* 3.275ff.) gets launched on its long literary career. Endless epigrams testify to the agonizing pains of unrequited passion, the heaven-on-earth of attainment. *Carpe diem:* a girl's concern for her virginity draws the brisk rebuttal that in Hades we're dust and ashes, no sex there, you can't take it with you (*Anth. Pal.* 5.85). Lovers from Asclepiades (*Anth. Pal.* 5.189) to Ovid (*Amores* 1.6) pine all night outside their beloved's door, or at least write stylized outside-the-closed-door-poems (*paraklausithyra*) claiming they did. If this literature is what most encourages the delusion that the Greeks 'lived in a rosy haze of uninhibited sexuality' (Dover GPM p. 205), it also, not by coincidence, abounds in poetical artifice, topos, and convention.

There is a nice paradox here. As the erotic element in literature shifted from the public to the private domain, it became less, rather than more, in touch with life as actually lived and loved: *graffiti*, epitaphs, and non-literary documents on papyrus (wills, marriage-contracts, private letters) reveal a far more stable world of touching, if humdrum, relationships. Humankind, as Eliot shrewdly remarked, cannot bear very much reality, an apothegm which the literary portrayal of sex tends to bear out in unexpected ways. One of the sillier judgements from antiquity was that which claimed not to know whether Menander (342/1–c. 290 B.C.) had imitated life, or life Menander. The world of pirates, foundlings, kidnapped heiresses and long-lost siblings he portrays, however tricked out with shrewd characterization and peppy aphorisms, belongs to folklore and popular romance: social realism has no part in it. This, clearly, did not bother Menander's audiences, who had no great liking for the world in which they found themselves, and preferred fantasy to fact, a psychological addiction which the Roman playwrights Plautus and Terence (who both adapted Menander's material) found as flourishing in their day as Sam Goldwyn or Norman Lear have done in ours. Cunning servants, manipulative pimps and bawds, irate fathers, wastrel sons, braggart soldiers and the rest no doubt did, and do, occur in real life; but for Menander (or Sheridan, or Coward, or Ayckbourne) they are no more than cardboard cutouts from a perennial pantomime. Sex and money remain the eternal prizes, but the girls, though constantly exposed to the regulation fate worse than death, all come through in the end as triumphantly inviolate as any Barbara Cartland heroine, getting Mr. Right *and* his father's cash at the very end of Act V. Greek novels explore this world of sexual fantasy in an even more grotesque manner: *Daphnis and Chloë*, for instance, depends on the notion of a young country couple too innocent to know about intercourse, the ultimate improbability to anyone brought up within reach of a real farm.

This gap in understanding between city and country is symbolized to perfection by what was perhaps the most characteristic literary development of the Hellenistic age: the pastoral idyll. Its ideals are bucolic; it romanticizes the shepherd's life, a mythical Arcadia (the real Arcadia was, is, barren, backward, mountainous); and it could only have been invented and practised by nostalgic urban intellectuals who had never herded sheep in their lives, but were hooked on the seductive dream of a lost rural Golden Age. Theocritus's herdsmen retain some semblance of earthiness: they bugger each other *al fresco* when bored (*Idyll* 5), carve wood, chase girls. But Polyphemus's outsize and milky devotion to Galatea (*Idyll* 11.19ff.) hints at the stylized sentimentality inherent in the *genre*. These shepherds are fair poets, but no one really believes in their sheep or goats. Virgil's blandly paederastic Corydon is a mere literary humour. The way is being prepared for Marie Antoinette and her idiot Court milkmaids. Unreason and fantasy are compounded by those implacable demands for instant gratification that stamp a consumer culture, and were directly responsible, throughout the Graeco-Roman period, for a quite startling explosion of erotic magic, reflected equally in the literature and in surviving magical formulae on lead tablets or papyrus[33]: spells to compel desire in cooled-off lovers (Theocr. *Idyll* 2), to punish infidelity, prevent impotence, and generally to bend the law for the attainment of private pleasures.

43

There is, of course, a close nexus between magic and pornography, which, again, seeks to reshape nature as *ad hominem* (or *ad feminam*) wish-fulfilment, by projecting fantasies of stakhanovite yet reductionist sexual athletics, all parts and no whole. Though true pornography was rarer in antiquity than we might guess from some modern bookshops, such beady-eyed practitioners as Sotades, Herodas, or, later, Martial, with their dildoes, scatology, and bisexual athletics suggest that the formula has stayed pretty constant down the ages. Yet it would be a mistake, again, to suppose that Graeco-Roman civilization evolved an increasingly permissive culture which only Christianity, in the end, could control or change. The sense of restraint, of social decorum was always there: the extent of its influence varied, but it was never a negligible force. The age that produced Catullus also produced that stupefyingly respectable bourgeois politician Cicero; of the two, Cicero was by far the more typical. The *Meditations* of Marcus Aurelius remind us that, at the very close of classical antiquity, a chaste Stoic spirit was not quite such an anomaly as we might suppose from skimming the more lurid passages of Tacitus or Suetonius. We hear a good deal about the sexual puritanism supposedly imposed on a cheerfully guiltless pagan culture by St. Paul's tight-lipped disciples: the monastic exodus to the Egyptian desert, the dirt, the fasting, the self-flagellation, the graphic temptations of St. Anthony. None of this in fact was new, or even specifically Christian. The instinct had been there from the beginning. It reaches its anti-romantic apogee in a passionate atheist, Lucretius (?94–?55 B.C.), who devoted a long section of his *De Rerum Natura* (4.1058ff.) to sex, piling detail on sickening detail, harnessing the rhetoric of disgust to biological exegesis, the 'cold friction of expiring sense'. Juvenal by comparison is mild; the old satirist may find women either bores or bitches (cf. above, p. 28), but his pragmatic solution is to sleep with a boy instead, on the, to us, curious grounds that a boy doesn't make demanding scenes in bed (*Sat.* 6.34ff.).

The literature of sex in antiquity is full of these paradoxes; its very unpredictability is what makes it so intriguing. If I believe—as I do, and as this essay should have made clear—that we might be well advised to study, and, hopefully, learn from, the archaic and classical Greek scene rather than indulge, yet again, our uneasy sense of self-identification with its more cosmopolitan Hellenistic and Roman successors, this does not mean I think that the latter have yielded up all their secrets, or that the former has all the answers. Sex *is* the ever-interesting topic (for once the cliché is right), not least because, in a matter of vital concern to each and every one of us, no consensus is attainable, by historians or anyone else. That, of course, does not relieve us of the responsibility for trying. The debate continues. Hence this volume.

NOTES

1. Just how far things have moved in a very short time may be deduced from C. J. Fordyce's edition of Catullus, published in 1961, which omitted no less than 31 poems because they 'did not lend themselves to comment in English'. Earlier evidence is abundant, ranging from the habitual suppression of the second and ninth satires of Juvenal from all exegetic commentaries to such *curiosa* as Pickard-Cambridge's habit of air-brushing out the erections from ancient representations of satyr-drama (to which he devoted a good proportion of his scholarly career), or W. W. Tarn's determined efforts to clean up Alexander's sex-life (for which see his *Alexander the Great*, Cambridge 1948, vol. 2, Appendix 18, pp. 319–26), or the habit—now at last abandoned—of translating Martial's more obscene epigrams, not into English, but into *Italian*, which managed, in different ways, to slur no less than three ethnic groups simultaneously.

2. E.g. Sir Kenneth Dover, *Greek Homosexuality* (London, 1978), and Sarah B. Pomeroy, *Goddesses, Whores, Wives and Slaves* (New York, 1975).

3. The value of this, of course, varies, as students of Claude Lévi-Strauss are well aware; perhaps the Freudian approach has done more than any other to obfuscate the historical issue by overlaying ancient fantasies with modern ones. See, e.g., Philip E. Slater, *The Glory of Hera* (Boston, 1968), and, for a fundamentally sane critique of these various approaches, G. S. Kirk, *Myth: Its Meaning and Functions* (Cambridge, 1970).

4. Homer's Ionian patrons: G. L. Huxley, *The Early Ionians* (London, 1966), p. 43; expurgations: G. Murray, *The Rise of the Greek Epic* (4th ed., Oxford, 1934), ch. v, pp. 120ff.; Achilles and Patroclus, Dover, op. cit. pp. 53, 197–98, and cf. note 8 below.

5. The double standard clearly applies to Odysseus. When he finds that twelve of the serving women in his palace have been putting out for the wooers he has just slaughtered, he tells Telemachus and Eumaeus, first, to have these girls remove the bodies and clean up the mess, and then to put them all to the sword (Telemachus, however, feeling that they do not deserve a 'clean death', partly because they put out, and partly because

they insulted his mother (? by putting out), hangs them all instead): *Od.* 22, 417–72, esp. 440–45, 461ff.

6. Helen is also, of course, a survivor: as MacNeice wrote, 'the whore and the buffoon will come off best' (a good classicist, he might have had Helen and Menelaus in mind), and Helen's reappearance in the *Odyssey* (4, 120ff.) after the war, every inch the respectable married society matron, is one of the great comic scenes in world literature.

7. Aeschylus, for one, was far more explicit: frs. 228–29 of his play *The Myrmidons* clearly refer to intercrural intercourse.

8. Dover, ibid., citing Aeschines 1.142 (the speech *Against Timarchus*). See also now the admirable article by W. M. Clarke, 'Achilles and Patroclus in love', *Hermes* 106 (1978), 381–96, esp. n.38, where Clarke observes that in the *Iliad* 'we see the reticence of the author, and presumably his audience, to label a love that, in any case, requires no name to be understood.'

9. I would not include in this category such phenomena as the temporary Athenian law, passed at a time during the Peloponnesian War when husbands were in short supply, permitting *de facto* bigamy (i.e. legitimizing offspring by concubines), or Plato's frigid notion that warriors who distinguished themselves on the battlefield should be given special sexual privileges when on furlough: see Diog. Laert. 2, 26, cf. D. M. MacDowell, *The Law in Classical Athens* (London, 1978), p. 90; Plato, *Rep.* 460b, 468b–c. Such measures are utilitarian rather than aimed at the pleasure principle; indeed, Plato's contempt for the sexual act is notorious, and his exposition of sexual eugenics in the *Republic* must rank—along with Lucretius's tirade, *De Rerum Natura* 4, 1030–287, cf. p. 44—among the most antaphrodisiac passages in all literature.

10. For an excellent analysis of the continuing tradition, which takes full advantage of the anthropological and sociological field-work carried out by such researchers as Campbell, Friedl, Peristiany and Sanders, see Peter Walcot, *Greek Peasants, Ancient and Modern: A Comparison of Social and Moral Values* (Manchester U.P., 1970), esp. chs. ii–iii.

11. One of Hesiod's fears is excessive sexual demands by a wife: WD, 704–5, and cf. 585–88, where he claims that in high summer women are most insatiable, but men dried out and at their lowest ebb, a generalization which should amuse *habitués* of Hellenic cruises. For the prevalence of such fears see H. R. Hays, *The Dangerous Sex: The Myth of Feminine Evil* (New York, 1964), esp. pp. 239ff.

12. Phocylides, fr. 2 Diehl, expresses similar sentiments, again praising the bee-wife. See now the admirable edition of Semonides's poem by Professor Hugh Lloyd-Jones, *Females of the Species* (Park Ridge, N.J., 1975): his introduction contains some illuminating general remarks (pp. 25ff.) on women in Greek literature.

13. By a kind of selective breeding process such chauvinistic attitudes also produced a few really powerful and sexually dominating matriarchs: the real-life analogues of mythical characters such as Clytemnestra or Medea would be Cimon's sister Elpinice and, in the fourth century B.C., Philip II's terrible wife Olympias.

14. We should beware, as Dover very properly reminds us, of assuming without question, in default of confirmatory evidence, that poems purporting to describe details of the writer's own life are, in fact, autobiographical: see 'The poetry of Archilochus', *Fondation Hardt Entretiens*, Vol. x, *Archiloque* (Vandoeuvres-Geneva, 1964), 183–212, esp. 206ff. But in Archilochus's case I suspect a kind of sexual exhibitionism that took especial pleasure in self-revelation, and was calculated to shock.

15. 'Kick the empty-headed rabble!' he snorts (*Theog.* 847); note also his significant complaint, common in an era when capital first began to erode traditional privileges, that 'money is what holds most power for all men' (*Theog.* 718). The bulk of his erotic addresses to Kyrnos are gathered at the end of the *Theognidea* (lines 1231ff.), perhaps a late act of sequestration by mediaeval Christian scribes who were disconcerted at finding homosexuality—in fact very characteristically—allied to moral protreptics: see Martin L. West, *Studies in Greek Elegy and Iambus* (Berlin, 1974), p. 43ff., and cf. the Suda s.v. Theognis (1).

16. Now conveniently catalogued by Dover, op. cit., pp. 206ff.; he also reproduces a good many of them. Cf. John Boardman, *Athenian Black Figure Vases* (London, 1974), p. 210: 'Male homosexual activity is so commonly shown that it acquires iconographic conventions of its own. . . . The scenes appear regularly from about 560 on.'

17. A seeming exception would be the famous temple prostitutes of Corinth, or Eryx in Sicily or Comana in Asia Minor: see Strabo 8.6.20, C.378, 6.2.6, C.272, 12.3.36, C.559; Athenaeus 13.573 *passim*; Diod. Sic. 4.83. But in the first place it is nowhere expressly stated that these prostitutes actually had intercourse *in the temple* of Ma or Aphrodite; and in any case there are few taboos of this sort that do not have a formalized ritual exception.

18. Cf. T. B. L. Webster, *The Tragedies of Euripides* (London, 1967), pp. 64ff.

19. Plato, *Symp.* 207b, 208e–209d *passim*, cf. *Phaedr.* 250e; well discussed by Dover, op. cit., pp. 163, 167; cf. also his excellent monograph *Greek Popular Morality* (Oxford, 1974), pp. 206–7. See below, n. 25.

20. On this fascinating topic see G. Devereux, 'Greek pseudo-homosexuality and the "Greek Miracle"', *Symbolae Osloenses* 13 (1967), 69–92, cf. Dover op. cit., pp. 81ff.

21. Most accounts of Alcibiades are still absurdly over-eulogistic: for a salutary corrective see E. F. Bloedow, *Alcibiades Reexamined* (Wiesbaden, 1973); and for Alcibiades's philosophic-erotic relations with Socrates, M. Gagarin, 'Socrates's *Hybris* and Alcibiades's Failure', *Phoenix* 31 (1977), 22–37. The standard biography is that by Jean Hatzfeld, *Alcibiade* (2nd ed., Paris, 1951). See also my article 'Alcibiades: a lion in the State', *Internat. Hist. Mag.*, 17 (1974), 8–23.

22. The paradoxes of the Athenian attitude to homosexuality become a little more manageable if one constantly bears in mind that *only* the courting of adolescent boys (in particular those whose beards had not yet begun to grow: a significant point, since this emphasizes their girlishness) by older—but normally not middle-aged or elderly—men was regarded as socially acceptable; whereas *all* homosexual activity *between adults*, above

47

all, *passive promiscuity* by adult effeminates (and indeed even over-eagerness on the part of an adolescent *eromenos*) provoked social disapproval or derision. Any male citizen who prostituted his favours was debarred from many civic rights, including that of addressing the Assembly. Cf. Dover ch. ii, pp. 19ff., analysing Aeschines's speech *Against Timarchos*.

23: See my article 'Strepsiades, Socrates and the Abuses of Intellectualism', *Greek Roman and Byzantine Studies*, 20 (1979), 11–21.

24. By a nice paradox, the two things about Plato that have always ensured his popularity, with post-Christian moralists and aesthetes alike, are, first, his hauntingly brilliant characterizations and crystalline prose style (which, like Proust's, can often reconcile the reader to illogical or antipathetical propositions); and second, his simultaneous obsession with Eros and disapproval of physical sex. What hair-splitting Augustinian could resist a preacher who both argued that *paiderastia* was the best route to philosophical appreciation of beauty, and damned homosexual intercourse as 'contrary to nature' (*Laws* 636a–c, 836d–e)?

25. K. J. Dover, *Greek Popular Morality in the time of Plato and Aristotle* (Oxford, 1974), p. 211. Hereafter 'Dover GPM'.

26. See, e.g., Antiphon 1.14–20; Aristoph. *Eccles*. 225–28, *Thesm*. 478ff.; Andocides 4.14, 4.33; Lysias 1.6–26, 14.29; and cf. Jeffrey Henderson, *The Maculate Muse: Obscene Language in Attic Comedy* (Yale U.P., 1975), pp. 183ff. On incest see R. and E. Blum, *Health and Healing in Rural Greece* (Stanford, 1965), p. 49.

27. Herodotus 1.8–10, 61; 2.89; 5.92 n.3; 9.112.

28. Cf. Pomeroy, op. cit. (above, n.2), 98–114.

29. Sappho might seem to present an early exception, and in ways I think she does; the island of Lesbos—small enough for isolation, large enough to sustain an independent world—was a natural enclave. Yet even Sappho often regards love as a plague to the senses: the student of mine who said that her famous list of symptoms (fr. 31 Lobel-Page, vv. 7–16)—sweat, pallor, voice-failure, and so on—sounded more appropriate for cholera than for passion (in the modern sense, understood) had a point. Evidence for passion as madness or an affliction: Dover GPM pp. 77, 125, 137, 208.

30. On Aphrodite Urania and Aphrodite Pandemos see Plato, *Symp*. 180e–181c, cf. Xen. *Symp*. 8.9, *Paus*. 1.22.3.

31. See Dover GPM, pp. 205–7.

32. See John Ferguson, *The Heritage of Hellenism* (London, 1973), pp. 27ff., and Lewis Mumford, *The Culture of Cities* (New York, 1938, repr. 1970), esp. chs. i–ii.

33. See A. Audollent, *Defixionum Tabellae* (Paris, 1904); S. Eitrem, 'La Magie comme motif littéraire chez les Grecs et les Romains', *Symbolae Osloenses* 21 (1941), 39–83; K. Preisendanz, *Papyri Graecae Magicae* (Leipzig, 1928–31); E. Tavenner, *Studies in Magic from Latin Literature* (New York, 1916); G. Luck, *Hexen und Zauberei in der Römischen Dichtung* (Zurich, 1962); A. M. Tupet, *La Magie dans la poésie latine* (Paris, 1976), esp. pt. ii, pp. 107ff.

2

'Last Night's Rambles': Restoration Literature and the War Between the Sexes

by ANGELINE GOREAU

1

The Restoration has long been considered the most bawdy chapter in the history of English literature. I propose in the following discussion to examine the nature of the 'revolution' in sexuality that produced this literature and determine what its effects were upon relations between the sexes. Ordinarily, it is difficult to assign a specific set of dates to the complex and often contradictory shifts in sexual mores, but the significant political forces at work in this case provide an unusually clear line of demarcation.

Charles II's return to the throne in 1660 effected an abrupt and deliberate reversal of Puritan ethic. His need to distinguish himself in every way from his predecessors—added to his natural inclination—created an atmosphere in which promiscuity, systematic frivolity, and extravagance were adhered to as a social norm almost as dogmatically as the more severe of the Puritan party had adhered to godliness. Part of the point, of course was to demonstrate one's loyalty to the royal cause: Francis North was advised that his sobriety might call his political sympathies into question and was counselled to 'keep a whore', because he was 'ill-looked upon [at Court] for want of doing so'.[1] Adultery was part of the calling of a gentleman, as essential to his place in society as fluency in French, a wig, or a sword at his side. The King set the tone by openly keeping several mistresses, carrying on numerous chance affairs, and bestowing titles, estates, and fortunes on his women and bastards. Royal libertinism does not necessarily engender promiscuity in the population at large—in fact the King may bring disapproval and disrespect upon himself; but there seems to have been a particularly vocal group that imitated Charles II's precedent. The movement primarily affected the fashionable society of London—the court and aristocratic circles, the playhouse, the taverns, coffee-houses, and ordinaries—but, as these were the most visible and the most influential groups, they seemed to dominate the rest. The Whiggish City merchants who were the moral and political inheritors of Puritanism were, as the constant taunting of Restoration dramatists indicates, very much in opposition to the Tory libertines, but it is hard to tell to what extent the new immorality filtered down to the rest of the population. Statistics indicate a slight rise in bastardy and prenuptial pregnancies during this period, and there seems to have been a remarkable increase in prostitution as well at the end of the seventeenth century; but those figures may just as well have been influenced by economic considerations and other changes in the social fabric as by revolutions in sexuality.[2] However widespread the practice of sexual freedom actually was in Restoration society as a whole, it was so much in evidence in the capital that even those contemporaries who disapproved often believed themselves to be in the minority—lonely voices of reason in an unruly and wicked age.

Countless references to the universality of the 'modern' social mode fill the poetry, plays, tracts, diaries, letters, and other documents of the period. A minor playwright named Joseph Arrowsmith even wrote a play (*The Reformation*, 1673) in which a mock Society for the Reformation of Male-Female Relations was created—to the purpose of assuring greater sexual freedom. Outside of the context of a general movement in that direction, the joke would not have been funny. John Wilmot, Earl of Rochester, wrote a poem called 'A Ramble in St. James's Park' which describes the fashionable scene in London in the early 1670s:

> Much wine had passed, with grave discourse
> Of who fucks who, and who does worse
> (Such as you usually do hear
> From those that diet at the Bear),
> When I, who still take care to see
> Drunkenness relieved by lechery,
> Went out into St. James's Park
> To cool my head and fire my heart.
> But though St. James had th' honor 't,
> 'Tis consecrate to prick and cunt. . . .
> Nightly now beneath [the] shade [of the trees there]
> Are buggeries, rapes and incests made.
> Unto this all-sin-sheltering grove
> Whores of the bulk and the alcove,
> Great ladies, chambermaids, and drudges,
> The ragpicker, and heiress trudges.
> Carmen, divines, great lords, and tailors,
> Prentices, poets, pimps, and jailers,
> Footmen, fine fops do here arrive,
> And here promiscuously they swive [fornicate].[3]

Rochester's poem was passed around in manuscript, copied, and sent to relatives and friends in the country to amuse them with the latest goings-on in London. No doubt some were offended by the grossness of the verses, but Rochester and the avant-garde wits only laughed at prudery. The Court, wits, players, and gentry flocked to Spring-Gardens, to Hyde Park and St. James, where they promenaded, flirted, told the newest gossip, looked over, and were looked over. Obscene poems were much in vogue, and wits tossed off lines conjuring their mistresses to be 'kind' (i.e. compliant), and insulting them if they refused. They wrote each other satires making fun of their more sober contemporaries, laughing at the women they had seduced and dropped, and recounting their 'last night's rambles' in sexual conquest: if you wish to be excused in society, wrote Lord Buckhurst, 'say that cunt detained thee'.[4]

The Restoration rake was the hero of most of the plays staged at the Theatre Royal or the Dorset Garden Theatre; he was never serious, frequently drunk, and systematically lusty, capricious, wild, and jesting. Above all, he was anti-romantic. He subscribed to the philosophy that based its rejection of the spiritual on the materialism of Hobbes and Lucretius and placed body over mind, sense over soul. Preoccupation with morality or the metaphysical were better left to Puritans; wits would choose, as Rochester put it, 'the readiest way to Hell'. The only principle that existed for them was the pleasure principle: 'For why should mankind live by rule and measure,' said Sir Francis Fane, 'since all his virtue rises from his pleasure?'[5] Any lie a gallant might tell in the pursuit of that pleasure was only a part of the game. When one character expresses surprise that the hero of Crowne's *The Country Wit* (1675), appropriately named 'Ramble', has sworn up and down on his soul, and then casually broken his word and followed his own desires, another character tells him: '. . . Ramble think he has a soul! Alas good man, he seldom sets his thoughts on those affairs: he loves his soul, but as he loves his bawd, only to pimp for pleasures for the body, and the, bawd-like it may be damned, he cares not.'[6]

Charles II himself had a reputation for cynicism and was sceptical of anyone who pretended to act out of any other motive than self-interest. According to Gilbert Burnet, he 'had a very ill opinion both of men and women; and did not think there was either sincerity or chastity in the world out of principle.'[7] In a play written by the woman playwright Aphra Behn, who represents the only female voice in Restoration drama, there is a passing reference to what was regarded as the general dissolution of morals: 'Art thou honest?' Philander asks Alcander, and the latter replies, 'As most men of my age. . . .'[8] The heroine of Aphra Behn's play *The Amorous Prince* is warned by her own brother not to believe anything her lover might say to get her into bed: '. . . beware of men,' he tells her in a letter, 'for though I myself be one, yet I have the frailties of my sex, and can dissemble too. Trust none of us, for if thou dost, thou art undone. We make vows to all alike we see, and even the best of men . . . is not to be credited in an affair of love.' The lover, a typical Restoration gallant, has promised to marry her and successfully made love to her on that condition, without the slightest intention of keeping his word.

2

The sexual 'revolution' and Restoration cynicism had made love obsolete. Charles II, in 1664, wrote to his sister, Minette, in France: 'I find the passion love is very much out of fashion in this country. . . .'[9] Earlier poets of the seventeenth century had placed their mistresses on the Petrarchan pedestal: their eyes were idealized to starry orbs, lips to coral, breasts to snow, cheeks to roses, teeth to pearls. . . . The unrequited lover of platonic convention threatened to expire from despair alone if his mistress would not condescend to return, even for a minute, his worshipping look. But the Restoration wits would have nothing of idealized love: any pretence of love at all they deemed nothing more than shallow hypocrisy. Their mistresses were advised to give up such ridiculous romantic day-dreaming and deliver up their 'charms'. Women who demurred or pro-tested modesty were as likely as not told that their beauty was not worth the pursuit when there were other women more easily to be had. Etheredge wrote that a man was an 'ass' to 'sigh and whine' for a woman; 'if she be not as kind [in the sexual sense] as fair, but peevish and unhandy,' he counselled, 'leave her, she's only worth the care of some spruce Jack-a-dandy.'[10] Wycherley, whose mistress evidently wanted him to declare his love before she would consider sleeping with him, told her: 'Fantastic Phyllis! Cease to please,/ Or else consent to give me ease [i.e. to make love]/ Pox! of your dull platonic schemes/ 'Tis wasting life in idle dreams/ And quitting solid joys, to prove/ What crowns the fairy land of love.'[11]

Libertine philosophy held that love was merely an illusion— an elaborate myth to cover what was really no more than sexual desire pressing to be satisfied. Rochester mocks the tradition of love songs written to women under the guise of a pastoral name, saying: 'A song to Phyllis I perhaps might make,/ but never rhymed but for my pintle's [slang for penis] sake.' A pamphlet describing the *Character of a Town Gallant* (1675), stated that 'his trade is making-of-love, yet he knows no difference between that and lust. . . .'[12] The same wisdom is repeated over and over again by contemporaries, including the gallants and wits themselves, who were not in the least averse to making their attitudes public. Sir George Etheredge, writing to Lord Buckhurst in a verse letter that was circulated to the amusement of all, tells of his sexual adventures and philosophically remarks:

> . . . This shows love's chiefest magic lies
> In women's cunts, not in their eyes:
> There Cupid does his revels keep,
> There lovers all their sorrows steep;
> For having once but tasted that,
> Their mysteries are quite forgot.

Woman's mystery could be reduced to just that. A woman was a 'cunt' and any man who was fool enough to respect her for other qualities was missing the point. Poems like the anonymous 'No true love between man and woman' proliferated in contemporary collections of verse: 'No, no—'tis not love—' the author begins, 'You may talk till doomsday,/ If you tell me 'tis more than mere satisfaction/ I'll never believe a tittle you say. . . .'

> When a man to a woman comes creeping and cringing,
> And spends his high raptures on her nose and her eyes;
> 'Tis Priapus inspires the talkative engine,
>   And all for the sake of her lilly white thighs.
>
> Your vows and protests, your oaths all and some,
> Ask Solon, Lycurgus both learned and smart;
> They'll tell you the place from whence they all come,
>   Is half a yard almost below the heart.[13]

If love was an unreasonable expectation on the part of a mistress, then so was fidelity. Desire must find its expression wherever and whenever it arises, the rhetoric went. When the young woman in love with Celladon, the rake hero of Dryden's *Secret Love* (1668), asks him if he could be faithful to one woman alone, he replies: 'Constant to one! I have been a courtier, a soldier, and a traveller, to good purpose, if I must be constant to one: give me some twenty, some forty, some a hundred mistresses: I have more love than any one woman can turn her to. . . . Yet for my part, I can live with as few mistresses as any man. I desire no superfluities, only for necessary change, or so, as I shift my linen.'[14]

Rochester, in a poem called 'Against Constancy' (1676), warns his mistress: 'Tell me no more of constancy,/ The frivolous pretence/ Of cold age, narrow jealousy,/ Disease, and want of sense.' He further informs her that he intends to change his mistress nightly until he is dead and is changed himself to worms. In another poem, on 'Love and Life' (1677), he replies to another young woman, who is evidently reproaching him for his falseness to her, that 'If I, by miracle, can be/ This livelong minute true to thee,/ 'Tis all that heaven allows.' In still another poem, when a shepherdess accuses her lover of betrayal, he answers that 'Since 'tis nature's law to change,/ constancy alone is strange.' He explains to her that it is the nature of love itself that once the object of desire is possessed it ceases to hold interest for the man who desired. The 'showers' of ecstasy kill the 'flame', the shepherd tells the nymph—man's nature is that satisfaction extinguishes love.

A great number of similar poems justifying masculine roving and attacking the ideal of constancy appeared in the miscellanies of the time and were passed from hand to hand. Usually they were written in reply to some demanding feminine voice in the poem who is either accusing the masculine 'I' of desertion or attempting to exact some promise of fidelity on his part. Etheredge's 'To a Lady, asking him how long he would love her', conjures her to refrain from asking for anything more than the pleasure of the moment. 'It is not, Celia, in our power/ To say how long our love will last,/ It may be we within this hour/ May lose the joys we now do taste,/ The blessed, that immortal be/ From change in Love are only free.' Celia is exhorted to sleep with her suitor while he is still in love with her, as his fancy will inevitably pass elsewhere before too long.

The proponent of the 'new sexuality' of the 1660s gave his mistress no commitments and no assurances—except that of his own capriciousness. The only pledge a woman might have in an affair with a wit was the certainty that he would sooner or later abandon her for some fresher adventure and probably prove unfaithful even before. Sir Charles Sedley, in a 'Song to Phyllis', tells her, 'I'll dote no longer than I can' and presents her with an ideal of liberated love in which each party, on tiring of the other, is free to part (as freely as they met), 'each one possessed of their own heart.'[15] One does not know what Phyllis answered, but the lady whom Charles Cotton wrote to charged him with loving her too little:

> . . . She cries I do not love her,
> And tells me of her honour;
> Then have I no way to disprove her,
> And my true passion to discover,
> But straight to fall upon her.
>
> Which done, forsooth, she talks of wedding,
> But what will that avail her?
> For though I am old dog at begging,
> I'm yet a man of so much reading,
> That there I sure shall fail her.
>
> No, hang me if I ever marry,
> Till womankind grow stauncher,
> I do delight delights to vary,
> And love not in one bulk to tarry,
> But only trim and launch her.[16]

Marriage was anathema to the Restoration gallant. To be forced to remain on terms of intimacy with a woman beyond the (avowedly short) term of his desire was an affront to his manhood. Though wives seldom succeeded in exacting any real restraint over their husbands' amorous activities, they could be a nuisance: 'A spouse I do hate,' wrote Wycherley, 'for either she's false or she's jealous.' A husband had to take care that he was not being cuckolded by another man and at the same time avoid arousing his wife's jealousy by concealing his own affairs. A wit needed, so the wits said, a woman who would give everything and ask nothing—for he could make no commitments, stand no obligations: 'Give us a mate,' said Wycherley, 'who nothing will ask us or tell us./ She stands on no terms. . . . But takes her kind man at a venture./ If all prove not right,/ Without an act, process or warning,/ From a wife for a night,/ You may be divorced in the morning.'[17]

3

To an exact perfection they have wrought,
The action, love; the passion is forgot.

—Rochester

The multiplicity of feminine voices in the wits' verses complaining of their behaviour seems to suggest that there was considerable female discontent with the state of affairs between the sexes. For women, the new sexual liberty, as it turned out, consisted primarily in the freedom to behave as cynically as the men; a woman who failed to understand the rules of the game and to play it to her advantage was likely to end in ruin. Casualties of the sexual ideology that the wits were celebrating in their verses as 'free love' were common.

The career of the actress Elizabeth Farley was not unusual. She first appeared on the stage at the opening of the theatres after the Restoration, in the season of 1660–61. Virginal, young, and reportedly very beautiful, she immediately caught the eye of the King, whose messenger summoned her to his bed chamber shortly thereafter. She held his fancy for a short time, and then he proceeded to other amorous interests—which were many. A few months later, Elizabeth Farley became the mistress of a lawyer of Gray's Inn, James Weaver, who kept her for almost a year. When his desire also began to wander, he threw her out of the house they had been living in together and requested the return of thirty pounds he had given her, for which he had (with what might be called cynical anticipation) previously extracted a written note from her. She was left entirely without resources, and to make matters worse, she was pregnant. Mrs. Farley continued to act with the King's Company as long as possible, but when the fact of her condition could no longer be disguised, she was forced to abandon her only source of income. As long as she was a 'servant of the King' (as all members of the King's Company were), she could not be arrested, but after her discharge from the theatre, debtor's prison threatened. In desperation, she applied to Charles (who had, after all, originally 'ruined' her). Thomas Killigrew, head of the King's Company, was ordered to reinstate her, but his collaborator, Sir Robert Howard, protested that 'women of quality' had promised to boycott the stage if such a woman were allowed on it in such a condition. Mrs. Farley weathered her disaster until her bastard was born and quietly took her place in the company again. The scandal had finished her reputation, however, and she was deeply in debt. An actress's salary was little enough to live on, much less to pay off debts. She had become too 'common' to attract another wealthy keeper. Hounded by debt and disgrace, she finally vanished into the slums of London when the theatres closed temporarily at the time of the Great Plague in 1665. Years later, Lord Buckhurst mentioned her in a bawdy verse letter to Sir George Etheredge—she had become a well-known prostitute. The market value of those ladies in the latter half of the seventeenth century, perhaps because of their rapid increase in number, was notoriously low, and the relatively few years of prosperity a young woman in that profession might have to trade on then gave way to a lifetime of poverty, disease, and abuse. A great many looked like old women before they were 35.

In James Wright's *Humours and Conversations of the Town* (1693), one woman warns another of the inevitable result of too easily trusting a wit or gallant in an affair of the heart. Once his object (seduction) has been attained, she says, he will find some excuse to break off with you or simply drop you without apology at all. The consequence of such an affair, in addition to a child, perhaps, 'is to be cast off by your relations, forced to prostitute yourself for a living, or marry some footman or soldier, follow the camp, and die in a hospital [a sort of dumping ground for the poor in the seventeenth century]; at best in an old tattered manto, carrying news about, from one acquaintance to another, for a meals-meat and a glass of wine. If there be anything delightful in the affair, 'tis but short, and full of fatigue, and attended with certain ruin of fortune and fame.'[18]

If the end for women of the Restoration game of love was inevitable, the time she could play it was short, only as long as her beauty lasted—'at twenty-five in women's eyes/ Beauty does fade, at thirty dies.'[19] Male attractiveness, on the other hand, went far beyond that age, and the libertines seduced girls at a progressively greater distance from their own age, while the young women who had been their contemporaries were discarded as no longer 'fresh'. This apparently was so widely and unquestioningly accepted that the wits even used it as a 'persuasion to enjoy' device in their poems, arguing that a woman ought to take full advantage of her brief moment of beauty, as all too soon she will no longer be desirable. She had to be careful, though, not to take *too* full advantage. Sexual experience reduced the value of a lady even as it served to make a gallant more charming. Too many love affairs inevitably branded her a whore.

The loosening of moral strictures that began in the 1660s had undoubtedly given women of a certain circle (that of fashionable London) a greater freedom of movement and possibility, but it had also split them off from the great majority of other women. The choice was limited: one could become a wife or a mistress. The fact that there was little possibility, financial or social, of a single woman's surviving on her own is supported by an interesting linguistic development that John Evelyn recorded in his diary for 1662—'Miss', which had previously simply indicated a young unmarried woman, came to mean a whore. The actress Roxolana had been taken away to become the Earl of Oxford's 'Miss', noted Evelyn, 'as at this time they began to call lewd women.'[20] Actresses and other women, whether married or not, had to begin to call themselves 'Mrs.' to avoid scandal.

Choosing to be a wife, despite the advantages of social respectability and financial security, usually meant lonely confinement in an isolated country estate for the better part of one's life; it was customary for Restoration gentlemen to leave their spouses safely out of the path of potential cuckolds and themselves free to do as they liked in libertine London, far from the jealous eyes of their wives. This practice became so common that it was even noted as an explanation by the early demographer John Graunt (1696) for the lower birth-rate in London than in the surrounding countryside.[21] The ideology that had come into fashion deemed wives hateful burdens and made them the butt of countless jokes, satires, and tirades. Only Presbyterian preachers superseded them as objects of ridicule.

Choosing to be a mistress, however, made one still more dependent, of course—unless one's 'keeper' could be outwitted by calculating tactic. In a world where men had grown accustomed to using women with ruthless egotism, the only way for a woman to survive was to behave even more cynically than her man.

Rochester, in 'A Letter from Artemesia in the Town to Chloë in the Country' (1679), gives, in the guise of a woman's voice, an account of the gossip of the town ('What loves have passed/ In this lewd town, since you and I met last') and describes the state of affairs between the sexes in London. Artemesia regrets the passing of 'that lost thing love' and blames it on feminine manipulation: 'Love, the most generous passion of the mind . . . is grown like play [gambling], to be an arrant trade/ The rooks creep in, and it has got of late/ As many little cheats and tricks as that./ But what yet more a woman's heart would vex,/ 'Tis chiefly carried on by our own sex. . . .' As illustration, she gives the story of Corinna, a young beauty who came to town and was courted, admired, loved and 'with presents fed' until she had the misfortune to fall in love with 'a man of wit, who found 'twas dull to love above a day;/ Made his ill-natured jest, and went away./ Now scorned by all, forsaken and oppressed,/ She's a *memento mori* to the rest;/ Diseased, decayed, to take up half a crown,/ Must mortgage her long scarf and manteau gown.' After six months' scrounging and skimping, Corinna collects the money to buy herself a new gown and sets out to turn the 'too dear-bought trick on men'. She finds a young heir just come up to town from the country and plies him with her charms. She sets up as his mistress, extracts a house (the deed in her own name), money, jewels and plate, and then poisons him before he begins to tire of her—having made sure that his will has been revised in her favour first.

A successful Corinna like Rochester's was not quite as common as he makes her out to be. His description of the circumstances that forced her into such behaviour, however, is substantiated by many other texts of the period. Marriage for money had quantified the relationship between men and women, devaluing it as well, and now 'free love' had become a 'trade'. The idea was current that any woman could be bought—it was only a question of price. An anonymous 'Song on London Ladies' published in a popular anthology of 1673 describes the phenomenon:

> A World 'tis of pleasure, one necklace or pearl,
> Will conjure the richest, or modestest girl.
> All trade is for gain, all commodities sold,
> Fear not; for thy coin thou mayst justly be bold.
> A pox on fine words; the contemplative fool
> Talks of love, and of shame; and oh! what misrule
> These keep in his heart. . . .
>
> Love is banished the world, and vertue is gone,
> To some private recess, to lament all alone;
> For now she grows barren, and none of her race
> Can be found either with, or without a good face;
> To the Mall, to the Park, to the Pit, to the Box;
> Where you will, you can't miss: there's meat for the cocks.[22]

In order to survive in such a world, women had to renounce love because it made them too vulnerable in a predatory sexual scheme where the law was to eat or be eaten.

4

> What is not a crime in men is scandalous and unpardonable in women. . . .
>
> —Mary Manley, 1696

The wits and libertines had announced the demise of feminine chastity and a fashionable following had ostensibly rejected traditional restrictions, but the influence of modesty had far from departed. It had, in a sense, gone underground. The libertine bent every effort to seduce a lady to his bed, but once she was there, he despised her for it. The expression of desire on the part of a woman still violated too many taboos— the woman who was kind (in both senses of the word) was sure to be rejected: 'My love she did retard, prevent,/ Giving too soon, her kind consent,' wrote Wycherley. A woman had to be distant in order to be attractive. 'The Forsaken Mistress' who speaks in Etheredge's poem of that name had understood too late the sexual politics behind the seduction she has given in to: 'Tell me, gently Strepthon, why,' she begs her lover, 'You from my embraces fly?/ Does my love thy love destroy?/ Tell me, I will yet be coy.' Whether it was fear of the emotional

61

commitment reciprocal love might involve or the threat that women would actively return desire rather than merely act as its passive instrument that motivated the wits, they generally took flight in the face of feminine response. Ismena, a young woman in Aphra Behn's *The Amorous Prince* (1671), remarks to a typical Restoration rake: '. . . as most gallants are, you're but pleased with what you have not; and love a mistress with great passion, 'till you find yourself beloved again, and then you hate her.'

A series of love lyrics exchanged between Rochester and his wife reveals a great deal about the sort of strategies this fact forced women to adopt. Rochester, in the first verses, pleads with his wife to be 'kind'. Her answer (still preserved in manuscript) reminds him that when she was kind, he only rejected, scorned, and abandoned her: 'I, to cherish your desire,/ Kindness used, but 'twas in vain./ You insulted in your slave;/ To be mine you soon refused. . . .' The only way to keep his love, she concludes, is to feign 'scorn and rigour'. Of course it might be argued that this phenomenon was by no means confined to Restoration sexuality but is universal. In that period, however, this mode of masculine perversity seems to have so marked relations between the sexes that contemporaries commented on it repeatedly.

Despite their profession of sexual liberty, the promiscuous gallants still more or less unconsciously held on to the very ideas about woman's modesty they had loudly repudiated. This double impulse put women in an impossible position. Aphra Behn, in a poem 'To Alexis, in answer to his Poem against Fruition', complained:

> Since Man with that inconstancy was born,
> To love the absent, and the present scorn,
> Why do we deck, why do we dress
> For such a short-liv'd happiness?
> Why do we put attraction on,
> Since either way 'tis we must be undone?
> They fly us if honour take our part,
> Our virtue drives 'em o'er the field.
> We lose 'em by too much desert,
> And Oh! they fly us if we yeild.
> Ye Gods! is there no charm in all the fair
> To fix this wild, this faithless wanderer?

Wycherley wrote of another lady who protested similarly in 'A Song sent to a Lady, who gave the subject for it, by complaining of the hard fate of Women; who, for refusing Love [i.e., sex], must be hated, yet for granting it, despised.' After listing all the lady's complaints, Wycherley twists them into an argument for sleeping with him—on the ground that she cannot win no matter what she does, so she may as well have the temporary satisfaction of sex. He does not say that he intends to treat her any differently from the other men she complains of.

The contradictory position that the demands of 'feminine modesty' had always put women in needed no external reinforcement from men, however, for whatever state of sexual freedom libertine ideology might proclaim, the 'fair sex' was still very much subject to them. Women of Aphra Behn's generation had been educated to modesty, and it remained a powerful force whether they chose to conform to its dictates or defy them. Countless remarks in letters, poetry, and drama suggest that it was rare for a woman to renounce entirely at least the appearance of feminine virtue—Wycherley's reference in a preface to one of his plays to that 'mask of modesty' all women 'promiscuously wear in public', is characteristic. This self-image was so deeply ingrained that often even women of notorious reputation made an attempt at pretence. If they acknowledged their own sexuality and acceded to it, they violated the essential element of what they had been brought up to believe was their femininity: virtue. On the other hand, if they held to honour, they sacrificed desire. Numerous poems written by the wits and libertines record this ambiguity on the part of their women—Wycherley's 'A Song to an incredulous dissident Mistress, who said, she was resolved to keep her reputation, in spite of her love', among them.

Since few seventeenth-century ladies discussed such matters in personal correspondence, it is difficult to document fully the feminine point of view, but what little survives testifies to the toll this conflict took on women. Aphra Behn wrote at the end of her life of the mind/body split that the feminine education of her age necessarily produced: '. . . 'tis the humour of our sex to deny most eagerly those grants to lovers, for which most tenderly we sigh, so contradictory are we to ourselves, as if the deity that made us with a seeming reluctancy to his own designs; placing as much discord in our minds, as there is harmony in our faces. We are a sort of airy clouds, whose lightning flash out one way, and the thunder another. Our words and thoughts can ne'er agree.'

Aphra Behn was not alone in her perception of the underlying structure of women's experience. About the time she wrote these lines, her fellow poetess, the anonymous author of *Sylvia's Complaint of her Sex's Unhappiness* (1688) wrote of the very same impulse:

> Hence 'tis, our thoughts like tinder apt to fire,
> Are often caught with loving kind desire;
> But *custom* does such rigid laws impose,
> We must not for our lives the thing disclose.
> If one of us a lovely youth has seen,
> And straight some tender thoughts to feel begin;
> Which liking does insensibly improve
> Itself to longing fond impatient love,
> The damsel in distress must still remain,
> Tortured and wracked with the tormenting pain:
> *Custom* and *modesty*, much more severe
> Strictly forbid our passion to declare.
> If we reveal, then decency's provoked,
> If kept, then we are with the secret choked.[23]

The scarcity of evidence itself argues that it was modesty, not passion, that emerged dominant in the struggle; if it did not always actually prevent women from indulging their desires, it at least kept them from talking about them. The one poem published by a woman under her own name—other than Aphra Behn herself—in Mrs. Behn's *Miscellany* of 1685 is by an otherwise unidentified Mrs. Taylor, whose contribution begins thus: 'Ye virgin powers, defend my heart/ From amorous looks and smiles. . . .' She leaves little doubt that virtue has not been compromised in her case and advises recourse to honour in circumstance of temptation: '. . . if through passion I grow blind/ Let honour be my guide. . . .'[24]

By 1696, when 'anon.' (female) was writing her *Essay in Defense of the Female Sex*, the bawdy Restoration had passed, and her statement on the subject reflects less conflict than resignation: 'Modesty and the rules of decency observed among us, not permitting to us the liberty of declaring our sentiments to those we love, as men may; we dare not indulge a wanton fancy or ramblin inclination, which must be stifled in our own breasts, and could only give us a hopeless anxiety. . . .'[25]

Sex in the seventeenth century, given the feminine education of that era, had in recent memory at least always involved a ritual of contradiction between instinct and education; it was part of the way love was carried on. But the new sexual modality of the 1660s had called the traditional structure into question while at the same time tacitly acting on many of its assumptions. The multiplication of conflicts that this engendered added to the real loss of material and emotional security for women and unleashed a war between the sexes that was to be so closely associated with the ethos of the age that it is remembered as one of its most central characteristics. In Restoration drama, a standard scenario of sexual battle is played out over and over again: the roving gallant attempts to seduce a young lady, or even several young ladies, without committing himself in any way, while the heroine usually witholds her favours and tries to hold his interest through a series of false promises, disguises, teasings, and other devices, wearing him down to a promise of either constancy or marriage itself before she takes the risk of sleeping with him. There are, of course, variations on the theme and varying degrees of self-consciousness in the action, differing terms on which the women are willing to concede, and more or less cynicism on the part of either the lover or the mistress. The struggle may be light-hearted or intense, but it is inevitably present—the Restoration war between the sexes made it unavoidable.

In addition to unleashing a war between the sexes, the sexual 'liberation' of the 1660s and 1670s seems to have set off a series of reactions which ultimately amounted to a counteraction of the original impulse: there was a considerable growth of misogyny, principally directed at those women who had imitated their male partners in their sexual voraciousness. Finally, there is evidence of an increasing disgust with the sexual act itself among the wits and libertines who had initiated the vogue for bawdy. In a sense, the rovers had been alienated by their own promiscuity: 'enjoyment dulled the appetite', as Wycherley put it.

The wits had urged their women to cast off old-fashioned coyness, but when they did, the emancipated rakes proved to be among the most threatened. The expression of desire—to say nothing of its realization—evoked disgust. It is apparent in the language itself. 'When your lewd cunt came spewing home/ Drenched with the seed of half the town,/ My dram of spérm was supped up after/ For the digestive surfeit water', wrote Rochester, railing at his promiscuous mistress. Her crimes were no more than his, but in a woman they were intolerable. He swears to 'plague this woman and undo her'. His revenge, he says, will be saved for when she is married; then he will 'pelt her with truth or lies/ And her poor cur [husband] with jealousies/ 'Till I have torn him from her breech [female sexual parts]/ While she whines like a dog-drawn bitch;/ Loathed and despised, kicked out o' the town/ Into some dirty hold alone,/ To chew her cud of misery/ And know she owes it all to me./ And may no woman better thrive,/ That dares prophane the cunt I swive.'[26]

Feminine promiscuity, even if it were nothing other than a mirror image of masculine behaviour, was intolerable. The wits wrote vicious satires cataloguing the sins of women who had a reputation for lust—including the King's mistresses. The anonymous author of 'A Faithful Catalogue of Our Most Eminent Ninnies' called the royal mistresses 'a brace of cherubs, of as vile a breed,/ As ever were produced of human seed'.[27] Nell Gwyn was called, among other epithets, the 'countess of the cockpit', and Louise de Kerouaille, Duchess of Portsmouth, 'the incestuous punk'. Countless satires vilipending the Countess of Castlemaine were passed around or even published, their subject inevitably on this order: 'When she had jaded quite/ Her almost boundless appetite/ Cloyed with the choicest banquets of delight/ She'll still drudge on in tasteless vice/ As if she sinned for exercise/ Disabling stoutest stallions every hour,/ And when they can perform no more/ She'll rail at 'em and kick 'em out of door.'[28] The wits had cheerfully promised their mistresses that they would do no less, but they did not like to have the tables turned.

The physical repulsion that feminine sexuality inspired in the male poets of Aphra Behn's generation is underlined repeatedly in the way they write about women. Charles Sackville, Earl of Dorset, wrote a mocking poem on Katherine Sedley, mistress of James II and daughter of his friend Sir Charles Sedley, deriding her efforts to disguise incipient wrinkles, 'the approaches of decay', with 'embroidery, fringe, and lace'. He taunts her: 'Wilt thou sparkle in the box,/ Still ogle in the ring?/ . . . So have I seen in larder dark,/ Of veal a lucid loin;/ Replete with many a brilliant spark,/ As wise philosophers remark,/ At once both stink and shine.'[29] Aphra Behn had at about the same time written a poem congratulating Dorset on his marriage to a woman twenty years younger than himself; Katherine Sedley was a little over 30.

The possibility that women might have sexual desires that were independent of their role as passive receptacle of male desire obsessed the wits. Frequent references to feminine masturbation and to the use of dildos testify to this preoccupation. Robert Gould, in *Love Given O'er* (1682), scourges the women of his age and tells how 'when into their closets they retire,/ Where flaming dildoes does inflame desire/ And gentle lapdogs/ To whom they are more kind and free/ Than they themselves to their own husbands be./ How curst is man/ When brutes his rivals prove/ Even in the sacred business of love.'[30] As the author of 'Our Most Eminent Ninnies' warns: 'Let no such harlots lead your steps astray./ Her clitoris will mount in open day. . . .' Is it possible, he questions philosophically, that 'man be plagued with a severer curse?'

Hardly, said the Earl of Rochester. In his characteristic role of spokesman for his age, he summed up the view that the gallants and wits of fashionable circles had come to have of women:

> Love a woman? You're an ass!
>   'Tis a most insipid passion
> To choose out for your happiness
>   The silliest part of God's creation.

> Let the porter and the groom,
>   Things designed for dirty slaves,
> Drudge in fair Aurelia's womb
>   To get supplies for age and graves.

Farewell, woman! I intend
  Henceforth every night to sit
With my lewd, well-natured friend,
  Drinking to engender wit.

Then give me health, wealth, mirth, and wine,
  And if busy love entrenches,
There's a sweet soft page of mine
  Does the trick worth forty wenches.

NOTES

1. Roger North, *Lives of the Norths* (London, 1826), vol. 2, p. 164.
2. The assumption, says Peter Laslett, 'that illegitimacy figures directly reflect the prevalence of sexual intercourse outside marriage, which seems to be made whenever such figures are used to suggest that beliefs, attitudes and interests have changed in some particular way, can be shown to be very shaky in its foundations' (*Family Life and Illicit Love in Earlier Generations*, [Cambridge, 1977]), p. 106.
3. John Wilmot, Earl of Rochester, *Complete Poems*, ed. David Vieth (New Haven, 1968), pp. 40–1. The date of this poem is uncertain, but evidence indicates that it was written sometime not long before March, 1673. All further quotes from Rochester's poems are from this edition.
4. George Etheredge, *Poems*, ed. J. Thorpe (Princeton, 1963), p. 42. All further quotes from Etheredge's poems are from this edition.
5. Sir Francis Fane, *Love in the Dark* (London, 1675), p. 77.
6. John Crowne, *The Country Wit* (London, 1675), p. 8.
7. Gilbert Burnet, *History of My Own Times* (London, 1883), p. 61.
8. Aphra Behn, *Works*, ed. Montague Summers (London, 1913). All further quotes from Aphra Behn's works are from this edition unless otherwise noted.
9. Julia Cartwright, *Madame: A Life of Henrietta, daughter of Charles I and Duchess of Orleans* (London, 1900), p. 153.
10. George Etheredge, *The Comical Revenge; or Love in a Tub* (London, 1664, repr. 1667), p. 24.
11. William Wycherley, *Works*, ed. Montague Summers (London, 1924), vol. 4, p. 237. All further quotes from Wycherley's plays or poems are from this edition.
12. *Character of a Town Gallant* (London, 1675), p. 2.
13. *Chorus Poetarum* (London, 1694), p. 23.
14. John Dryden, *Dramatic Works*, ed. Montague Summers (London, 1931–32), vol. 2, pp. 14–15.
15. Sir Charles Sedley, *Works*, ed. V. de Sola Pinto (London, 1928), vol. I, p. 6.

16. Charles Cotton, *Selected Poems*, ed. Gregory Grigson (London, 1975), pp. 88–9.
17. From Wycherley's *Love in a Wood*, produced in 1671.
18. Janes Wright, *Humours and Conversations of the Town* (London, 1693), p. 136.
19. *A New Collection of Poems* (London, 1674), p. 76.
20. John Evelyn, *Diary*, ed. E. S. de Beer (Oxford, 1959), p. 433, January, 1662.
21. John Graunt, *Natural and Political Observations on the Bills of Mortality* (London, 1662), p. 62.
22. *A Collection of Poems by Several Persons* (London, 1673), pp. 178–79.
23. *Sylvia's Complaint of her Sex's Unhappiness* (London, 1688), p. 12.
24. Aphra Behn, *Miscellany* (London, 1685), pp. 69–70.
25. *An Essay in Defense of the Female Sex* (London, 1696, repr. 1721), p. 118.
26. There was a tradition going back to the Middle Ages of anti-feminist tracts written to demonstrate women's carnal nature and warn un-suspecting male victims of their instability, but this vituperation came from moralists for the most part. What the wits and libertines were writing had a very different source, tone, and vocabulary.
27. *Poems on Affairs of State*, ed. George de F. Lord (New Haven, 1963–76), vol. 4, p. 194.
28. British Museum, Harleian Ms. 6913, fol. 36b.
29. Charles Sackville, Earl of Dorset, in *The Works of the Most Celebrated Minor Poets* (London, 1749), p. 131.
30. Robert Gould, *Love Given O'er; A Satyr Against Women* (London, 1682), p. 5.

Extracts from *Reconstructing Aphra: A Social Biography of Aphra Behn* by Angeline Goreau (1980) are reprinted by kind permission of the Oxford University Press, Oxford.

3

The Secret Nexus: Sex and Literature in Eighteenth-century Britain

by PAUL-GABRIEL BOUCÉ

If the public life of eighteenth-century Britain is a field well covered by swarms of scholars, the same can hardly be said of the people's private life, which, especially in the case of the lower classes, is very sparsely documented, as Lawrence Stone makes abundantly clear in his pioneering study of such matters, *The Family, Sex and Marriage in England 1500–1800*.[1] On the contrary, in our so-called 'permissive' society, it is but a commonplace observation to remark that one cannot open either a popular magazine nowadays, or a scholarly journal,[2] not to mention the daily newspapers, without finding there articles or references to sex and its manifold implications. There are even national or international conferences of sexology. This is what Michel Foucault, in a most apt phrase, calls 'le grand prêche sexuel'[3]—'the great sexual preaching'. In spite of the thick blanket of modest silence which has endeavoured to muffle, if not stifle, sexuality in past centuries, Foucault puts forward the most provocative idea that sexual repression in the last three centuries simply did not exist, but that, on the contrary, ever since the early seventeenth century, our Western civilization has been marked by 'une véritable explosion discursive',[4] 'une fermentation discursive qui s'est accélérée depuis le dix-huitième siècle'.[5] In Foucault's view, sex is omnipresent as a patent or a latent discourse, whether in the Roman Catholic confession-box, or in the dormitories of English public schools, not to mention universities, big cities or small villages. Foucault's at first startling contention is that this immense preoccupation with sex, even in times of overt repression such as those of seventeenth-century Puritanism, or Victorianism, was in fact required and organized by society itself, for political, economic and technical reasons.

After such abstract speculations, it is somewhat of a relief to return to Lawrence Stone's book with its solid basis of historical documentation. Stone sees in what he calls 'Affective Individualism', 'perhaps the most important change in *mentalité* to have occurred in the Early Modern period, indeed possibly in the last thousand years of Western history.'[6] The rise of 'Affective Individualism' is connected with the progressive emergence of 'the Closed Domesticated Nuclear Family'[7] in the late seventeenth century and its predominance in the eighteenth. The keystone of this new type of family was more personal autonomy and greater privacy within the home. One of the sociological, but also ethical, corollaries of the rise of 'Affective Individualism' was, against the declining, but at times still strong, currents of Christian restraint, a glorification of sensuality and sexual activities, or, as Stone puts it 'Freedom of sexual expression was one of the many by-products of the eighteenth-century pursuit of happiness.'[8] This release of long-repressed libido could assume very modern forms, as, for example, the advertisements in respectable London newspapers in the late eighteenth century quite openly 'soliciting female friendships'.[9] A far less familiar instance in our days of oral contraceptives and planned parenthood would be the procreative record of the well-named Augustus the Strong, Elector of Saxony and King of Poland, who could boast 354 *acknowledged* bastards![10]

The object of this essay will be to venture, away from the well-trodden literary tracks, into the thick scrub and undergrowth of what might be called 'subculture',[11] and more precisely 'subliterature' and 'paraliterature', *subliterature* covering miscellaneous productions of little or no literary value, whereas *paraliterature* will be used to designate scientific, or pseudo-scientific, works with no avowed literary aim. It is hoped thus to assess, at least tentatively, what some of the prevailing attitudes towards sex in mid-eighteenth-century Britain were. Pope's Belinda, Richardson's Pamela and Clarissa, Fielding's chaste but much assaulted heroines Fanny, Sophia, and Amelia, although at one point or another of their glorious literary careers faced with the ugly realities of violent sex, tell us little directly about the *mentalité* of their times. My contention is this: if we do more research into such fields, usually little familiar to the literary scholar, as medical lore, with its stringent advice and interdicts, or into the ill-famed purlieus of erotic or pornographic subliterature, much valuable knowledge will thus be gained, which will shed new and revealing light on the above-mentioned heroines. Fictional heroes should certainly be included too, such as Fielding's Joseph Andrews and Tom Jones, Smollett's Roderick Random and Peregrine Pickle, Richardson's Lovelace, Sterne's Yorick, since their amorous adventures—or non-adventures—lie at the core of the several novels. It is obvious that many dangers beset the explorer as he reads his weary way through a tangled jungle of sub- or para-literary material such as contemporaneous medical handbooks or tiresomely repetitive erotica. To what extent, for instance, were such works actually known, read, and the medical advice of the manuals duly regarded? This is well-nigh impossible to assess with a degree of certainty, except through usually faint contemporary echoes, and the number of successive editions as a possibly misleading token of their popularity. What sort of a readership was there for erotic or pornographic subliterature? What was readily available in mid-eighteenth-century London, would probably be much more difficult to get hold of in the provinces. Some may well object that the study of such material bears little, if any, relevance to major literary works. To which I would reply that the dividing line between 'major' and 'minor' works is a largely artificial product of critical hindsight. No 'great' literature can exist 'in vacuo', but must be rooted in the rich socio-cultural subsoil of the times, exactly as a plant of the most exquisite beauty and vigour thrives on a bed of leaf-mould or compost.

First, some considerations on the *medical* knowledge of sexuality in the eighteenth century will illuminate our ancestors' current attitudes to female virginity, impregnation and pregnancy, and lastly barrenness.

By *sexuality*, female sexuality mostly is meant here, for the simple, but inescapable reason that practically all the books, manuals, treatises, pamphlets devoted to the subject were the productions of male doctors, more concerned with the mysteriously intricate workings of their female partners' sexuality than with their own (apparently) less recondite sexual physiology and impulses.

As a representative example of medical knowledge in the mid-eighteenth century, Dr. Robert James's *A Medicinal Dictionary* in three folio volumes, published in 1743–45 in London is convenient enough. Dr. Robert James (1705–76) was no obscure quack, but an old school-fellow of Johnson's at Lichfield, and his lifelong friend. Fielding also referred to Dr. James in his first edition of *Amelia* (1751) as his 'worthy ingenious Friend [who] would in almost any country but this, have received public Honours and Rewards', a flattering reference subsequently expunged from the novel. Johnson helped Dr. James to write the *Proposals* for his *Dictionary* in 1741, and actually wrote the 'Dedication' to Dr. Richard Mead. There are about half a dozen more or less complimentary allusions to Dr. James made by Johnson and reported in Boswell's *Life*. Dr. James remains famous for his widely used fever powder and pill for which he took out a patent in 1746, the composition remaining a jealously guarded secret until his death in 1776. Poor Oliver Goldsmith is said to have died of an overdose of Dr. James's powder, which probably did little more than aggravate his condition. Dr. James's *Dictionary* is over five million words long, the preface alone running to some 130,000 words; it was translated into French by Diderot and others in 1746–48. The judgement of the *D.N.B.* on Dr. James's *Medicinal Dictionary* is sound enough: 'The articles are well written and contain much information compiled from books, but very little original information.' Thus, Dr. James's *Dictionary* may safely be assumed to reflect current mid-eighteenth-century medical opinion, with perhaps already at the time of its publication in 1743–45 a slight tendency towards obsolescence, the inevitable fate anyhow of all dictionaries as soon as they are published.

A very moot and much controverted issue in eighteenth-century medicine was the existence or absence of the hymen. Virginity then was not only invested with a socio-religious and ethical value, but in the property-minded world of eighteenth-century Europe appeared as the much-prized hallmark of chastity, enforced for reasons of genealogical purity. As Samuel Johnson, often the guardian of conservative morals, once remarked to Boswell: 'Consider of what importance to society the chastity of women is. Upon that all the property in the world depends. We hang a thief for stealing a sheep; but the un-chastity of a woman transfers sheep, and farm and all, from the right owner.'[12] The 'virgo intacta' was thus the frail, but indispensable, rampart against the misappropriation of estates and capital. After giving an anatomical description of the elusive membrane Dr. James indulges in one of his rare personal comments: 'With respect to the Hymen, upon which the *Jewish* Test of Virginity depends, it must be remark'd, that this Membrane is frequently not to be found in Girls a Month old, and very seldom in those of a more advanced Age. This I thought myself obliged to take notice of, because I have, some-times, known Families render'd unhappy by a Disappointment, as to some unreasonable and ill-grounded Expectations, which, however it may happen in *Judea*, and the warmer Climates, ought to raise no Suspicions of Incontinence in ours' (s.v. 'Hymen'). Such was the price set on virginity—which sheds much socio-cultural light on the Richardsonian struggles of poor Pamela with Mr. B., and of the vanquished Clarissa with Lovelace—that recipes, or prescriptions, were quite current in eighteenth-century manuals, describing the sly but not un-necessary art of 'repairing' damaged maidenheads. A good poetic instance is to be found in Dr. John Armstrong's *The Oeconomy of Love* (London, 1736), where the deflowered girl:

> . .'. with painful hand collects
> The sylvan store. The lover *Myrtle* yields
> Her Styptick Berries, and the horrid *Thorn*
> Its Prune austere; in vain the *Caper* hides
> Its wand'ring Roots; the mighty *Oak* himself,
> Sole Tyrant of the Shade, that long had 'scaped

The Tanner's rage, spoil'd of his callous Rhind,
Stands bleak and bare. These, and a thousand more,
Of humbler Growth and far inferior Name,
Bistort, and *Dock*, and that way-faring Herb
Plantain, her various Forage, boil'd in Wine
Yield their astringent force, a Lotion prov'd
Thrice powerful to contract the shameful Breach.

(ll. 221–33)

A commercial corollary of the virginity-cult was that maiden-heads being a rare commodity were to be sold at a high price by wise old bawds offering second-hand patched up 'virgines intactas' to lecherous but unsuspecting gentlemen, as is illustrated in Smollett's *Roderick Random* (Chap. XXII) where the not-so-innocent Miss Williams's already shattered hymen is sold for one hundred guineas to a foolish judge. The trick, with rather more gory technical details, is also practised in Cleland's *Memoirs of a Woman of Pleasure*.

Impregnation and pregnancy, in a century haunted by the antithetic and at times overlapping dreads of over-population and de-population, naturally receive careful and detailed attention in such medical manuals as *The Ladies Dispensatory, or, Every Woman her Own Physician* (London, 2nd ed., 1740),[13] and in Dr. James's *Dictionary*. In spite of the Dutch scientist Leeuwenhoek's microscopic examination of spermatozoa in the mid 1670s, and of his animalculist theory, whereby he postulated that the spermatozoa actually penetrated the egg, a process he was technically unable to observe, both the unknown author of *The Ladies Dispensatory* and Dr. James cling, with unscientific nostalgia, to the outdated effluvium theory, which had prevailed for many years, whereby fertilization resulted from vapours arising out of the seminal fluid.[14] The author of *The Ladies Dispensatory* declares he is aware of the 'universal modern Observation' concerning the 'Animalcula' or 'Homunculi' (p. 177) in male seed; he even refers to the process of the fertilization of the ovum, but raises what he considers a devastating objection, viz. the biological problem of cross-breeding. Dr. James's objections to the well-known observations of the Italian scientist Francesco Redi (1626–97 or 98), and those of Leeuwenhoek are more of a theological than a physiological nature. He declares himself, at the end of the article entitled 'Generatio', dissatisfied with all the current theories of reproduction, and he accuses Leeuwenhoek and his followers of having 'deduc'd a new system of Generation, as it should seem, utterly romantic, and inconsistent with the Conduct of Providence, observable in all natural Productions', a way of thinking that neither Pope nor Fielding, with their confidence in an all-powerful and benevolent Providence, would have rejected. Dr. James believes in a well-ordered— and all-ordering—thrifty Providence, as a sort of 'primum mobile' in the 'Great Chain of Being', tolerating no waste of those millions of animalcules: 'Besides, we must suppose, that Providence aims very ill, if obliged to load her Engine so enormously, in order to be able to hit the Mark propos'd.' A striking metaphor, hallmarked by physicotheology, but scientifically, a woefully inaccurate one!

A certain sign of conception for the anonymous author—'a Physician'—of *A Rational Account of the Natural Weaknesses of Women*[15] is post-coital orgasmic pleasure, described in purely mechanistic terms, as though the penny had dropped: 'The falling of one of the little Eggs from its [*sic*] Cell in the Ovaria, through one of the Womb Trumpets, into the Womb, often occasions an uncommon Sensation and gentle shivering of the Body after the Conjugal Act, which is therefore a Sign of Conception.'[16] As Stone has noted, it was a commonly held belief in the seventeenth century that 'female sexual pleasure was needed in order to open the mouth of the womb to receive the male sperm.'[17] If, as Stone asserts, one of the consequences of the 'Rise of Affective Individualism' was the greater—and better—care given to infants and children, his theory may be buttressed by the importance of the additional material to be found in the eighth edition of *The Ladies Physical Directory* (London, 1742) when compared with the same author's 1716 *A Rational Account*. To the eight chapters of *A Rational Account* are annexed two new chapters directly relevant to pregnancy and child-rearing.

Equally interesting in *A Rational Account* are the chapters dealing with barrenness (Chap. VII) and with male infertility and impotency (Chap. II of the *Practical Discourse* annexed to *The Ladies Physical Directory*). Obviously, the author is much concerned with the fecundity of his female readers, and barrenness appears as a sort of implicit curse: 'As being the Mother of Children is the highest Honour, and most exalted State of Satisfaction, that the Fair Sex can attain to in a married life; so on the contrary Barrenness, of all other Misfortunes is by much the greatest, producing the most severe Affliction that can attend a Family, and causing the deepest secret Grief in a Woman that is possible to be imagined. . . .'[18] It would certainly not be amiss to bear in mind such widely held beliefs when coming across the apparent fictive cliché which closes so many eighteenth-century novels (and later ones as well): 'They married, had many children, and were happy ever after.' Our highly aseptic and ruthlessly contraceptive times can easily make fun of such stereotyped endings. But if the critic is aware of the vital nexus linking subculture and 'great' literature he will realize that in times of poor obstetric and gynaecological care, to conceive a child, give birth to it and bring it up was no easily dismissed cliché but a tough and hazardous struggle in which countless mothers and infants lost their lives. Thus, to give but one example, the last sentence of *Roderick Random* (1748) is typical of both the *mentalité* of the age and of its fiction. Roderick, somewhat smugly, rejoices that his 'dear angel [Narcissa] has been qualmish of late, and begins to grow remarkably round in the waist; so that I cannot leave her in such an interesting situation, which I hope will produce something to crown my felicity.' It is highly significant that the last word of the novel should be 'felicity': Roderick, in spite of a nasty brush with venereal disease during his pre-marital amours, has proved fertile, and so has his beloved and beautiful Narcissa. As Smollett also writes on the last page of his first novel, Fortune indeed and at last 'seems determined to make ample amends for her former cruelty'.

No reader therefore should be surprised to find, both in *A Rational Account* and *The Ladies Physical Directory*, prescriptions—which rather read like elaborate recipes—for remedies to either male or female infertility, such as the 'Prolifick Elixir', the 'Powerful Confect', or the 'Stimulating Balm'. The commercial purpose of both manuals is patent enough as the following advertisement, appearing in both books, makes quite clear: 'All the Medicines mentioned and prescribed in this

Book, are Sold only by the Gentlewoman at the TWO BLUE POSTS, near the Square in HAYDON YARD, in the MINORIES, LONDON.' On the last page of both editions the price list appears remarkably stable over a period covering a quarter of a century (1716–42): five shillings for the 'Hysterick Julep' (to dispel catamenial pains); three shillings and sixpence for 'Uterine Drops', and five shillings for the well-named 'Powerful Confect', the composition of which oddly reads like a magic incantation to the Goddess of Fertility: 'Take of the best treble-refin'd Loaf-Sugar, six Ounces; the best Damask Rose Water, four Ounces; Juice of Kermes, Berries, twelve Ounces; boil them to the Consistence of a thick Syrup, and then add of the choicest MALAGA Wine, three Ounces and half; Syrup of candied Ginger, fifteen Ounces; mix them well together, and then stir in the following ingredients, first reduced into fine Powders and Pulps, as they severally require, viz. Mace, Nutmegs, Cardamons, Seeds of Nettles, Grains of Paradise, of each a Dram. Benjamin, long and black Pepper, Galangals [i.e. *galingale*, the aromatic root of certain East Indian plants formerly widely used in medicine and cookery], Cloves, Seeds of Ash, of each a Dram and an half; fine ENGLISH Saffron, two Drams; Xyloales [wood of aloes], two Drams and a half; Cinnamon, three Drams and an half; candied Ginger, Eringo candied, Pulp of Dates, Pine and Pistach Nuts, sweet Almonds, of each half an Ounce; Satyrion Root, fresh gathered, two Ounces; Musk, a Scruple; Ambergrease (dissolv'd in some Drops of Oil of Cinnamon) two Scruples. Incorporate all very well together according to Art, and then add, of Powers [i.e. the active principles?] of Vipers, an Ounce; of my stimulating Essence, half an Ounce; and make a Confect according to Art, which may be kept in Pots of about three Ounces each.'[19] One may well wonder how efficient such 'aids to venery'—as they were then technically known—may have proved: probably no more nor less so than the much publicized and more chemically noxious 'rejuvenators' currently sold in our sex-shops.

One last look at Dr. James's *Dictionary*, under the heading 'Venery' will be enough to show that the Augustans took their sex-lives seriously, like good thrifty Britons who abhorred any wanton waste of the most precious of all life-moistures, viz. sperm. The 'Venery' article, although fairly short—half a

folio-column long—reveals Dr. James's very cautious, com-
monsensical, attitude towards sex, with always at the back of
the good doctor's mind the notion that sexual activities necessarily imply an expenditure of vital energy, which might be
more wisely saved up against times of great physical need,
especially illness. Dr. James's ambivalent, and hence ambiguous, attitude may be perceived in his definition of 'venery' as:
'an Action which may either promote or destroy Health,
according as it is regulated: For it is certain, from Experience,
that too great a Retention of the Semen induces a Torpor and
languid State of the Body, and often lays a Foundation for
terrible nervous Disorders. And whereas the Semen is, as it
were, the Flower and choicest Part of the Blood, and nervous
Fluid, so Venery ought to be only moderately used, lest too
great an Evacuation of this Substance should prove prejudicial
to Health.' People who are too weak, too old, too young, or
convalescent are advised to abstain, as well as . . . scholars:
'Nor should Persons indulge themselves in Venery after strong
Application of Mind, or long Watchings; because these Things
have a Tendency to weaken the Body.' Finally, sexual intercourse should take place preferably in spring, whereas winter
and summer are considered—in the article 'Ver' (spring)—
'more dangerous; but the most dangerous of all the four, by
many Degrees, is the Autumn.' Ever since the Roman medical
compiler Celsus (c. A.D. 25) abstinence from sexual intercourse
in summer had been deemed highly desirable because at that
time of the year it was only too likely 'to throw the Humours
into too violent Commotions'. No 'Sun, Sand and Sex' then for
our supposedly vital energy-saving eighteenth-century fore-
bears. One last remark: sperm is not only to be treasured and
'spent'—the sexual denotation of the verb *spend* is symbolic
enough—sparingly as a precious life-giving liquor, but it is
reckoned by Dr. James and his contemporaries as a sort of
miraculous balm capable of curing most female disorders.
Sperm appears as the great gynaecological and psychosomatic
healer, a belief widely reflected in eighteenth-century European literature—marriage as a miracle cure for chlorosis and
generally poor health in females—: 'It is, also, certain from
Experience, that Venery both alleviates and removes various
Disorders incident to Women: for the male Semen, consisting

of a fine elastic Lymph, rarefies and expands not only the Eggs, but, also, the Blood and Juices in the Vessels of the Uterus, the Fibres of which it likewise strengthens. Hence the Reason is obvious, why Venery, or Coition, cures Women, rendered cachetic by a Suppression of the Menses, and generally restores that salutary Evacuation.' A fairly cheap, and readily available remedy!

Although the limited scope of this essay precludes any exhaustive study of so vast a topic as sex and literature in eighteenth-century Britain, it would be decidedly inappropriate to conclude this rapid exploration without even a brief glance at a few aspects of erotic and pornographic subliterature. Such great 'classics' as John Cleland's *Memoirs of a Woman of Pleasure* (1749), better and internationally known as *Fanny Hill*, will not be examined here, as they have already received plenty of critical and scholarly attention, as, for instance, Sade's works in France. Why then should erotic or pornographic subliterature be examined, even briefly? Although much of it is intolerably dreary—such works seem to obey the mechanical theorems of what I would be tempted to call 'invariable geometry'—and makes for dull reading, the spread of native erotic literature and prints by mid-eighteenth century is a somewhat distorted, but nonetheless significant, indication that a new sensibility was spreading fast, and as such cannot be dismissed as an irrelevant phenomenon.

Roland Barthes's definition of eroticism, in his *Sade Fourier Loyola* has the merit of stressing the essential allusiveness of eroticism, as opposed to the grossly overt explicitness of pornography. For Barthes, eroticism is 'nothing but a kind of speech, since the practices can only be codified if they are known, that is to say, spoken out; but our society never enunciates any erotic practice, only desires, preambles, contexts, suggestions, ambiguous sublimations, so that for us eroticism can be defined but by a kind of perpetually allusive speech.'[20] It is interesting to compare Barthes's tentative definition with Peter Hughes's concept of 'erotic heroism' in eighteenth-century literature, which he views as the 'constant pushing of the sexual and amorous beyond itself into the language of power, of masters and victims, of self-consciousness that turns into the sacrifice and even the destruction of self',[21] a notion fairly close to Georges Bataille's as expressed in *La Littérature et le Mal* (Paris, 1957). What is latent in Barthes's definition—the all pervasive power of the word in society—is forcefully brought out by Peter Hughes who behind the time-hallowed analogy of love and war in such vastly different works as Pope's *The Rape of the Lock* (1712–14) and Richardson's *Pamela* (1740) detects the harsh realities of an invidious class-struggle.

Captain Samuel Cock's *A Voyage to Lethe* (1741) is a sustained erotic maritime allegory, teeming with more or less allusive double entendres and heavy sexual innuendoes. It relies throughout on wearisomely onomastic punning, Samuel's father being '*Sampson Cock* of *Coney-Hatch*' and his mother a member of the 'Laycock family, settled at *Cunnington* in *Huntingdonshire*',[22] after which cocky pedigree, the author valiantly indulges in a piece of topo-eroticism, when he describes his manor, unavoidably called 'Allcock', which is 'most singularly curious for its Shape, and situate withal in a very pleasant and fertile Part of the Country, being a long Neck of Land, shaded by a Grove of Trees, and supported by a couple of Hills, impregnated according to the Virtuosi, with a white sort of Metal, which being liquify'd, is deem'd an excellent Restorative. Its Figure towards the End is in the Form of a large Nut; and there is an Aqueduct thro' it, that terminates in a *jette d'Eau*, as often as it is properly supply'd with Water' (p. 8). The same technique had been used by Thomas Stretzer (or *Stretser*) one of Curll's hacks, who produced that often reprinted classic of the second row, *A New Description of Merryland* (1740), quickly followed in 1741 by a mock-indignant counter-blast, entitled *Merryland Displayed: Or, Plagiarism, Ignorance, and Impudence, Detected*, written by Stretzer himself at Curll's request in order to fan commercial interest in the *New Description*.[23] Obviously, the link there between erotic subculture and literature—of a rather low degree, but highly popular, as these pamphlets went through many editions—is decidedly commercial, a phenomenon not unknown in our times either. . . . Thus, in *A New Description of Merryland*, what the French call 'Terre Gaillarde' is 'situate in a *low* Part of the Continent, bounded on the upper Side, or to the Northward by the little Mountain called MNSVNRS, on the East and West by COXASIN and COXADEXT, and on the South or lower Part it lies open to the TERRA FIRMA.'[24] The use of judicious abbreviations was meant less to puzzle the readers than to protect the author against any accusation of obscenity, the shortest way to gaol, the pillory and a swinging fine.

It is interesting to notice how the erotico-nautical metaphor takes over for practically the rest of the eighty-four pages of *A Voyage to Lethe*. This is how Captain Cock's ultimate preparations of his ship, the *Charming Sally*, are described before launching on the matrimonial waters: 'The Main-Mast being a Long-side, we strove to heave it in, but found much difficulty; indeed I thought once I should never have got it righted in her, being somewhat of the largest; but by greasing and working it to and fro, the third Day it went tolerably plumb into the Socket. I work'd Night and Day upon the rest of her Rigging . . .' (p. 13). The only slight merit of this erotico-nautical metaphorical voyage is that the author, like John Cleland in *Fanny Hill*, never uses any coarse four-letter words, apart from the ubiquitous *cock*. This is no more than sustained, somewhat heavy-handed at times, schoolboyish badinage, yet, it remains interesting on two accounts. First, for its very moral and genuinely shocked rejection of such 'vices' as masturbation or homosexuality, a characteristic certainly not to be found in Sade's deliberately amoral writings some decades later. Second, for the devious light it sheds on the supposedly repressed sense of sexual fun since Puritanism had swept over England in the second half of the seventeenth century, which subsisted in deep recesses of the national psyche in spite of the liberating explosion of the Restoration. The arch sexual allusions of Pope's 'And maids turn'd bottles, call aloud for corks' or 'Oh hadst thou, cruel! been content to seize/ Hairs less in sight, or any hairs but these!' in *The Rape of the Lock* find their subliterary counterparts in such works as *A Voyage to Lethe*. Likewise, Commodore Trunnion's very nautical epitaph in *Peregrine Pickle* (1751), or Tabitha Bramble's and Win Jenkins's most enjoyable, if at times somewhat salacious, verbal distortions in *Humphry Clinker* (1771) assume even deeper literary resonance when read against a popular background of a shared and lively subculture. Another example will perhaps serve to illuminate further the secret but life-giving nexus between subliterature and 'great' literature. To return once more to Pope, Shock, Belinda's cherished lap-dog in *The Rape of the Lock*,

> . . . who thought she slept too long,
> Leap't up, and wak'd his mistress with his tongue

in Canto I, ll. 115–16. This is innocent enough, or so it seems. Yet, it is highly probable that the first readers of Pope's poem must have chuckled at the mere mention of Belinda's lap-dog, since these pampered pets were often accused in coarser subliterature of abetting their mistresses' sexual whims. Ned Ward in his *The Secret History of Clubs* (London, 1709) is quite explicit about this in his essay on 'The Scatter-Wit Club'. Lady Fizzleton's lap-dog, the well-named Jewel, has:

> A lovely Mouth, well arm'd with *Ivory* Twangs,
> Whose Lips are honour'd oft with kind Salutes
> To Man deny'd, tho' granted thus to Brutes:
> A Mouth whose Tongue my Lady's Wants supplies,
> But never tells the Freedom it enjoys;
> Pleases much better than the *Spanish* Art,
> Tickles at once and mundifies the Part.[25]

Even more specific are the following lines:

> Stroak'd as thou slumberst 'twixt thy Lady's Knees,
> As if thou hadst some secret Power to Please;
> Fondled all Day, and then at Night prefer'd
> To sleep in Holland, and be Honour's Guard,
> That none without thy Notice should approach
> The Seat of Joy, which thou hast Leave to touch,
> And with thy icy Nose presum'st to kiss,
> Without Offence, the very Gates of Bliss.[26]

Whether Pope had read or not Ned Ward's *The Secret History of Clubs* before composing his *Rape of the Lock* is totally irrelevant. What matters is that Pope should delicately allude to a practice of deviant sex more coarsely and explicitly satirized in a subliterature which reflects and crystallizes the current beliefs and attitudes of the period, without the screens and verbal decorum of more polished works.

Decidedly of a more sexually provocative nature is *A New Atalantis* (London, 2nd ed., 1758), a book of libidinous potted biographies. But the moral pretence is still there, in the preface, where the authors make a very specious plea that 'As men of morality, we have for a long time been highly displeased at the illicit pursuit of pleasures *a posteriori*; which are not only unnatural, but also inconsequential. While those from *a priori*, the only genuine source of pleasures, all laudable effects are derived for the support and ornament of society' (p. 11). Far from being lecherous corrupters of innocent youths, the authors view themselves as worthy initiators and guides in the bewitching fields of Venus, 'ad majorem *Britanniae* gloriam': eroticism flying to the help of a population-obsessed patriotism. This is a constant trait of subliterary satire against the homosexuals, as for instance in Ned Ward's lively essay, 'The Mollies Club' in the already quoted *The Secret History of Clubs* (1709), or in an apocalyptic pamphlet entitled *Hell upon Earth: or the Town in an Uproar* (London, 1729). Also in the thunderingly vocal *Satan's Harvest Home: or the Present State of Whorecraft, Adultery, Fornication, Procuring, Pimping, Sodomy and the Game at Flatts* (London, 1749), the effeminate sodomites appear as a sort of treacherous 'fifth column'—to use a sadly anachronistic term—more or less planted in Britain by its corrupt and corrupting arch-enemies, the Italians and the French, in order to ruin the virile life-strength of the country. These references to subliterature can but deepen the reader's understanding of such notorious homosexual characters—probably among the first to appear in English fiction—as Captain Whiffle, the effeminate, powdered, scented and gloved commander of *The Thunder* who replaces the crusty old tar Captain Oakhum in Chapter XXXV of Smollett's *Roderick Random*, and also the rapacious and insidious Lord Strutwell in Chapter LI of the same novel. In such cases subliterature provides an attentive twentieth-century reader with the kind of relevant background information which was immediately accessible to his mid-eighteenth-century counterpart.

Quite different is John Wilkes's notorious *Essay on Woman*, a pornographic parody of Pope's *Essay on Man*, of which only a dozen copies or so were printed in the autumn of 1763.[27] Apart from its complicated publication history, and the weighty part it played in Wilkes's tumultuous political troubles of 1763–64, *The Essay on Woman* has little in it to retain scholarly attention for long. As its modern editor, Adrian Hamilton, rightly remarks, 'It managed to be obscene, libellous and blasphemous at the same time.'[28] The poem is inscribed to Fanny Murray (*c.* 1729–79), the mid-eighteenth-century reigning queen of Covent Garden harlots. Here, pornography may be—tentatively—defined as the deliberate and explicit intention to sully or destroy commonly received moral concepts of sexuality, and the wilful degradation of man and woman to their mere physiological functions. The first eight lines of the poem with their liberal use of obscene words, certainly set the tone for this most objectionable production of low parodic wit:[29]

> Awake, my Fanny, leave all meaner things,
> This morn shall prove what rapture swiving brings.
> Let us (since life can little more supply
> Than just a few good fucks, and then we die)
> Expatiate free o'er that lov'd scene of Man;
> A mighty Maze! for mighty Pricks to scan;
> A wild, where Paphian Thorns promiscuous shoot,
> Where flowers the Monthly Rose, but yields no Fruit.

In spite of the fairly close parody of the *Essay on Man*, and the mock-critical apparatus of pseudo-notes which pastiche Warburton's edition of Pope, Wilkes's *Essay on Woman* is of scant literary interest. Yet, for the sexologist and the historian of ideas it can be analysed as an important development in the increasingly liberated and 'permissive' attitude of the 1760s towards sex, just before a phase of repression got under way in the early 1770s, still overlapping with the 1670–1810 great central period of permissiveness.[30] Also, for once, it is 'great' literature which sheds light on its subliterary parody, a deliberate inversion of the normal process.

Halfway between erotic writings and pornography stands what might be termed, for lack of a better phrase, 'pragmatic erotica', such as Harris's *List of Covent Garden Ladies for the Year 1788*,[31] 'Containing the Histories and some curious Anecdotes of the most celebrated Ladies now on the Town, or in keeping, and also many of their Keepers.' This annual directory of prostitutes lists seventy-four meretricious beauties, with a quick erotic sketch of their physique, education, amorous abilities and sexual specialities, not forgetting their professional addresses and expected fees. Whenever possible, reassuring prophylactic information is given. Most of these pragmatic portraits are preceded by rather ornate and highly laudatory verse: this is a sales-catalogue of prostitutes couched in Augustan poetic diction of apparently impeccable origin. In other words, the secret nexus linking literature and subliterature does not function one way only. Subculture may well steal the gold of major poetry and debase it into tinny pinchbeck. Thus, for instance, the description of Miss Lister's charms at No. 6 Union Street, Oxford Road:

> The *tell-tale eyes* in liquid pools sustain'd,
> The throbbing breast now rising, now suppress'd;
> The *thrilling bliss* quick darting thro' the frame,
> The *short fetch'd sighs*, the snow white twining limbs,
> The sudden gush, and the extatic [sic] oh. (p. 15)

The prose description is even more graphic, but no four-letter words are ever used, and the diction remains uniformly periphrastic, as in *A New Atalantis*, where the female pudendum is referred to by means of half a dozen coy periphrases such as for instance 'the magic circle', 'Cupid's grotto', 'the procreative ring', 'Cytherea's cell', 'Venus's *camera obscura*', which at least proves that subliterary hacks were well-grounded in classical mythology. In Harris's *List*, Miss Lister's lips 'display a casket of snow white pearls, ranged in the nicest regularity, the *neighbouring hills* below full ripe for manual pressure, firm; and elastic, and heave at every touch. The *Elysian font*, in the centre of a *black bewitching grove*, supported by two pyramids white as alabaster, very delicate, and soft as turtle's down. At the approach of their *favourite lord* [they] unfold, and for three guineas he is conducted to this *harbour* of never failing delight. Add to all this, she sings well, is a very chearful companion, and has only been in *life* nine months' (pp. 16–17). At three guineas, Miss Lister must have been rather choice game, prices ranging from a mere crown to five guineas. In the lists for the following years (1789, 1790, 1793), a five guineas' fee becomes the usual payment for the better class of prostitutes. When one bears in mind the countless tales of 'whore's progresses' in eighteenth-century European literature, it is striking how often drinking (especially gin, some prostitutes being called 'juniper-girls') and swearing are denounced as the bane of the profession. The compiler never fails to commend abstemious and well-spoken girls, for instance Miss Williams in the 1790 *List*: 'She is seldom guilty of those vices which we have so frequently censured, and which defile the sex more than any other; we mean drinking and swearing' (p. 7). Such deviant proclivities as flagellation—exploited *ad nauseam* by Sade—were catered for, and in the 1793 *List* 'the birchen operation' (p. 86) is advertised at no less than half a guinea, but such practices were well-known already by mid-eighteenth century, as a 1752 print reproduced in Stone's book (illustration No. 34 of a gentleman being birched for pleasure) tends to prove.

This all too rapid exploration of an immense and protean topic focused chiefly on the middle years of the eighteenth century, will at least have revealed a few glimpses of a usually little known chiaroscuro world of medical lore, not to mention the more rarefied, and at times oppressive, atmosphere of erotic or pornographic subliterature. The real world in which Pamela and Clarissa, Roderick Random and Tom Jones, might have moved, had they been actual persons, was one where human sexuality could be sublimated into the scintillating gems of Pope's mock-heroic wit in *The Rape of the Lock*, and denounced as a horrifyingly repulsive experience by Swift's Gulliver in Brobdingnag and among the subhuman—but all too human—Yahoos. Sexual impulses could also be channelled into the relatively distinguished, or at least immensely successful, eroticism of Cleland's *Fanny Hill*, or into the gross parody of Wilkes's *Essay on Woman*.

The ways, literary and otherwise, of human libido are certainly inscrutable, at times erratic, often unpredictable. But it would be wrong for tempting reasons of convenient and intellectually satisfactory classification to separate the great mid-eighteenth-century authors from 'the other Augustans', those who have never achieved literary, political, scientific, artistic or economic fame. These obscure, often nameless, 'other

Augustans', peopling a Popean 'universal darkness', are in fact, when placed in their literary and socio-cultural contexts but one of the manifold, often objectionable, but always fascinating aspects of that creature, Man,

> Sole judge of Truth, in endless Error hurl'd:
> The glory, jest, and riddle of the world!

NOTES

1. Published by Weidenfeld and Nicolson, London, 1977, pp. XXXI + 800. Hereafter referred to as 'Stone'.
2. See *TLS*, 18 July 1980, review by Peter Redgrove and Penelope Shuttle, pp. 819–20.
3. Michel Foucault, *La Volonté de Savoir* (Paris: Gallimard, 1976), p. 15. Hereafter referred to as 'Foucault'.
4. Foucault, p. 25.
5. Foucault, p. 26.
6. Stone, p. 4.
7. Stone, p. 6.
8. Stone, p. 529.
9. Stone, p. 532.
10. Stone, pp. 532–33.
11. For a definition of 'subculture' see Pat Rogers, *Grub Street: Studies in a Subculture* (London: Methuen, 1972), pp. 279–81.
12. Boswell's *Life of Johnson*, ed. G. B. Hill, rev. L. F Powell, vol. V, 2nd ed. (Oxford: Clarendon Press, 1964), p. 209.
13. Pp. XVI + 324 + Index [6 pp.]. *The Wellcome Medical Library Catalogue* lists a first edition dated 1739. The book was translated into German in 1741, and *The British Library Catalogue* lists another London edition tentatively dated 1770.
14. On this fascinating controversy see Joseph Needham, *A History of Embryology* (Cambridge, 1959), pp. 179–229, and Pierre Darmon, *Le Mythe de la procréation à l'âge baroque* (Paris: Pauvert, 1977), *passim*.
15. 2nd ed., London, [1716], 79 pp. Republished as early as 1727, 3rd ed., London, as the revised and augmented *The Ladies Physical Directory*.
16. *A Rational Account*, 2nd ed. (London, [1716]), pp. 60–1.
17. Stone, p. 490.
18. *A Rational Account*, p. 55.
19. *The Ladies Physical Directory*, pp. 56–7.
20. Roland Barthes, *Sade Fourier Loyola* (Paris: Le Seuil, 1971), pp. 31–2, my translation.
21. Peter Hughes, 'Wars within Doors: Erotic Heroism and the Implosion of Texts', *English Studies*, 60 (1979), 403.

22. Captain Samuel Cock, *A Voyage to Lethe* (London, 1741), p. 4.

23. On Stretzer, see Ralph Straus, *The Unspeakable Curll* (London: Chapman & Hall, 1927), pp. 308–14.

24. [Thomas Stretzer], *A New Description of Merryland*, 2nd ed. (Bath, 1741), p. 3.

25. Ned Ward, *The Secret History of Clubs*, 1st ed. 1709. The reference is taken from the seventh edition, *A Compleat and Humorous Account of all the Remarkable Clubs and Societies in the Cities of London and Westminster* (London, 1756), p. 245.

26. Ibid., p. 246.

27. See Adrian Hamilton, *The Infamous Essay on Woman, or John Wilkes Seated Between Vice and Virtue* (London: A. Deutsch, 1972), p. 256. Hereafter referred to as 'Wilkes'.

28. Wilkes, p. 92.

29. For a recent study see Calhoun Winton, 'John Wilkes and *An Essay on Woman*', in Donald Kay, ed., *A Provision of Human Nature* (University, Ala., 1977), pp. 121–32.

30. See Stone, pp. 543–45.

31. London, 1788, pp. XI + 146.

4

Victorian Erotica

by PETER WEBB

1

In the October 1873 issue of the *Contemporary Review*, Thomas
Maitland published a violent attack on what he termed 'The
Fleshly School of Poetry'. His main targets were Dante
Gabriel Rossetti and Algernon Charles Swinburne, and his
criticisms reflected informed opinion as to what was accept-
able in the high Victorian period.

Rossetti's paintings of *Beata Beatrix* (*c.* 1863) and *Proserpine*
(1874) are haunting visions of powerfully sexual women whose
eroticism depends upon an uneasy balance between spiritual
and worldly love. Such images are paralleled in the poems
'Blessed Damosel' and 'Nuptial Sleep', both of which were
criticized by Maitland in his article. Of the latter, which
Tennyson is said to have found 'the filthiest thing he had ever
read',[1] Maitland wrote that it contained 'the most secret
mysteries of sexual connection and that with so sickening a
desire to reproduce the sensual mood, so careful a choice of
epithet to convey mere animal sensations that we merely
shudder at the shameless nakedness'.

Rossetti's images in these paintings and poems reflect his
obsessive love for Elizabeth Siddall and Jane Morris, and it is
the intensely personal involvement with the subject matter
that gives them their power of erotic attraction. Similarly, the
poems of Swinburne are charged with a heavy eroticism which

reflects their author's predilection for masochistic pleasures. Writing in defence of his much criticized *Poems and Ballads* (1865), he pointed to 'those violent delights which have violent ends in frank and free sensualities' as his inspiration, and it is no surprise that Maitland objected to the subject matter of poems like 'Anactoria', 'Hermaphroditus' and 'Dolores' ('Oh bitter and tender Dolores, Our Lady of Pain').

Swinburne's prose writings also reflect his obsession with physical punishment. In the autobiographical novel *Lesbia Brandon* (1877) there is a vivid description of a boy being flogged by his tutor, and the privately published *Whippingham Papers* of 1887 contained a contribution by Swinburne entitled 'Hints on Flogging' ('one of the great charms of birching lies in the sentiment that the flogee is the powerless victim of the furious rage of a beautiful woman').

Swinburne's idiosyncratic sexual pleasures were far removed from the infatuation with young girls shared by Lewis Carroll and John Ruskin, but the intensity of such personal tastes colour the writings of all three. Carroll's stories, which originated as amusements for his little girl friends, are often thinly veiled sexual fantasies, and his beautiful photographs of girls with little or no clothing are further expressions of his personal inclinations.[2] Similarly, Oscar Wilde's taste for homosexual love underlies his novel *The Picture of Dorian Gray* (1891) as well as poems such as 'Wasted Days' of 1877, though without any explicit incidence of homosexuality. For this, one must turn to *Teleny*, privately published in 1893, which it seems probable was edited and partly written by Wilde.[3]

Teleny is one of the few examples of Victorian erotica which is entirely concerned with homosexual love. The unusual frankness is allied to some real insight into the central relationship, and the emotional development, though marred by some dreadful passages, lifts it well above the usual standard of explicit Victorian erotica.

The sexual themes in Victorian literature which we have discussed tend to involve extremes: the obsessive infatuations of Rossetti, the masochism of Swinburne, the love of little girls experienced by Carroll and Wilde's homosexuality.[4] These themes were explored by men who were at odds with the accepted moral standards of the day and who made a conscious or subconscious attempt to reject those standards. Their work seems the most convincing among Victorian erotic literature because they had the necessary motivation, the courage and the artistic talent to express *themselves*; it is in this respect that their work contrasts so strongly with the pornographic novels which circulated surprisingly widely during this period. These had few literary aspirations; their authors were simply appealing to a sexual appetite and writing what they knew would sell.

There are thus two classes of Victorian erotic literature. On the one hand, the writings of Wilde and Swinburne are imbued with the personal expression of deeply held obsessions. On the other, coldly calculated indulgence in male fantasy provides the impetus for the multiple rapes in Hugues Rebell's *Dolly Morton* and the endless flagellation of Edward Sellon's *New Ladies Tickler*. The latter have a common degree of insensitivity in their male-orientated world where women are sexual objects, continually at the mercy of their male aggressors. And yet behind both categories we can see the same world of sexual repression.

Victorian overground literature for the most part reflects the moral codes of the day. In George Eliot's *Middlemarch* (1871) we find the accepted pattern of marriage and family life. *Jane Eyre* (1847) may be about a passionate woman, but Charlotte Brontë, who was no sexual rebel,[5] makes her submit in the end to a powerful man in marriage. For Charles Dickens, passion usually means aggression which leads to self-destruction, an obvious example being Quilp in *The Old Curiosity Shop* (1840). In Dickens's world the male is superior, the woman is dominated.[6] Both men and women seek fulfilment in marriage, which is the haven in a storm of animal instincts. Sex is not an important part of marriage, for sex is not a pleasure.

The strict code of morality that lay behind this world of literature was in real life being breached continually. Sophisticates and intellectuals, in their private rather than their public lives, were giving rein to their sexual needs, and if the brothels provided the opportunities, the pornography catered for the fantasies. As officialdom warned against masturbation and the harmful effects of sexual excess,[7] so the pornographic novel provided the male reader with fuel for endless sexual fantasies, in a world where sex was of paramount importance. The genre hardly constitutes good literature, but nevertheless it deserves examination for the insight it gives into the effects of sexual repression in Victorian England, even if this is rarely accomplished with any degree of probing analysis or subtlety of sexual arousal.

These sexually orientated novels had their prototypes in the eighteenth century, the world of *Moll Flanders* and *Fanny Hill*, of *Liaisons Dangereuses* and *Justine*. But these were works of merit as literature, whether the language was delicate or coarse and whether the material was carefree or disturbing. Their nineteenth-century descendants show the conventions without the skill, with rare exceptions such as *Venus and Tannhauser*, *Teleny*, *Gamiani* and *Venus in Furs*.

2

Even though the raw material is not easy to obtain, there has been no shortage of commentators on these Victorian pornographic novels. Henry Spencer Ashbee made copious bibliographical notes in the 1870s, though his research led him to few books that he could actually persuade himself to praise.[8] More recent commentators have either followed his general line of disapproval (Hyde, Pearsall, Young[9]), or found a secret world of insight and fascination (the Kronhausens, Fryer[10]). Steven Marcus has perhaps shown the greatest insight into this material.[11] While severely criticizing the literary quality of all the examples he knew, he nevertheless found the best of them worthy of critical evaluation and valuable as clues to Victorian sexual morality.

These novels certainly constitute a genre of their own. If the Victorian novel attempts to represent the whole range of human experience, the pornographic variety presupposes a world where all human experience is concerned exclusively with sex. This is a world without conscience, where character development is minimal, a world in which human conflict is merely sexual conquest. But it clearly underlines the lack of real sexual analysis and investigation in the Victorian novel. The range of sexual activities in this genre is wide, from incest to male and female homosexuality, but the most frequently found are rape and flagellation. This in itself is revealing of a sexually repressed and totally male-dominated society.

A very average example may be taken to typify these most common themes: *Raped on the Railway* of 1894. The full title gives a good idea of its contents: *Raped on the Railway, A True Story of a Lady who was First Ravished and then Chastised on the Scotch Express*. The author states his position at the outset: 'To get a strong-bodied wench, in the prime of health, down on her back, and triumph over her virtue, in spite of all her struggles, is to my mind the height of delightful existence, the sum of all human ambition.' He then relates the story of Robert Brandon whom we meet at Euston Station as he boards the Glasgow train. Seeing a lady whose face is concealed behind a veil, he takes a seat in her compartment, and manages to keep other passengers from joining them. Once the journey has begun he loses no time in making sexual advances towards the unknown lady. She refuses even to show her face, and so he snatches at the veil and finds her to be extremely beautiful. She then threatens him with a revolver but collapses in a faint as the train comes to a sudden halt. He immediately lifts her skirt and petticoats and reveals her sexual charms: 'uttering an exclamation of joy, he tore open his trousers, and there sprang out, ready for the fray, his huge member rearing aloft at the end of the big straight hard column of muscle the round red gland which had hunted love through so many soft, damp velvety caverns, and though exhausted by the chase, was ever ready to begin again after a short rest. At that moment the lady opened her eyes, and the first thing she caught sight of was the big machine prepared to impale her.'

A vigorous battle ensues, the outcome of which is never in doubt: 'as she arched up her buttocks that she might better be able to twist sideways and get rid of the intruder, Brandon gave a powerful downward lunge, and as the head of his tool was already within her lips the double force sent two thirds of his big column into her vulva. She knew then that he had won the game, and woman-like burst into a flood of tears.' After he has completed the rape, Brandon proceeds to apologize, blaming his behaviour on her extraordinary beauty. The lady is flattered and forgives him, realizing that she has quite enjoyed the experience.

During a stop at a station, another passenger is tipped off by the guard about what has happened and recognizes the lady as his brother's wife. He and his three male friends presume that she had invited the assault and determine to punish her, being members of the Society of National Purity. They enter her compartment, tie up Brandon, and then proceed to immobilize the lady and lay bare her buttocks. She is subjected to a severe beating: 'Down came the cane again, and another weal marked her bottom, and the woman, in her vain efforts to shield her cruelly treated bottom, turned completely on her side. Rage and shame made her forget modesty and she did not know that she was displaying to the enraptured eyes of the men a large triangular fleece of golden chestnut hair, which covered the whole of the lower part of her belly, and beneath which could be seen the pink lips of her dainty coynte. Pretty as the spectacle was, the men quickly turned her on her belly again, and down came the cane a third time. There was another attempt at a scream; through the handkerchief could be heard her voice in a hoarse whisper, saying: "Oh you wretches! Oh, you curs! Oh, you beasts!" '

Brandon and the lady are released, and to avoid a scandal, decide to keep quiet about the attack. At Glasgow they go their separate ways. The lady is visited by the brother-in-law who had beaten her on the train. When he tries to rape her she manages to resist and dislocates his penis, which proves fatal. Brandon and his wife Maud learn the pleasures of flagellation but later she dies in childbirth. He then goes to South Africa and enlists in the Army where he becomes friendly with a Captain Sinclair. The Captain is severely wounded in action and before dying gives Brandon a letter to be delivered to his wife in Glasgow. The widow proves to be the lady from the Scotch Express, and so the protagonists finally become man and wife.

The two most common themes of Victorian pornography—rape and flagellation—constitute a very large proportion of the material of *Raped on the Railway*. The story is seen typically from an entirely male point of view: 'the sum of all human ambition is to rape a woman.' The woman is portrayed solely as a sexual object for men's pleasure. Sex is performed as rape, and rape is a game: 'she knew then that he had won the game,

95

and woman-like burst into a flood of tears.' The whole tone is that of a man writing for other men: when Brandon apologizes for raping her, the lady forgives him; the brother-in-law automatically presumes that she had invited the assault.

The punishment inflicted by the brother-in-law and his friends is only one of many flagellation scenes in the book. The author expresses a common male fantasy when he has Brandon's wife Maud tell him: 'there is nothing makes a woman so randy as a good flogging, and nothing so much excites a man as flogging a woman or seeing her flogged.' The second point is clearly illustrated during the railway compartment scene by the men's reactions: 'their eyes sparkled with delight and their lips wore a grim smile of enjoyment.' Even the trussed-up Brandon finds he has a strong erection during the flogging. Maud herself demonstrates the efficacy of punishment by giving Brandon a night of undreamt-of passion after he has severely whipped her. She goes further and in turn flogs Brandon to revive his wilting penis: 'Twice more she brought down the strap, and then quickly skipped out of the way, as Brandon stood upright, faced round with his magnificent engine boldly rearing its huge red head, and tried to grasp her.'

This last sentence demonstrates another typical aspect of the Victorian pornographic novel, the concentration on sexual organs rather than personalities: The penis becomes a huge weapon or a powerful machine: the penis becomes the man. We have already seen this in the account of the railway compartment rape: 'ready for the fray, his huge member . . . ever ready to begin again after a short rest . . . the big machine prepared to impale her.' During a bout with Maud, we read that he 'opened the soft pink lips of her rosy love-cleft with his fingers, and inserted the head of his huge tool . . . the enormous engine was buried up to the roots, and still her insatiable coynte was unsatisfied.' After this session, Maud remarks with curious logic; 'Five times! And your great thing is fully nine inches long! that makes nearly four foot of tool that you drove with all your might into my poor little belly.'

Raped on the Railway clearly does not constitute good literature. It lacks invention, is endlessly repetitive and heavily adjectival. It has no humour, ends entirely unconvincingly, and represents a straightforward male fantasy that could easily be adapted to fit other situations. In fact a variant was published in America entitled *Raped on the Elevated Railway, a True Story of a Lady who was First Ravished and then Flagellated on the Uptown Express, illustrating the Perils of Travel in the New Machine Age.* And it has little social comment other than the implication behind the description of the cruel brother-in-law as a member of the Society of National Purity. In order to fulfil its purpose of male sexual arousal, it needs to concentrate on erotic events with few distractions, and so has little room for the overground novel's analysis of relationships and motives. But of course it meets a need which the novel rarely meets.

3

From our discussion of *Raped on the Railway*, we can make certain general points about Victorian pornographic novels. They have a structure consisting of a succession of erotic scenes with as few distractions as possible, and so contain little character analysis or philosophical discussion. Rather than reflecting the basic realities of life, they concentrate on stimulating an erotic response by means of simplified psychological mechanisms. Thus the male reader is presented with tailor-made sexual fantasies: scenes of rape and flagellation combine erotic and sadistic impulses; penises of exaggerated size and ability give reassurance about the limitless nature of sexual potency. These fantasies may involve incestual relations, the sexual attraction of little girls, homosexual and lesbian encounters, but most characteristically rape and flagellation. It will be instructive to examine each of these fantasies in turn.

One of the most consistently popular English underground novels of the nineteenth century was *The Lustful Turk: a History Founded on Facts, containing an interesting narrative of the cruel fate of two young English ladies named Silvia Carey and Emily Barlow.* First published in 1828, it was reprinted in 1829, then republished twice by William Dugdale in the 1860s and again by Leonard Smithers in 1893. The book consists of a series of letters between Silvia and Emily recounting their misadventures as prisoners of the Dey of Algiers. Emily is captured on her way to India in 1814, and the Dey wastes no time in deflowering her: 'My petitions, supplications and tears were of no use. I was on the altar, and, butcher-like, he was determined to complete the sacrifice; indeed, my cries seemed only to excite him to the finishing of my ruin, and sucking my tits and breasts with fury, he unrelentingly rooted up all obstacles my virginity offered, tearing and cutting me to pieces, until the complete junction of our bodies announced that the whole of his terrible shaft was buried within me. I could bear the dreadful torment no longer, but uttering a piercing cry sunk insensible in the arms of my cruel ravisher.' This sets the tone of the story, which becomes a series of descriptions of violent rapes. Emily relates the experiences of other ladies of the Dey's harem, and also of her maid Eliza, and then receives a letter from her friend Silvia expressing disgust at her behaviour. The Dey hears about Silvia, and has her kidnapped from Toulon, whereupon he subjects her to the same fate as Emily. For a time he enjoys the two of them together, until a new member of the harem castrates him. He survives this setback and has his penis and testicles preserved in two glass vases, which he gives to Silvia and Emily as he releases them.

The Lustful Turk is an early example of the pornographic genre and shows clear literary influences. The epistolary style is a poor copy of Richardson's *Pamela* or Laclos's *Liaisons Dangereuses*, but the first person narrative gives it an authenticity which adds considerably to the power of the sexual fantasy. There are strong flavours of Byron in the stories related by the harem girls, and the Dey himself can perhaps be seen as a Byronic hero, though one without a conscience. The book relates closely to the Romantic Movement and yet we can already see certain pornographic conventions making their appearance. The speed with which both Emily and Silvia are transformed into willing victims of their rapist betrays the fact that the book was written by a *man* for the pleasure of other *men*: 'I was lost to everything but the wonderful instrument that was sheathed within me. I call it wonderful, and I think not improperly; for wonderful must that thing be that in the midst of the most poignant grief can so rapidly dissolve our senses with the softest sensations, spite of inclination, so quickly cause us to forget our early impressions, our first affections, and in the most forlorn and wretched moment of our existence make us taste such voluptuous delight and lust-ful pleasure.' And the use of the term 'wonderful instrument' is a sign pointing the way to the deification of the penis: 'You, Silvia, who are yet I believe an inexperienced maid, can have no conception of the seductive powers of this wonderful instru-ment of nature—this terror of virgins, but delight of women.... I was soon taught that it was the uncontrolled master-key of my feelings.'

The rape fantasy that underlies *The Lustful Turk* and *Raped on the Railway* is commonplace in the genre. In *A Man with a Maid* (*c.* 1893), Jack has been jilted by a virgin called Alice, and lures her to a soundproof room in order to get his revenge: ' "My God!—no, no!" she shrieked, frantically wriggling her buttocks in an attempt to thwart me. But the contact of my prick with Alice's flesh maddened me: thrusting fiercely forward, I, with very little difficulty, shoved my prick half-way up Alice's bottom with apparently little or no pain to her; then falling on her, I clasped her in my arms and rammed myself well into her, till I felt my balls against her and the cheeks of her bottom against my stomach! My God! it was like heaven to me! ... I shall never forget it! ... "Ah! Ah!" she gasped, as she felt herself inundated by my hot discharge! ... she had lost the maidenhead of her bottom!!!' Buggery adds a little variety to the usual deflowering ceremony, but the debased literary standard is sadly typical of many Victorian pornographic novels. *A Man with a Maid* is also typical in its concentration on the curious fantasy of female ejaculation: 'then Alice spent frantically, plentifully bedewing my finger with her virgin distillation!' and 'I spent deliriously into her with my hot discharge at the same moment feeling the head of my prick christened by the warm gush that burst from Alice as she also frantically spent, punctuating the pulsations of her discharge by voluptuous upheavings of her wildly agitated bottom.'

Rape and flagellation fit all too neatly together, as *Dolly Morton* demonstrates. This famous book was trumpeted by its publisher Carrington as 'the most wonderful romance of flagellation in existence'. It appeared in 1899 as *The memoirs of Dolly Morton. The Story of a woman's part in the struggle to free the slaves. An account of the whippings, rapes and violences that preceded the Civil War in America. With curious anthropological observations on the radical diversities in the conformation of the Female Bottom and the way different women endure Chastisement.* Long explanatory titles were common for books of this sort, and the point was thus made on the title page that this tale had an important setting in recent history. Great claims have been made for *Dolly Morton*: the bibliographer C. R. Dawes described it as being 'among the very few good erotic books of the period . . . by far the best of all the books whose main theme is Flagellation',[12] and Hyde declares in *A History of Pornography* that it 'recaptures the plantation atmosphere, even more graphically and convincingly than *Uncle Tom's Cabin*'.[13]

Charles Carrington was an extremely successful publisher of English erotica in Paris towards the end of the century, and it seems that *Dolly Morton* was written with an eye to a new market rather than as an eye-witness account of history. It first appeared as *En Virginie* and its author was 'Georges Grassal', pseudonym of Hugues Rebell, who was a friend of Carrington and an enthusiast for flagellation. He was well-read in nineteenth-century American literature and thus well suited to write a pornographic novel with an American setting and with redeeming social value in addition. The English translation included a pious introduction by Carrington drawing attention to the exploits of brave women in the cause of emancipation, but the real intention behind the book becomes plain in the first few pages.

Dolly Morton is an 18-year-old orphan who travels to Virginia with an older lady to set up a centre for aiding escaped slaves. A rich plantation-owner named Randolph discovers her secret and when she resists his sexual advances he sends his men to punish her: 'He went on whipping me very slowly, so that I felt the full sting of each stroke before the next one fell; and every stroke felt as if a red-hot iron was being drawn across my bottom. I winced and squirmed every time the horrid switch fell sharply on my quivering flesh. . . . The feeling of shame again came over me as I began to notice the way the men were looking at my naked body, and I tearfully begged them to pull down my clothes. No-one did so however, and Stevens pointing to me said: "There, boys, look at her bottom. You see how regularly the white skin is striped with long red weals; but there is not a drop of blood. That's what I call a prettily whipped bottom." '

To save herself from further pain, Dolly agrees to live with Randolph on his plantation. Her deflowering follows swiftly: 'After toying with me a moment or two longer, he laid me on my back, saying: "Now, Dolly, I am going to do the job. To use plain words, I am going to poke you. You will feel a little pain, but you must bear it. Every woman suffers more or less, the first time she is poked by a man; but afterwards she feels no pain at all, but only pleasure when in the arms of her lover." The fatal moment had come! . . . I shuddered and uttered a low cry. My martyrdom had commenced!' Although deeply shocked by the experience, Dolly realizes she must submit to Randolph whenever he wishes; indeed it soon becomes easier for her: 'I discovered that there was a strain of voluptuousness in my disposition.'

Dolly is horrified by the continual whippings to which the slaves are subjected, for as Randolph explains: 'You are a Northern girl, so you don't understand how we Southerners look upon our slave women. When they take our fancy we amuse ourselves with them, but we feel no compunction in whipping them whenever they misbehave. Their bodies belong to us, so we can use them in any way we please. Personally, I have no more regard for my slaves than for my dogs and horses.' As Dolly becomes better acquainted with plantation life, her disgust at the way the slaves are treated increases, but when she catches two black children stoning a kitten to death, she gives them each a good spanking which gives her 'a glow of satisfaction'.

Soon after this incident, Randolph spanks her and her reaction has changed: 'Strange to say, the slight spanking had excited a voluptuous feeling in me, and I was anxious to receive the stroke. He unbuttoned his trousers, and then making me separate my legs slightly, he clasped his arms round my body, as stooping a little he thrust his "thing" into the "spot" between the cleft of the thighs. . . . He worked away in fine style, and I gave him every assistance, so in a few seconds the supreme crisis arrived.'

The Civil War breaks out, and while Randolph is away, the Yankees take over the plantation. Dolly falls in love with the Captain and seduces him, but soon he is called away and she hears he has been killed in action. Randolph sends for her and she travels to Richmond, though she is brutally raped by three ruffians on the way. Randolph then takes her to New York and after a few weeks, buys her a house and says farewell. Dolly then takes up a life of prostitution.

Dolly Morton is interesting on several accounts: it is narrated in the first person by a female, has a historical setting, and seems to have been written with great care. The style is not tedious like so many of the type, and the book contains material of interest in addition to the usual flagellation scenes. Admittedly Carrington intends his English readers to feel outraged by American barbarism while at the same time being sexually stimulated by the incidents of rape and violence. But nevertheless the historical detail does give the story a social value that lifts it far beyond the level of *Raped on the Railway*.

At many points in the narrative, *Dolly Morton* professes to be written by a female: 'I thought it strange at the time, but I have since found out that men's passions are inflamed by whipping the bottom of a female till she cries and writhes with pain, and if they can't do it themselves, they like seeing it done. This is a curious, but undoubted fact, and it shows what cruel creatures you men are.' And the philosophical digressions tend to follow the same anti-male position: 'I think that a man always enjoys poking a woman whether he loves her or not: but I am sure that a woman never really enjoys a man's embrace unless she loves him. . . . I think a man copulates with the woman he loves differently to the way he pokes the woman he merely lusts for.' These digressions are curiously conventional, and the anti-male tone does not for one moment disguise the fact that the book is a male fantasy throughout.

Dolly Morton's author, Hugues Rebell, wrote another flagellation tale, *Frank & I* (1902). This is the story of a wealthy young man named Charles Beaumont who meets a runaway boy called Frank and invites him to stay at his house. All goes well until the boy misbehaves and so is given a beating, at which point a discovery is made: 'He drew up his legs one after the other and then kicked them out again, he jerked his hips from side to side, and rolled about in pain, half turning over on to his side for a moment, so that I saw the front part of his naked body. And what I saw paralysed me with astonishment, causing my uplifted arm to drop to my side, and the rod to slip from my grasp. In that momentary glimpse, I had caught sight of a little pink-lipped cunt, shaded at the upper part with a slight growth of curly, golden down. "Frank" was a girl!'

It is only a matter of time before the girl is deflowered: ' "What I am going to do to you, will give you a little pain at first; but afterwards, you will experience nothing but pleasure when I do it to you." I stretched out her legs as widely as possible, then after placing myself in position to make the assault, I separated with my fingers the tightly-closed lips of her little cunt and inserted the tip of my prick. . . . I thought the membrane would never yield. I paused for a moment to recover my breath; then taking a fresh hold on her bottom, I recommenced fucking her with increased vigour, making her quiver all over; but she managed to gasp out between her squeaks and groans: "Oh! Oh! You—are—hurting—me— dreadfully!" At last I felt the thing beginning to yield, and after a few more powerful thrusts, her maidenhead gave way; she uttered a sharp cry of pain, and my prick buried itself to the roots of her cunt. Then, a few short digs finished the affair; the supreme spasm seized me, and I spent profusely, pouring out a torrent of boiling sperm, while she gasped, squirmed, and wriggled her bottom furiously, uttering little squeaks of mingled pleasure and pain as the hot stuff spurted in gushes up her lacerated cunt. And when all was over, she lay trembling in my arms, her breath coming and going quickly, her bosom heaving tumultuously, and the flesh of her bottom twitching nervously; her cheeks were scarlet, and there was a languorous look in her moist eyes.' It is worth quoting this passage at length, because not only is it almost identical to the same scene in Rebell's other book *Dolly Morton*, but it is echoed in almost every Victorian pornographic novel. It is the typical, obligatory deflowering: first reassurance, followed by physical difficulty, vain resistance, and the inevitable triumph leading via a cry of pain to the copious discharge. It is of course seen entirely from the male point of view since it is a male fantasy that is being presented to the readers: the man is the aggressor, the woman is the willing or unwilling victim. And at the end: 'there was a languorous look in her moist eyes'; the act of deflowering has unlocked the woman's true being.

Frank and I continues in the conventional manner. Charles educates the girl into the various excitements of sex, most of which involve physical punishment. Especially interesting is a visit to a London brothel where the couple enjoy a series of *Tableaux Vivants*, one representing *The Birching of a Nihilist in a Russian Prison*, followed by *Punishment in a Boarding-School for Young Ladies*, *Venus Rising from the Ocean*, *The Three Graces*, and *A Lesbian Kiss*. This scene has the ring of truth, as does the later one in the whipping-room of the same brothel: 'there were cushioned "horses", and sloping benches; long and short ladders; whipping blocks, and posts with rings for securing the victim's wrists and ankles. And, hanging in rows on the tapestry-covered walls, were birch rods of all sizes, whips of various kinds, leathern tawse, straps of all lengths and breadths and flat, round, wooden "spankers", with long handles.' One is reminded of Mrs. Theresa Berkley and her brothel at 28 Charlotte Street where she made her fortune with her 'Berkley Horse' and her correction room, described so vividly by Ashbee in his *Index* of 1877.[14] It also recalls the incident in the extraordinary sexual autobiography *My Secret Life* (*c.* 1890) when 'Walter' visits a flagellation brothel and watches a man being flogged until he reaches orgasm.

During the Victorian period, flagellation was known abroad as 'the English vice', and its popularity in both pornography and the brothels of London is sometimes explained as a consequence of experiences at boys' boarding schools. Certainly there was a vast amount of flagellation literature, and it took a wide variety of forms: novels, dialogues, lectures, plays, poems, letters, comic operettas and medical tracts. The titles always reveal the contents: *Lady Bumtickler's Revels* (1866), *Madame Birchini's Dance* by Lady Termagant Flaybum (1866), *Quintessence of Birch Discipline* (1870), *With Rod and Bum, or Sport in the West-End of London* (*c.* 1890), *The Birchen Bouquet* (*c.* 1896). One of the most disturbing of these books is *The Experimental Lecture of Colonel Spanker on the Exciting and Voluptuous Pleasures to be derived from crushing and humiliating the spirit of a beautiful and modest young lady, as delivered by him in the Assembly Room of the Society of Aristocratic Flagellants, Mayfair* (1878–79). Ashbee describes this as 'the most coldly cruel and unblushingly indecent of any [book] we have ever read'.[15]

104

For the most part, however, these books represent the schoolboy fantasy of being whipped by dominating women, as the titles and names suggest. We have already noted Swinburne's predilection for masochistic pleasures: 'One of the great charms of birching lies in the sentiment that the flogee is the powerless victim of the furious rage of a beautiful woman.' Swinburne learned to enjoy a whipping at Eton, and in later life would visit 7 Circus Road, St. John's Wood in North London where two ladies were adept at chastizing gentlemen guests.[16] The quotation is from one of his contributions to *The Whippingham Papers* (1887), a miscellany edited by St. George Stock who also wrote the flagellation tale *The Romance of Chastisement* (1866), one of the most articulate of the genre.

Victorian flagellation pornography therefore reflects the tendencies on the one hand of de Sade, but more often those of Sacher-Masoch who wrote *Venus in Furs* (*c.* 1880). This auto-biographical novel relates the experiences of Severin, a wealthy young man who allows himself to become the slave of a heartless woman named Wanda, whom he encourages to whip him while wearing nothing but a fur coat: ' "Perhaps after all, there isn't anything so very unique or strange in all your passions, for who doesn't love beautiful furs? And everyone knows and feels how closely sexual love and cruelty are related".... "Whip me", I begged, "Whip me without mercy". Wanda swung the whip, and hit me twice. "Are you satisfied now?" "No." ' Over the years, the story has become fair game for caricature, but it is written with an intensity that gives it an authentic feeling, and it has contributed a new word to our language.

Masochistic pleasures had been part of religious observances for centuries, and Dr. E. P. Pusey's *Manual for Confessors* of 1878 recommended whipping as a penance: 'for mortifications, the Discipline for about a quarter of an hour a day.' But one of the most interesting examples of Victorian masochism is *Gynecocracy: Narrative of the adventures and psychological experiences of Julian Robinson (afterwards Viscount Ladywood) under petticoat rule, written by himself* of 1893. We have seen that *Frank and I* involved transvestism in a small degree, though 'Frank' is soon revealed as a girl and remains totally female throughout the story. *Gynecocracy* concerns role-reversal, a theme previously

105

touched upon by André de Nerciat in *Mon Noviciat* (1780) and more fully explored in *Monsieur Venus* by 'Rachilde' (1888). Julian Robinson is sent as an adolescent to his uncle's estate where he is subjected to strict discipline and dressed as a girl: 'And now Julian, you shall be deprived of your trousers. Take a long leave of them. When you will see them again, I do not know; they teach you all sorts of resistance and naughtiness, and make you assume airs of ridiculous superiority which you do not possess. We must make a girl of you. Elise, make him stand up and take them off.' Julian is tightly corseted, birched and locked up. At one point he is urinated upon; later he is threatened with castration though in the event merely circumsized. Finally, he learns to enjoy being a girl and dressing in female clothing, and this remains so even after his eventual marriage.

The transsexual fantasy in *Gynecocracy* is an extreme example of the dominance-submission theme. The sex-role reversal becomes a symbol of male humiliation, just as Julian has to lose his trousers as they represent a symbol of male superiority. Petticoat rule can therefore be seen as a rejection of the *status quo* in which to be a man is to be superior.

4

Flagellation pornography can be seen as a reversal of the ideal Victorian personal standards of manliness and moral uprightness as promulgated by public school education. It assumes that its audience has had such an education, and indeed boarding schools and aristocratic circles provide the setting for most examples. Public school experience of both flagellation and homosexuality contribute to the effect of this literature. The powerful and dominant female chastiser can be seen at times as a surrogate mother. She is often represented as being very masculine. The ambiguity of sexual identity can extend to the figure being punished, and this seems to strengthen the fantasy. The material is written by men for other men, and many examples have strong homosexual overtones. Marcus in *The Other Victorians* goes much further when he states categorically: '[The] fantasy is a homosexual one: a little boy is being beaten—that is, loved—by another man. And we must conclude, I believe, that the entire immense literature of flagellation produced during the Victorian period, along with the fantasies it embodied and the practices it depicted, represents a kind of last-ditch compromise with and defence against homosexuality.'[17]

The homosexual overtones in certain examples are presented in an all-female setting: *The Merry Order of St. Bridget, Personal Recollections of the Use of the Rod* (1868) concerns the activities of a closed order of female flagellants. Edward Sellon's *New Ladies Tickler, or the Adventures of Lady Lovesport and the Audacious Harry* (1866) consists of a series of letters from Emily to her friend Lucy describing how she was initiated into the pleasures of chastisement by her aunt, Lady Lovesport: 'It usually happened that between my struggles and her endeavours to retain me on her knee, her clothes would also be tossed up, and before the conclusion of my punishment, her thighs were generally as bare as my own, and I lay with my naked belly and thighs pressed against her naked person. On these occasions I could not but admire the softness and beauty of the charms which were thus exposed to me.' And two of Emily's letters deal exclusively with the homosexual activities that take place between a younger and an older boy. These scenes recall similar activities in *Adventures of a Schoolboy or the Freaks of Youthful Passion* (1866) by Ashbee's friend James Campbell Reddie, with illustrations by Edward Sellon: two Eton schoolboys seduce their young female cousins but when excited by reading *Fanny Hill* they have sex with each other.

Another example of flagellation literature betraying homosexual feelings is the poem entitled '*The Rodiad*' (*c.* 1820s). The author is trying to demonstrate that 'the schoolmaster's joy is to flog':

> For want of better sport, I hold with glee
> Some naughty urchin tight across my knee;
> And while his puny pike for pardon begs,
> Stripe the whole skin between his straddling legs.
> Oh, hour that comes too late and goes too soon,
> My day's delight,—my flogging hour at noon,
> When I count up the boys that stay behind,
> And class their bottoms in my cheerful mind!

And homosexual overtones can be found quite frequently in other varieties of pornography: in *Rosa Fielding, or a Victim of Lust* (1867), two men enter a woman at the same time, while in *La Femme Endormie* (translated as *The Benumbed Woman*) of 1899, two men copulate with a life-sized female doll at different times, leaving notes for each other in her underwear, thus having a sexual relationship with each other via the doll they share.

Famous examples of explicit homosexual pornography include the Earl of Rochester's amusing play *Sodom* written for Charles II in 1684; a scene in John Cleland's *Fanny Hill* of 1784; and the poem *Don Leon* published by Dugdale (implausibly attributed to Byron) in 1866. One of the most interesting nineteenth-century books relating to homosexuality is *The Phoenix of Sodom, or the Vere Street Coterie* of 1813. This is a shocked account of the sexual happenings at the White Swan public house in Vere Street, which was raided by the police in 1810, leading to the execution of two soldiers and the imprisonment of seven men. The book describes the furnishings of the various rooms and the mock marriages and other activities that took place, and gives details about the inhabitants: 'It seems the greater part of these reptiles assumed feigned names, though not very appropriate to their calling in life: for instance, Kitty Cambric is a Coal Merchant; Miss Selina a Runner at a Police Office; Black-eyed Leonora, a Drummer; Pretty Harriet, a Butcher; Lady Godina, a Waiter; the Duchess of Gloucester, a gentleman's servant; Duchess of Devonshire, a Blacksmith; and Miss Sweet-Lips, a Country Grocer.'

Another homosexual scandal, the Boulton and Park case of 1871, was the inspiration for two specifically pornographic tales, *The Sins of the Cities of the Plain, or the recollections of a Mary-Anne* (1881) and *Letters from Laura and Eveline giving an account of their mock-marriage, wedding trip etc.* (1883). The former is the story of a man who picks up an 'effeminate, but very good looking young fellow' in Leicester Square, takes him back to his rooms for sex, and then hears his story of life in London as a 'Mary-Anne'. The book seems to be based on fact, and gives a convincing account of one aspect of sexual life in Victorian London which is largely ignored in *My Secret Life* of *c.* 1890.

Among known admirers of *The Sins of the Cities of the Plain* was Oscar Wilde. We have already noted his probable involvement in *Teleny or the Reverse of the Medal* published by Smithers in 1893, the best-known example of Victorian homosexual pornography. Opinions of *Teleny* have ranged from 'the most pretentious clandestine homosexual fantasy' (Fryer[18]) to 'better written than the vast majority of English erotic books' (Dawes[19]).

The story tells of the passionate love felt by Camille de Grieux for the famous pianist René Teleny. Camille is saved from suicide by his idol, and they masturbate each other in the cab on the way home: 'Our fingers hardly moved the skin of the penis; but our nerves were so strained, our excitement had reached such a pitch, and the seminal ducts were so full, that we felt them overflowing. There was, for a moment, an intense pain, somewhere about the root of the penis—or rather, within the very core and centre of the veins, after which the sap of life began to move slowly, slowly, from within the seminal glands; it mounted up the bulb of the urethra, and up the narrow column, somewhat like mercury within the tube of a thermometer—or rather, like the scalding and scathing lava within the crater of a volcano. It finally reached the apex; then the slit gaped, the tiny lips parted, and the pearly, creamy, viscous fluid oozed out—not all at once in a gushing jet, but at intervals, and in huge burning tears. At every drop that escaped out of the body, a creepy almost unbearable feeling started from the tips of the fingers, from the ends of the toes, especially from the innermost cells of the brain . . . a tremendous shock took place; a convulsion which annihilated both mind and matter, a quivering delight which everyone has felt, to a greater or lesser degree—often a thrill almost too intense to be pleasurable.'

Teleny teaches the inexperienced Camille the delights of homosexual love, and for a time life is perfect. They go to parties and concerts together, and take part in an orgy in an artist's exotically furnished studio: 'A thousand lamps of varied form filled the room with a strong yet hazy light. There were wax tapers upheld by Japanese cranes, or glowing in massive bronze or silver candlesticks, the plunder of Spanish altars; star-shaped or octagonal lamps from Moorish mosques or Eastern synagogues. . . . Though the room was very large, the walls were all covered with pictures of the most lascivious nature . . . on faded old damask couches, on huge pillows made out of priests' stoles, worked by devout fingers in silver and gold, on soft Persian and Syrian divans, on lion and panther rugs . . . men, young and good-looking, almost all naked, were lounging there by twos and threes.'

Camille soon learns to enjoy to the full his new-found life with Teleny: 'He took hold of my rod and pressed it against his gaping anus. The tip of the frisky phallus soon found its entrance in the hospitable hole that endeavoured to give it admission. I pressed a little; the whole of the glans was engulfed. The sphincter soon gripped it in such a way that it could not come out without an effort. I thrust it slowly to prolong as much as possible the ineffable sensation that ran through every limb, to calm the quivering nerves and to allay the heat of the blood. Another push, and half the phallus was in his body. . . . I pressed forward again, and the whole of it, down to its very root, was all swallowed up . . . so keen was the bliss that overcame me, that I asked myself if some ethereal, life-giving fluid were not being poured on my head, and trickling down slowly over my quivering flesh? Surely the rain-awakened flowers must be conscious of such a sensation during a shower, after they have been parched by the scorching rays of an estival sun. Teleny again put his arm round me and held me tight. I gazed at myself within his eyes, he saw himself in mine.'

Camille begins to suspect his lover of having an affair with a lady, and to his horror discovers his own mother in the arms of Teleny. He throws himself in the river but is saved. Teleny, who has made love to Madame de Grieux solely in order to pay off his debts, stabs himself but survives long enough for Camille to find him. After their reconciliation Teleny dies in Camille's arms.

Teleny distinguishes itself from most Victorian pornography because it is not written to be enjoyed at the expense of women. The partners in the scenes of homosexual love are equals, enjoying a mutually pleasurable activity. There is no rape or flagellation, no partnership of dominance and submission. And the sexual scenes involve not merely activities but emotions and feelings. These scenes go into much more detail about the effects of sexual arousal than is usual, and show an attempt to escape from the usual hackneyed phraseology. In parts, especially towards the end of the story, the literary standard is very uneven, but the flavour of the Decadent period runs throughout, and like *The Picture of Dorian Gray* (1891) it shows the influence of Huysman's *À Rebours (Against Nature)* of 1884.

The most famous examples of homosexuality and lesbianism in nineteenth-century literature both involve mysterious author-ship. We can be reasonably sure that Oscar Wilde edited and inspired *Teleny*, though whether he wrote any of it is less certain. Research has however demonstrated that Alfred de Musset wrote *Gamiani* in 1833, perhaps with the involvement of George Sand.[20] The book was translated as *Gamiani or Two Nights of Excess*, and has been frequently republished. The language remains polite throughout, in spite of incidents involving rape, flagellation, bestiality with a dog, an orang-utan and an ass, an orgy in a convent and numerous lesbian encounters, all accomplished in a mere sixty pages. The style is deliberately frenetic and lacking in all pretentiousness; clearly the author has no desire to be taken seriously, and the result is one of the most entertaining of all nineteenth-century pornographic novels. The climax is a love-death that parodies the world of high Romanticism: the lesbian Countess Gamiani has given her lover poison and swallowed the rest herself, and they die in a passionate embrace: 'I have known all the excesses of sensuality in the torments caused by the poison. I am dying in the rage of passion, mad, quite mad. Don't you understand? I only wanted to know if there was something more to be enjoyed in the agonies of death.'

5

Humour is rarely found in Victorian pornography. The fantasies are deadly serious, and the authors have no desire to show how absurd much of it is. But touches of humour occur in the underground magazines of the period, which had the added bonus of spicy engravings. The earliest was *The Exquisite* (1840s), followed by *The Boudoir* (1860) and *The Cremorne* (1882). The most famous was *The Pearl* (1879–80), which included serials (*Miss Coote's Confession, or the voluptuous experi-*

ences of an old maid; Lady Pokingham, or they all do it), readers' letters, parodies, limericks, poems and jokes: 'The Rev. Newman Hall will lecture on *The Conduct of Lot and his Daughters*, December 20th. Illustrated with Dissolving views of the Paternal Pego entering the Daughters' cunts. Also January 7th: *Solomon in All his Glory*, with 700 wives and 300 concubines; being an attempt to elucidate the mystery of how he gave satisfaction to them all.'[21]

An anti-religious note creeps into much Victorian pornography, as in *Cythera's Hymnal, or Flakes from the Foreskin* of 1870, a collection of cleverly written parodies of popular ballads and hymns:

> See him rise, with pride ascending,
>   Oft in favoured sinners lain,
> Thousand thousand crabs attending
>   Swell the triumph of his train;
>   Hallelujah! Hallelujah!
> Rises prick to fall again.
>
> Virgin eyes with fear behold him
>   Rise in dreadful majesty;
> Claps that set at nought and sold him,
>   Pox that burned him grievously,
>   Never fears he, never fears he,
> In the bliss of venery.

One is reminded of Dr. E. P. Pusey's already quoted *Manual of Confessors* by another poem which begins:

> The Reverend Pimlico Poole was a saint
>   Who averted from sinners their doom,
> By confessing the ladies until they felt faint,
>   All alone in a little dark room.

Rather less conscious humour can be found in the poems published by Aleister Crowley in 1898 as *White Stains: the literary remains of George Archibald Bishop, a neuropath of the Second Empire*. His subjects included venereal disease, a taste for human excrement, sex with a menstruating woman, bestiality with a dog, and necrophilia:

Yea, thou art dead. Thy buttocks now
   Are swan-soft, and thou sweatest not;
   And has a strange desire begot
In me, to lick thy bloody brow;

To probe thy belly, and to drink
   Thy godless fluids, and the pool
   Of rank putrescence from the stool
Thy hanged corpse gave, whose luscious stink

Excites these songs sublime. The rod
   Gains new desire; dive, howl, cling, suck,
   Rave, shriek, and chew; excite the fuck,
Hold me, I come! I'm dead! My God!

Mark Twain wrote an inspired satire in 1882 entitled: *1601—
a conversation as it was at the social fireside in the time of the Tudors*,
which represents a discussion between Queen Elizabeth I and
various courtiers arising from an unfortunate incident: 'In ye
heat of ye talk it befel yt one did breake wind, yielding an
exceeding mightie and distresfull stink.' The Queen asks
Master Shaxpur if he is responsible, but he denies it: 'the pit
itself hath furnished forth the stink, and heaven's artillery hath
shook the globe in admiration of it.' Another famous writer of
the day, George Augustus Sala, was the probable author of a
clever satirical play or pantomime entitled *Harlequin Prince
Cherrytop and the Good Fairy Fairfuck* of 1879. Inspired by
Rochester's *Sodom*, it tells of the struggle between Demon
Masturbation and the Good Fairy Fairfuck to control the
sexual habits of Prince Cherrytop. It is a playful satire which
laughs at the vices of Victorian England. Fairy Fairfuck wins,
and it has the traditional happy ending:

You, Prince, relieved from solitary vice,
May now enjoy each hole you fancy nice.

The most polished and sophisticated example of Victorian
sexual humour must be Aubrey Beardsley's *Venus and Tannhauser*, first published as *Under the Hill* in the *Savoy* magazine in
1897 and later issued in a more complete but still unfinished
version by Smithers in 1907. It contains no four-letter words or
explicit scenes of copulation and flagellation; instead, it is a

delicately risqué parody of the legend of Tannhauser and the Venusberg which seems much closer in spirit to eighteenth-century France than Victorian England: 'Tannhauser, pale and speechless with excitement, passed his gem-girt fingers brutally over the divine limbs, tearing away smock and pantaloon and stocking, and then, stripping himself of his own few things, fell upon the splendid lady with a deep-drawn breath!'

Beardsley allows his sexual imagination full rein: homo-sexual activities with little boys, erotic enjoyment of urination and other bodily functions, clothing fetishism, masturbation, transvestism and bestiality all play a part in the story and yet are described in witty and delicate language: 'After the first charming interchange of affectionate delicacies was over, the unicorn lay down upon his side, and, closing his eyes, beat his stomach wildly with the mark of his manhood! Venus caught that stunning member in her hands and lay her cheek along it; but few touches were wanted to consumate the creature's pleasure. . . . Venus knelt where it had fallen, and lapped her little aperitif!' We are far from the aching giant phalluses of Beardsley's *Lysistrata* illustrations of 1896, but both of his erotic projects give insight into his own sexuality as well as demonstrating artistic tastes in the 1890s. *Venus and Tannhauser* has nothing in common with the world of *Moll Flanders* or *Fanny Hill* where a life of wickedness is absolved by quick repentance. Nor does it share the Victorian pornographer's desperate attempt at sexual stimulation through endless descriptions of rape and flagellation, incest and homosexuality.

Incest is a fantasy that abounds in erotic literature, and *The Loves of Venus: or the Young Wife's Confession, a true tale of real life* of 1881 is an interesting example. In a series of letters, Fred recounts his experiences with his new wife Ada to his sister Frederica, with whom he has had an incestuous relationship. It transpires that Ada had been seduced by her brother Ferdie, who is now invited to join the couple and their maid Sophy for sexual pleasures: 'Isn't it lovely, dear, to see such a pretty pair in action? Look at Ferdie's beautiful prick as it slips in and out of his sister! Don't you wish you had a brother to fuck you, Sophy?' The story ends with an apologia for the practice of incest.

A much longer and more tedious book with a similar theme is

The Romance of Lust, or early experiences. Four volumes were published between 1873 and 1876, the first three having been written by Ashbee's friend William S. Potter, a pornographer and collector of erotica. The story tells of the sexual initiation and later exploits of Charles Roberts, written from the usual chauvinistic point of view, and concerns his sexual behaviour alone, to the rigorous exclusion of every other consideration. The book is thus a seemingly endless description of people having sex: heterosexual, homosexual, incestuous, flagellant. All the usual elements can be found, from ritual deflowering of virgins to descriptions of women spending copiously. The result is a positively anti-erotic exercise in which sex becomes a series of mechanical activities: 'The Count next took the Benson in cunt while I blocked the rear aperture, and the Frankland once more enculed the Egerton, who dildoed herself in cunt at the same time; all of us running two courses. We then rose, purified, and refreshed. When our pricks were ready it was the Egerton who took me in front and the Count behind, and the Benson, who had grown lewd on the Frankland's clitoris, was sodomised by her and dildoed by herself.'

Charles has early incestuous relationships with his two sisters and also his aunt and uncle. Towards the end of the book, he marries an Italian girl by whom he has a daughter. After his wife's death he initiates his daughter into sexual pleasure and then marries her. They have a son, and the three fuck together through his declining years: 'We are thus a happy family, bound by the strong ties of double incestuous lust.'

We have already noted the infatuation with young girls shared by John Ruskin and Lewis Carroll. Child prostitution was one of the saddest effects of sexual repression in Victorian London,[22] and pornography catered for this interest as well. *Flossie, a Venus of 15, by one who knew this charming goddess and worshipped at her shrine* (1899) recounts the extraordinary affair between Captain Archer and a young girl who lives in a personal dream-world. Captain Archer willingly plays the role required by Flossie's fantasies: 'Thrusting my yard between her lips, the Great White Queen of the Game Huchi Islands sucked in the whole column to the very root, and by dint of working her royal mouth up and down and applying her royal fingers to the neighbouring appendages, soon drew into her throat a tribute to her greatness.' The author makes a point of stressing that it is proper to initiate girls into sexual pleasures very early in life as long as intercourse is delayed until they reach maturity.

Flossie's dream-world is a useful gimmick and gimmickry pervades Victorian pornography. For instance, the narrator of *The Amatory Experiences of a Surgeon* (1881) by James Campbell Reddie is able to achieve the sexualization of all reality through the metaphor of his medical practice. He specializes in young ladies with menstruation and puberty problems, and at one stage concentrates his attentions on a 13-year-old called Mary who has a spinal complaint. This means she has to keep still, yet she implores her doctor to 'fuck me with real energy, if only for once; do let me feel what the extasies of sexual conjunction are really like; let me die of love for once, if I am never able to bear it again.' Never at a loss for ideas, the doctor invents a special couch onto which the girl is tied down, and the result is more than satisfying to each. In fact, 'the fucking etc. had such a salubrious effect upon my young patient that she eventually quite got the better of her spinal complaint, and was married at the age of eighteen.'

James Campbell Reddie was a collector of pornography and Ashbee's main informant. Besides *The Amatory Experiences of a Surgeon* he also wrote the previously noted *Adventures of a Schoolboy*. Ashbee's circle included most of the known authors of the mainly anonymous world of Victorian pornography, such as William S. Potter, part-author of the already discussed *Romance of Lust*, and Edward Sellon. Sellon was the author of the most famous fantasy concerning the defloration of young girls, *The New Epicurean or The delights of sex* of 1865. This relates the experiences of Sir Charles who lives on a country estate where he can satisfy his desires thanks to the kind services of a friendly neighbourhood school-mistress: 'We were soon naked, and sporting in the water; then only was it that I could take in all their loveliness at a glance. The budding small pointed breasts, just beginning to grow; the polished ivory shoulders; the exquisite fall in the back, the tiny waists, the bulging voluptuous hips, the dimpled bottoms, blushing and fresh, the plump thighs and smoothe white bellies. In a moment my truncheon stood up hard and firm as a constable's staff.' By showing the girls the mating activities of the animals on his farm, he easily arouses their desires for sexual experimentation, and his wife has no objections: indeed, at one point she succeeds in seducing a young boy.

Edward Sellon was probably the most interesting member of Ashbee's circle. He spent ten years in the Indian army, taught fencing, drove the London to Cambridge mail coach, translated Martial's *Epigrams* and Boccaccio's *Decameron* and illustrated James Campbell Reddie's *Adventures of a Schoolboy*. In addition to *The New Ladies' Tickler* and *The New Epicurean*, which have already been discussed, he also wrote two books on Hindu literature and archaeology, and an autobiography entitled *The Ups and Downs of Life* of 1867. He blew his brains out in a London hotel shortly after selling the manuscript to the publisher Dugdale. He was 48 years old.

The Ups and Downs of Life is a readable and entertaining account of Sellon's life, the concentration being on his sexual exploits. The first half concerns his years in India, and includes interesting accounts of the behaviour of native women: 'They have one custom that seems singular to a European, they not only shave the Mons Veneris but take a clean sweep underneath it, so that until you glance at their hard, full and enchanting breasts, handsome beyond compare, you fancy you have got hold of some unfledged girl. The Rajpootanee girl plucks out the hairs as they appear with a pair of tweezers, as the ancient Greek women did, and this I think a very preferable process to the shaving. It is impossible to describe the enjoyment I experienced in the arms of these syrens. I have had English, French, German and Polish women of all grades of society since, but never, never did they bear any comparison with those salacious, succulent houris of the far East.' After his return to England, he marries and enjoys a love-hate relationship with his wife. Periods are spent as 'a gentleman at large in London' and these alternate with wedded bliss in the country: 'Augusta would strip naked, place herself in any attitude, let me gamahuche her, would gamahuche in her turn, indulged all my whimsies. . . . I was faithful for three years.'

The most extraordinary sexual autobiography of the nineteenth century must be Walter's *My Secret Life* of *c.* 1890, in which an anonymous gentleman of the upper middle class describes his sexual experiences from childhood to late middle age. The book runs to eleven volumes, about 4,200 pages, and towards the end, the author declares that he has 'probably fucked now . . . something like 1,200 women. . . . I find I have had women of 27 different Empires, Kingdoms or Countries, and 80 or more nationalities, including every one in Europe except a Laplander.' An early encounter takes place in a village church-yard: 'I stripped off my coat, made it into a bundle, and placed it for her head. "There—there," I said, and pulled her down. She made no resistance. I saw white thighs and belly, black hair on her cunt; and the next minute I was spending up her. "Shove on," said she, "I was just coming"; and she was wriggling and heaving, "go on". I could always go on pushing after a spend in those days; my prick would not lose its stiffness for minutes afterwards; so I pushed till I thought of doing her a second time: but her pleasure came on, her cunt contracted, and with the usual wriggle and sigh she was over, and there were we laying in copulation, with the dead all around us; another living creature might that moment have been begotten, in its turn to eat, drink, fuck, die, be buried, and rot."'

We can see here the similarities between *My Secret Life* and more usual examples of Victorian pornography: the concentration on the details of the sexual act, the totally male viewpoint, the woman presented merely as an extension of the penis. But the author more than once expresses a dislike of pornography for its fantastic exaggerations and falsifications, and his own work differs considerably. There is a straightforwardness about his descriptions, and a lack of embellishment, which gives them authenticity and demonstrates a total lack of desire to stimulate. And his philosophical musings strengthen the feeling of authenticity. Nothing seems to escape his attention: he discusses sadism, masochism, menstruation, voyeurism, urination, defecation, venereal disease, crabs, lice. He experiments with homosexuality, enjoys copulating with a woman in another man's semen, experiences the pleasure of deflowering young girls. He gives information about brothels, public lavatories, women's underwear. What we have here is the record of a real existence, which in turn adds to our total picture of Victorian life.

There is no formal structure to *My Secret Life*. The information is neither presented as an analysis of social history, nor arranged in the cultivated literary style of a Casanova. But the book bears comparison with the Victorian novel. We have earlier discussed the lack of real sexual investigation in the works of Eliot and Dickens; Walter's powers of observation add the missing dimension. Of course he lacks Dickens's creative ability and appears to have no conscience at all. Nevertheless, his writing can be seen to have a value as an additional context for the study of Victorian literature.

6

Pornography is fantasy. The Victorian pornographic novel represents the fantasy of the Victorian male: all men are sexual athletes, all women flow with the juices of love. Jealousy and possessiveness have little part to play in this fantasy, for here, everything is for the best in the best of all possible worlds. It would seem that this must be a supremely happy world, yet behind the sybaritic pursuits, we can feel a desperation, an anxious search for something which real life could not provide. We do not necessarily have to agree with Marcus's view that 'inside of every pornographer there is an infant screaming for the breast from which he has been torn',[23] but all these mechanical couplings, these frenzied repetitions, this desperate search for endless pleasure, all the characteristic elements of Victorian pornography betray a secret need for sexual fulfilment. And that fulfilment is sought by the male, usually at the expense of the female.

We have discovered no unknown masterpiece in our discussion, although certain examples have shone out from the dross. But by means of reading between the lines and following the sign language employed, we have outlined a genre of the Victorian novel which complements the concerns of Dickens and Eliot and which reflects the obsessions of Swinburne and Rossetti, of Carroll and Wilde. It presents us with a mine of information on the most intimate activities of mankind, and adds considerably to our sense of the reality of life in Victorian England.[24]

NOTES

1. Quoted in G. H. Fleming, *That Ne'er Shall Meet Again* (Michael Joseph, London, 1971), p. 362.
2. Carroll's infatuation with little girls is discussed further in Peter Webb, *The Erotic Arts* (Secker & Warburg, London, 1975), pp. 193–96.
3. Wilde's involvement with Teleny is discussed in Montgomery Hyde, *A History of Pornography* (Four Square, London, 1966), pp. 149–53.
4. These obsessions are discussed further in Barry Curtis, *Erotic Themes in Victorian Literature*, in Peter Webb, op. cit., Chapter 5, section B.
5. Cf. 'you will know how to choose the good, and to avoid the evil; the finest passages are always the purest, the bad are invariably revolting; you will never wish to read them over twice.' Charlotte Brontë to Miss Lewis, advice on reading Shakespeare and Byron, letter dated 16 March 1839, quoted in Ronald Pearsall, *The Worm in the Bud* (Penguin, Harmondsworth, 1971), p. 518.
6. The part played by sex in the works of Dickens is discussed in Jennie Calder, *Women & Marriage in Victorian Fiction* (Thames & Hudson, London, 1976).
7. Official Victorian attitudes to masturbation are discussed in Alex Comfort, *The Anxiety Makers* (Nelson, London, 1967).
8. Ashbee published his researches in *Index Librorum Prohibitorum*, 1877; *Centuria Librorum Absconditorum*, 1879; *Catena Librorum Tacendorum*, 1885.
9. Montgomery Hyde, op. cit.; Ronald Pearsall, op. cit.; Wayland Young, *Eros Denied* (Corgi, London, 1968).
10. Drs. Phyllis and Eberhard Kronhausen, *Erotic Fantasies* (Grove Press, New York, 1969); Peter Fryer, *Private Case, Public Scandal* (Secker & Warburg, London, 1966).
11. Steven Marcus, *The Other Victorians* (Corgi, London, 1969).
12. C. R. Dawes, *History of English Erotic Literature*, 1943, unpublished, typescript in British Library.
13. Montgomery Hyde, op. cit., p. 141.
14. H. S. Ashbee, *Index*, op. cit., entry on *Flagellation*.
15. H. S. Ashbee, *Index*, op. cit.
16. Swinburne's enjoyment of flagellation is discussed in Philip Henderson, *Swinburne* (Routledge & Kegan Paul, London, 1974), Chapter 7.
17. Steven Marcus, op. cit., p. 263.
18. Peter Fryer, op. cit., p. 113.
19. C. R. Dawes, op. cit.
20. The authorship of *Gamiani* is discussed in the Kronhausens, op. cit., p. 130.
21. *The Pearl*, No. 17, November 1880.
22. Child prostitution in Victorian London is discussed in Ronald Pearsall, op. cit., Chapter 6.
23. Steven Marcus, op. cit., p. 277.
24. Certain works discussed in this essay have been published in recent editions: H. S. Ashbee, *Index of Forbidden Books* (Sphere, London, 1969),

and *Forbidden Books of the Victorians*, edited by Peter Fryer (Odyssey, London, 1970); *The Pearl, a Journal of Facetiae and Voluptuous Reading* (Grove Press, New York, 1968); *The Memoirs of Dolly Morton* (Brandon House, North Hollywood, 1968); *The Romance of Lust* (Grove Press, New York, 1968); *A Man with a Maid* (Grove Press, New York, 1968); *Gamiani* in *The Erotic Trio, Three Centuries of Sex* (Holloway House, Los Angeles, 1972); *Frank & I* (Grove Press, New York, 1968); *Venus in Furs* (Sphere Books, London, 1969); *Raped on the Railway*, no publisher, London, no date (1970s); *1601*, privately printed, Hackensack, 1968; *Teleny* (expurgated, Icon, London, 1966, and unexpurgated, Brandon Books, California, 1966); *The Story of Venus and Tannhauser* (Award Books, New York, and Tandem Books, London, 1967), and *Under the Hill*, completed by John Glassco (Grove Press, New York, 1959); *White Stains* (Duckworth, London, 1973); *My Secret Life* (Castle Books, New Jersey, 1966). See also: the Kronhausens, *Pornography and the Law* (Ballantine Books, New York, 1970); Robert Reisner (editor), *Great Erotic Scenes from Literature* (Playboy Press, Chicago, 1972); Patrick J. Kearney, *The Private Case* (Jay Landesman, London, 1981): this includes bibliographical details and catalogue numbers of many rare works discussed above which are now in the British Library Restricted Collection.

5

Sexual Fiction in America, 1955–80

by MAURICE CHARNEY

According to Spector's law, the amount of sexual activity in any given society is a constant and varies only in degrees of covert or overt expression. Although we cannot invoke the wraithlike Spector for further reasoning on this dictum, we can see that it applies with alarming relevance to American sexual writing of the past twenty-five years. The Sexual Revolution, so called, has not changed anything fundamentally, but only altered the ratios of covert to overt expression. Even the most blatantly overt forms of eroticism and pornography have their saturation point, so that the relaxation or disappearance of censorship does not have the cataclysmic effects attributed to it. It is still possible for X-rated movie theatres to go out of business for lack of patronage or for the most sexual of books to be remaindered for lack of readers. Sexuality is definitely not a growth industry of limitless potential. The sexual awareness of the '60s is already blunted, and a counter-movement for the return of innocence and 'family' values is well under way. This does not, however, shake Spector's redoubtable law, which would deny any net decrease in sexual interest—sexuality is well adapted to go underground. In movies, for example, it is no longer fashionable to have an obligatory and mostly irrelevant nude scene, but this doesn't mean that the powerful mixture of sex and violence has in any way abated. It is now spruced up to satisfy the objective criteria of 'family entertainment'.

George Steiner's plaintive outcry against dirty words and pornography in his *Encounter* piece, 'Night Words: High Pornography and Human Privacy' (and in public lectures of that period) is not only anachronistic but pointless. Steiner attacks Norman Mailer's novel, *An American Dream* (1965), for its crudely overt sexuality, yet the novel fails as sexual writing not because of its dirty words or its graphic description of sadistic anal sex, but because it is so unrealized in its sexual imagination. Cherry, particularly, is a sentimentalized whore with a heart of gold, and Mailer has never been able to recapture the aggressive sexual intensity of his short story, 'The Time of Her Time' (in *Advertisements for Myself*, 1959). Steiner's call for reticence in sexual writing seems to me entirely irrevelent to the genre. The skill and the accomplishment do not lie in degrees of overt or covert expression but in the ability to evoke erotic transcendence. Despite Mailer's admiration for Henry Miller, he has not been able to reproduce Miller's easy exuberance. *Tropic of Cancer* (1934) was such a wonderful sexual book because it was so light-hearted and so much insisted on sexuality as part of that good life lived only by artists and expatriates.

It is not possible in a short essay to summarize sexual writing in America in the past twenty-five years. There is virtually no recent novel that does not have some sexual scenes to satisfy the imaginary reader's demands. These need not be overt, as the enormous success of harlequin romances can testify, which, although chaste by the strictest standards, are nevertheless dripping with unrequited lust. We recall that the great English classic of sexual fiction, *Memoirs of a Woman of Pleasure* (1749)—also called *Fanny Hill*—has not a single dirty word in its highly euphemized pages. I would like to concentrate on what I consider the four most important sexual books of our period (1955–80): Philip Roth's *Portnoy's Complaint* (1969) and Erica Jong's *Fear of Flying* (1973), which are related to each other in many important assumptions; Nabokov's *Lolita* (1955) and Southern and Hoffenberg's *Candy* (1958), both published by the Olympia Press in Paris, which may be

123

even more closely related as model and parody. After these four novels, I would like to consider three characteristic sexual fictions of the '70s: William Kotzwinkle, *Nightbook* (1974); Gael Greene, *Blue Skies, No Candy* (1976); and Scott Spencer, *Endless Love* (1979).

Desire is the energizing element of all sexual fiction—not gratified desire but desire that is blocked, frustrated, and diverted; in other words, desire that has become part of imaginative projection. These motivating concepts have been skilfully acknowledged by Leo Bersani in *A Future for Astyanax: Character and Desire in Literature*, and by René Girard in *Deceit, Desire and the Novel: Self and Other in Literary Structure*. Desire evokes an eroticized reality; desire seeks correlatives, gestures, and rituals of satisfaction; desire creates a world that is the object of desire. In sexual literature, of course, the flow goes both ways and the created world of desire echoes back on the subject in a series of sexual correspondences.

These dynamics are evident in Philip Roth's exuberant novel, *Portnoy's Complaint*, published in 1969. For the author the novel represents an important breakthrough in the form of a psychoanalytic, 'autobiographical' outpouring that is highly explicit in its Yiddishized sexual expression. The novel purports to be a record of Portnoy's inflamed psychoanalytic sessions with Dr. Spielvogel—a series of therapeutic soliloquies in verbatim transcript. Thus, 'Portnoy's Complaint' is defined as a psychological disorder 'in which strongly-felt ethical and altruistic impulses are perpetually warring with extreme sexual longings, often of a perverse nature' (p. vii). It expresses itself in 'acts of exhibitionism, voyeurism, fetishism, auto-eroticism and oral coitus', and although the feeling of sexuality is intense, there is no 'genuine sexual gratification', but rather 'overriding feelings of shame and the dread of retribution, particularly in the form of castration'. The disorder has its origin in the feelings of guilt created by the mother-child relationship.

Mrs. Portnoy, the archetypal Jewish mother, looms large in *Portnoy's Complaint*. She is preoccupied with obsessive rituals of food and hygiene that will control a sexualized and anxiety-laden reality. The koshering of meat by salting it and letting the blood drain out is a symbol to Portnoy of emasculation, whereas the eating of unclean, unkosher meats like lobster releases for him 'the whole slimy, suicidal Dionysian side of my nature' (p. 79). All the prohibitive dietary rules and regulations were only designed 'to give us little Jewish children practice in being repressed' (p. 79). That's why Portnoy exclaims with such capitalized anguish: 'LET'S PUT THE ID BACK IN YID!' (p. 124) and why he strives so manfully to be 'the Raskolnikov of jerking off' (p. 20).

Masturbation is the symbol of the instinctual life and thus of one's sexual identity, and one's sexual identity is an exact equivalent of one's personal identity and integrity set apart from mother, father, and Old Testament God. Portnoy's whacking off is a strenuous and even painful assertion of his identity in the face of his mother's repressive control:

> I tear off my pants, furiously I grab that battered battering ram to freedom, my adolescent cock, even as my mother begins to call from the other side of the bathroom door. 'Now this time don't flush. Do you hear me, Alex? I have to see what's in that bowl!'
>
> Doctor, do you understand what I was up against? My wang was all I really had that I could call my own. (p. 33)

So Alex, striving to be the archetypal Bad Boy and commit the Unpardonable Sin, masturbates with a piece of liver at 3.30 p.m. that his family eats for dinner at 5.30 p.m. 'So. Now you know the worst thing I have ever done. I fucked my own family's dinner' (p. 134). The violation of food is for Alex the ultimate taboo.

Portnoy's world is deeply polarized between mythical Jews and Christians (*goyim*, and, especially, *shikses*, or Christian girls). Shikses are heavily erotic because they are forbidden, like the unclean meats prohibited by the dietary laws (the link between food and sex is everywhere assumed). Thus the lovely Christian girls ice-skating on the lake in Irvington Park illuminate for Portnoy the meaning of the words 'longing' and 'pang', themselves part of a heavily clichéd Gentile vocabulary: 'the sight of their fresh cold blond hair spilling out of their kerchiefs and caps' (p. 144) renders Portnoy 'ecstatic'. 'I am so awed that I am in a state of desire *beyond a hard-on*. My circumcised little dong is simply shriveled up with veneration. Maybe it's dread. How do they get so gorgeous, so healthy, so *blond?*' (pp. 144–45). Naturally, all of Portnoy's sex partners are shikses: Bubbles Girardi, Kay the Pumpkin, Sarah Abbott Maulsby, and especially The Monkey, so called for some special, unnamed perversion she has mastered. Jewish and Christian values are amusingly polarized as Portnoy and his partners avidly and romantically seek out contrary qualities: 'in this Monkey's estimation it was my mission to pull her up from those very abysses of frivolity and waste, of perversity and wildness and lust, into which I myself have been so vainly trying all my life successfully to sink . . .' (pp. 134–35). Portnoy and the Monkey educate each other in opposites.

In Alex's vision of America the Christian world is darkly sexual. It is his own 'heart of darkness' that he must penetrate, or, as he puts it,

> I don't seem to stick my dick up these girls, as much as I stick it up their backgrounds—as though through fucking I will discover America. *Conquer* America—maybe that's more like it. Columbus, Captain Smith, Governor Winthrop, General Washington—now Portnoy. As though my manifest destiny is to seduce a girl from each of the forty-eight states. (p. 235)

This is Portnoy as picaresque hero, but a *picaro*/seducer who needs to triumph over an alien world. The Jew is defined as an unheroic, comic sexual adventurer, whose victories are as much educational as sexual. His romantic quest takes a sexual turn, since it is *only* through fucking that Portnoy can possibly discover that other America that lies outside his Newark ghetto. He wants what's coming to him, his American birthright, '*My* G.I. bill—real American ass! The cunt in country-'tis-of-thee! I pledge allegiance to the twat of the United States of America . . .' (p. 236). All these hysterical declamations are only, of course, part of Portnoy's confessional soliloquy to his psychoanalyst. They are fantasies of power and dominance. Portnoy desperately needs Christian America, and especially the White Anglo-Saxon Protestant (W.A.S.P.) ideology, to release his heavily repressed sexual impulses; in Israel he is impotent.

Behind *Portnoy's Complaint* lies Freud's essay, 'The Most Prevalent Form of Degradation in Erotic Life' (1912), which is the title of the chapter beginning on p. 184. Freud's dynamics energize Portnoy's deeply dichotomized sexual life, which is split between his powerful, loving attachment to his ambivalent mother and his equally powerful but guilty feelings of lust. As Freud puts it, 'Where such men love they have no desire and where they desire they cannot love. In order to keep their sensuality out of contact with the objects they love, they seek out objects whom they need not love' (p. 177). In other words, the women desired for sex must be as unlike the mother as possible; if they are not, they must be 'degraded' in order to function as sexual objects: 'As soon as the sexual object fulfils the condition of being degraded, sensual feeling can have free play' (p. 178). The problem with this system is that its opposite poles never function independently of each other, so that love and lust are hopelessly confused and the whole mechanism is drenched in guilt.

But guilt fuels sexuality, and contemporary writing about sex would be impossible without guilt. The sex of *Brave New World*, for example, is both guiltless and joyless, and the pornotopia of science fiction is admirable for its ingenuity and effortlessness but not for its excitement. Portnoy cultivates his guilt because he cannot conceive desire without guilt: it is warm, sticky, forbidden, and almost inevitably connected with masturbatory fantasy. Sex cannot exist without fantasy, and the violation of taboos provides a necessary atmosphere for desire. For Portnoy and for many other essentially adolescent sexual heroes (or anti-heroes), sex must be dirty in order to be vital.

Erica Jong's *Fear of Flying* (1973) is in many ways a companion novel to *Portnoy's Complaint*. In both, guilt plays a large role and Alex and Isadora are trying to find themselves and establish their identity through sexual experience. Sexuality is central to understanding the world. Flying becomes a metaphor for orgasm through the drug link of being high, being free, unrepressed, open, euphoric. Through her adventures in Europe and England, our heroine moves to conquer her fear of flying. Her picaresque affair with the Laingian anti-hero, Adrian Goodlove—it is an affair that is literally 'on the road'—frees her from the restraints and stereotypes of a middle-class, married propriety, so that she can not only rediscover herself but also her husband. That is the happy ending promised in the final chapter (or epilogue): a Nineteenth-century Ending, which is self-consciously ironic.

Isadora's fantasy of the Zipless Fuck sums up the kind of romantic sexuality she is seeking: 'I wanted some ultimate beautiful act of love in which each person becomes the other's prayer wheel, toboggan, rocket' (p. 257). The Zipless Fuck is always identified as an American pop-culture fantasy that combines wish-fulfilment clichés with a desire to break through the clichés to an apocalyptic personal experience. This is, of course, a paradox, and Isadora is constantly referring to D. H. Lawrence, and especially the Lawrence of *Lady Chatterley's Lover* (1928), for a half-amused support: 'Until I was twenty-one, I measured my orgasms against Lady Chatterley's and wondered what was *wrong* with me. Did it ever occur to me that Lady Chatterley was really a man? That she was really D. H. Lawrence?' (p. 24). But the Zipless Fuck opposes Lawrence and Freud's 'phallocentrism' with strongly matri-archal images. It is not the phallus but the cunt that is central. The male lovers are reduced in importance by being deper-sonalized and anonymous strangers, who exist only to satisfy a women's endless longings. Sex is an uninvolved, uncommitted, purely physical experience, with the male lovers functioning as entirely casual and replaceable studs:

> For the true, ultimate zipless A-1 fuck, it was necessary that you never get to know the man very well. I had noticed, for example, how all my infatuations dissolved as soon as I really became friends with a man, became sympathetic to his prob-lems, listened to him *kvetch* about his wife, or ex-wives, his mother, his children. After that I would like him, perhaps even love him—but without passion. And it was passion that I wanted. (p. 11)

Once the man has 'a face' the infatuation is over.

As fantasy, the Zipless Fuck disposes of guilt, remorse, and technical difficulties: 'Zipless because when you came together zippers fell away like rose petals, underwear blew off in one breath like dandelion fluff. Tongues intertwined and turned liquid. Your whole soul flowed out through your tongue and into the mouth of your lover' (p. 11). It is a 'platonic ideal' in the sense that it converts real sexual experience into the archetypal models on which it depends, thus endowing the powerful fantasy with greater validity than any imperfect enactment of it. In this sense, both Roth and Jong are busy translating sexual experience into discourse and literature, where they can contemplate it with satisfaction according to the dictates of Barthes and Foucault. In the form of fantasy/discourse, sexual experience becomes a manageable intellectual entity that can be conceptualized with dream-like grace:

> The zipless fuck is absolutely pure. It is free of ulterior motives. There is no power game. The man is not 'taking' and the woman is not 'giving'. No one is attempting to cuckold a husband or humiliate a wife. No one is trying to prove anything or get anything out of anyone. The zipless fuck is the purest thing there is. And it is rarer than the unicorn. And I have never had one. (p. 14)

It is obvious that *Fear of Flying* must move away from the fear of flying embodied in the fantasy of the Zipless Fuck, which in itself is a refusal to accept a sexual reality that is in any way compromised by human beings.

Erica Jong is trying to write a distinctively feminine sexual fiction. Isadora's consciousness is different from the male point of view that prevails in most sexual writing. Whether Jong is entirely successful may be open to question; her heroine always needs men to complete her being and she has many other characteristics of the traditional woman of male fantasy. Yet *Fear of Flying* is a noble experiment that impressed its first readers with an enormous feeling of liberation. Isadora not only thinks about her own body and her own sexual needs, but she also thinks dirty thoughts and uses dirty words abundantly. Many women reading the book when it first appeared felt a lifting of cultural taboos.

The fact that Isadora menstruates is in itself a great breakthrough for sexual writing. Menstruation is a forbidden topic in all but the most kinky of erotic books; it is considered inherently anti-erotic. Isadora not only menstruates, but also thinks of menstruation as a physiological expression that is triumphantly female:

> It's funny how in spite of my reluctance to get pregnant, I seem to live inside my own cunt. I seem to be involved with all the

changes of my body. They never pass unnoticed. I seem to know exactly when I ovulate. In the second week of the cycle, I feel a tiny *ping* and then a sort of tingling ache in my lower belly. A few days later I'll often find a tiny spot of blood in the rubber *yarmulke* of the diaphragm. A bright red smear, the only visible trace of the egg that might have become a baby. (p. 47)

At the end of the novel, the heavily menstruating Isadora becomes a symbol for everything that flows, as in the spring finale of Thoreau's *Walden*, as she repossesses her own body and her own integrity as a woman.

Both Isadora and Alex are bathed in guilt, but the sort of guilt that is warm, tender, and infinitely self-indulging. Guilt circumscribes pleasure, which would otherwise be too overwhelming to bear. Isadora's husbands and lovers are all wrong for her, so that her sexual relations are strongly tinged with masochism and accommodation. Her first husband, Brian, makes impossible demands on her and eventually goes mad. Her next husband, Bennett, is an inscrutable and coldly passionate oriental:

> Long thin fingers, hairless balls, a lovely swivel to his hips when he screwed—at which he seemed to be absolutely indefatigable. But he was also mute and at that point his silence was music to my ears. How did I know that a few years later, I'd feel like I was fucking Helen Keller? (p. 32)

Isadora cannot resist the 'sick' Helen Keller joke, even though the sexes are reversed. Being married to Bennett becomes bland and predictable like eating Velveeta cheese, and Isadora seeks romantic escape with the English psychiatrist, Adrian Goodlove, a Bunyanesque allegorical lover with whom all is permitted.

But Goodlove is so intensely narcissistic that he can only love himself, which puts Isadora face to face with the paradox of the limp prick:

> The ultimate sexist put-down: the prick which lies down on the job. The ultimate weapon in the war between the sexes: the limp prick. The banner of the enemy's encampment: the prick at half-mast. The symbol of the apocalypse: the atomic warhead prick which self-destructs. *That* was the basic inequity which could never be righted: not that the male had a wonder-

130

ful added attraction called a penis, but that the female had a
wonderful all-weather cunt. . . . And at that moment, I fell
madly in love with him. His limp prick had penetrated where a
stiff one would never have reached. (p. 90)

But Adrian Goodlove remains forever unattainable like the
platonic ideal of the Zipless Fuck. Isadora's guilt seems to
dictate that she must always choose wrong, that she is not
intended to be sexually fulfilled and happy. Like Portnoy, for
Isadora guilt and desire are mutually motivating systems.
When guilt disappears in *How to Save Your Own Life*, the sequel
to *Fear of Flying*, the fiction assumes the sick-joke complacency
of fucking Helen Keller.

Nabokov's *Lolita* and Southern and Hoffenberg's *Candy* have
a family relationship to each other. Both were published by
Maurice Girodias' Olympia Press in Paris in the Traveller's
Companion Series, one in 1955 and the other in 1958. Both are
deeply ironic and parodic fictions ridiculing the sexual clichés
of popular culture. They are both very displaced and very
detached examinations of sexual mythology. Any personal
involvement is replaced by a self-conscious distancing from
'real life', and they both confirm Nabokov's dictum that 'sex is
but the ancilla of art' (p. 261). In other words, art precedes
and masters sexual expression; sex fulfilled or unfulfilled is
only the handmaiden of art. These assumptions are very
different from the bubbling of hot experience in *Portnoy's
Complaint* and *Fear of Flying*. Art as control could easily tame
the febrile neuroses of those novels. *Lolita* and *Candy* are
insulated by art from the pain, friction, and irritation of more
frankly autobiographical and confessional novels. But it is
significant that all four fictions need grotesque comedy to
carry their sexual themes. The comedy avoids a direct confrontation with sexual experience that might undermine the
fiction. In this sense, the great model for all sexual fiction is
Cleland's *Fanny Hill*, which is a triumph of sexual hyperbole
and euphemism. It is a triumph of art rather than believa-
bility; its pastoral and poetic eroticism is not meant to carry
conviction.

Humbert Humbert's nymphets in *Lolita* are eminently
creatures of the observer's imagination. They exist only in the
eye of the beholder, who endows them with all the folklore

131

characteristics of the changeling and the demon child. Thus there is always a profound dualism between the nymphet as she is and the nymphet as sexual object:

> What drives me insane is the twofold nature of this nymphet— of every nymphet, perhaps; this mixture in my Lolita of tender dreamy childishness and a kind of eerie vulgarity, stemming from the snub-nosed cuteness of ads and magazine pictures, from the blurry pinkness of adolescent maidservants in the Old Country (smelling of crushed daisies and sweat); and from very young harlots disguised as children in provincial brothels; and then again, all this gets mixed up with the exquisite stainless tenderness seeping through the musk and the mud, through the dirt and the death, oh God, oh God. (p. 46)

The nymphet cannot exist without artifice, as in the riddling doubleness of 'very young harlots disguised as children in provincial brothels.' The children are always ambiguous, *fausses naïves*, girl-boys poised between childhood and the beginnings of sexual maturity. They wear costumes rather than clothes and without a deliberate theatricalization of the effects there can be no sexual attraction at all. Thus disguise figures importantly in the sexual landscape of *Lolita*.

When Humbert Humbert manages to have his first orgasm with Lolita, it is a purely solipsistic experience in which the nymphet is totally unaware of what is happening:

> I felt proud of myself. I had stolen the honey of a spasm without impairing the morals of a minor. Absolutely no harm done. The conjurer had poured milk, molasses, foaming champagne into a young lady's new white purse; and lo, the purse was intact. Thus had I delicately constructed my ignoble, ardent, sinful dream; and still Lolita was safe—and I was safe. What I had madly possessed was not she, but my own creation, another, fanciful Lolita—perhaps, more real than Lolita; overlapping, encasing her; floating between me and her, and having no will, no consciousness—indeed, no life of her own. (p. 64)

In the midst of all this elaborate euphemizing and metaphorizing, Lolita remains a virginal art object who does not—and cannot—participate in the fantasies of her lover.

The real Lolita is a vulgar, strident, energetic, pre-teenage girl without the vaguest hint of reciprocation in Humbert

Humbert's sexual imaginings. 'A combination of naïveté and deception, of charm and vulgarity, of blue sulks and rosy mirth, Lolita, when she chose, could be a most exasperating brat. . . . Mentally, I found her to be a disgustingly conventional girl' (pp. 149–50). But all of that is beside the point. The vulgarity is an essential component of the grandeur, one is folded inside the other, and the revolting grossness of sex must be fully appreciated before one can experience its transcendence. That is, of course, the literal point of transcendence, that something solidly perceived and established must be transcended.

Thus, as Humbert Humbert obscenely dreams of seducing his stepdaughter nymphet while she has been subdued into a drugged sleep, little Lo takes the lead and engages her fumbling step-father in strenuous erotic play:

> Suffice it to say that not a trace of modesty did I perceive in this beautiful hardly formed young girl whom modern co-education, juvenile mores, the campfire racket and so forth had utterly and hopelessly depraved. She saw the stark act merely as part of a youngster's furtive world, unknown to adults. What adults did for purposes of procreation was no business of hers. My life [an Old World euphemism for penis] was handled by little Lo in an energetic, matter-of-fact manner as if it were an insensate gadget unconnected with me. (pp. 135–36)

The significance of this passage is that the physical relations are 'irrelevant matters' and that Humbert Humbert is 'not concerned with so-called "sex" at all. Anybody can imagine those elements of animality. A great endeavor lures me on: to fix once for all the perilous magic of nymphets' (p. 136). This is the union of heaven and hell to which *Lolita* is particularly devoted, the mixture of boredom and beatitude, vulgarity and refined sensation: 'The beastly and beautiful merged at one point, and it is that borderline I would like to fix' (p. 136). These are typical concerns of all of Nabokov's work.

Like Portnoy's grandiose impulse through fucking to 'discover America', Nabokov acknowledges in *Lolita* 'the task of inventing America' (p. 314). Humbert Humbert's erotic odyssey with Lolita is played out in an America of the mind drenched with kitsch. It is the sort of kitsch that exactly analogizes the tawdry bliss of the nymphet attraction, so that the reader is intensely aware that the travelogue is the objective correlative of the heavily sexual narrative. Both run in mirroring parallels. As Nabokov explains in his postscript, *Lolita* is staged on 'a number of North American sets. I needed a certain exhilarating milieu. Nothing is more exhilarating than philistine vulgarity' (p. 317). In this section of the novel the motel stands as bastion of forbidden sex, and Nabokov has a good eye for cinematic detail:

> To any other type of tourist accommodation I soon grew to prefer the Functional Motel—clean, neat, safe nooks, ideal places for sleep, argument, reconciliation, insatiable illicit love. . . . We came to know—*nous connûmes*, to use a Flaubertian intonation—the stone cottages under enormous Chateaubriand-esque trees, the brick unit, the adobe unit, the stucco court, on what the Tour Book of the Automobile Association describes as 'shaded' or 'spacious' or 'landscaped' grounds. The log kind, finished in knotty pine, reminded Lo, by its golden-brown glaze, of fried-chicken bones. (p. 147)

And what could be more archetypally American than fried chicken? *Lolita* becomes an apocalyptic vision of America like Henry Miller's *Air-Conditioned Nightmare* and Nathaniel West's *Day of the Locust*.

Candy, in Southern and Hoffenberg's novel, is a spiritual and sexual sister of Lolita, although *Candy* is more directly a parody than *Lolita*: of the already parodied optimism of Voltaire's *Candide*, of the benevolent banalities of the Eisenhower era, of the titillating clichés of slick magazine fiction, and, most obviously, of the mindless, heavy-breathing illogicalities of drugstore pornography. Both Lolita and Candy are essentially naïve and blank American heroines, who are concerned with sex not for itself but only as it relates to others. They are both comic-strip, pop art characters depicted in bold primary colours without shading. As artifacts of cultural mythology, they express the dominant male values of our society, especially the wildly contradictory clash between primness and lewdness. Neither heroine has much space or freedom in which to manoeuvre, so that they must necessarily respond to male needs in a predetermined way. Regardless of their cute protestations, they are predictably passive and masochistic.

Candy seems most strikingly to resemble Little Orphan Annie (and her Daddy and Daddy-surrogates are much like Daddy Warbucks). She uses an old-fashioned, comic-strip colloquial that is supposed to resemble honest, hearty, small-town speech, especially in the Mid-West. Her favourite exclamation is 'Good Grief', but we also have 'Great Scott', 'Good Heaven', 'Good Night', and 'Oh gosh'. Among the more colourfully dead expressions are: 'What in the world', *'I'll* say', *'And how', 'How could* you', 'Oh, it's simply a nightmare', and 'N-O spells *no*'—all appropriately underlined for emphasis. Candy's emotional and psychological life is radically simplified into the formulas of popular fiction. Her overwhelming impulse to be benevolent and give of herself establishes her need to be needed, which always expresses itself in a frantically sexual form.

So long as Candy only gives pleasure (and does not take any for herself), all is permitted, and her wild nymphomania is perceived as a self-sacrificing, philanthropic activity. Thus, with the kinky hunchback in Greenwich Village whom Candy names Derek, our sweet heroine offers herself in an atmosphere of maternal protection:

> his stubby fingers were rolling the little clitoris like a marble in oil. Candy leaned back in resignation, her heart too big to deprive him of this if it meant so much. With her head closed-eyed, resting again on the couch, she would endure it as long as she could. . . . It means so much to him, Candy kept thinking, *so* much, as he meanwhile got her jeans and panties down completely so that they dangled now from one slender ankle as he adjusted her legs and was at last on the floor himself in front of her, with her legs around his neck, and his mouth very deep inside the fabulous honeypot. (pp. 144–45)

'Fabulous honeypot' is only one among an enormous lexicon of euphemisms for Candy's cunt: her sugar-scoop, her seething thermal pudding, her sweet-dripping little fur-pie, her pink candy clit with slick lips all sugar and glue, her marvellous spice-box, her pulsing jelly box, her tight little lamb-pit. This sexual poeticizing is a direct imitation of Cleland's *Fanny Hill*, from which dirty words are banished and in which sexual expression is always in the high style, whose amused self-consciousness falls well short of the sublime. This endows both

135

Candy and *Fanny Hill* with a rhetorical extravagance that is both bathetic and ridiculously charming.

Candy always manages to avoid anything that could even vaguely resemble a peer relationship. She is either involved with her father and a whole series of father surrogates (Uncle Jack, Professor Mephesto, Dr. Irving Krankeit, Dr. Howard Johns, Pete Uspy, Grindle, and Buddha himself) or she is placed in an unequivocally maternal role (as with Emannuel the Mexican gardener and Derek the hunchback). Actually, the roles are confused by Candy's imperious desire to take care of everyone, to nurture them, and to minister to their aching need of her. With the redoubtable Dr. Krankeit (né Semite), author of the anti-Lawrentian tract, *Masturbation Now!*, Candy fantasizes needs of which the good doctor has not yet become aware:

> And this meant that *she*, in turn, must be the instrument of *his* release, though he hadn't as yet sensed it of course. This fact, that Krankeit was still unaware of their looming, destined love, only endeared him to her the more. The poor darling ninny, she thought, little did he realize the stark, aching need he had for her. She almost laughed aloud thinking of this obtuseness of his—so like a man too. There he was, all wrapped up in thoughts of his work, never dreaming what his heart held in store for him. She felt like pinching him, or playfully giving him a push, just to break through his absurd masculine numbness. . . . (p. 110)

But Dr. Krankeit is protected by his *real* mother, Sylvia Semite, a prototype for Mrs. Portnoy, who has taken a job washing floors in the hospital to shield her nubile Jewish son from rampant shikses like Candy. Candy is, therefore, easily scared off. Southern and Hoffenberg have a marvellous ear for the emotional clichés of soap opera and popular magazine fiction—clichés that touch the heart and arouse laughter at the same time. The stereotype of the small-town Christian girl— Candy's Christian name is indeed Christian, as in *Pilgrim's Progress*—who finds an unlikely happiness with an introverted, ghetto-derived Jewish doctor makes for deliciously sentimental good fun: 'Candy Krankeit, she thought with a bittersweet thrill—so that was how it was to be!' (p. 109)

Candy is played out against a matrix of popular culture, and especially the patronizing, do-gooder's culture of the Eisen-hower era of the '50s. The Third World peoples are not yet the intractable revolutionary group they will become, but rather the underprivileged, who with a little kindness and patience can easily be persuaded to join the dominant white middle-class society. In Candy's mind, strenuous sexual intercourse is a political gesture to the downtrodden that they are just as good as US—sexual capacity is clearly a symbol of mental and spiritual resources. With Emannuel, her family's Mexican gardener, Candy offers herself both out of Anglo guilt and the desire to make a statement: ' "I know you don't think Daddy— Mr. Christian—likes you. But I want you to know that we aren't all like that, I mean that *all* human beings aren't like that! Do you understand?" ' (pp. 37–8). Emannuel, of course, understands only that Candy is presenting her delicately nurtured, white Anglo-Saxon Protestant body to him, and he punctuates Candy's babble with a series of highly significant grunts, 'Whot?'. Candy always acts out of the highest principles, but she is sometimes surprised by the funny turns Real Life takes:

> 'Oh, you do need me so!' the closed-eyed girl murmured, as yet not feeling much of anything except the certainty of having to fit this abstraction to the case. But when the gardener's hand closed on her pelvis and into the damp, she stiffened slightly: she was quite prepared to undergo *pain* for him . . . but *pleasure*— she was not sure how that could be a part of the general picture. (p. 44)

When Candy's daddy bursts in on the copulating, racially mixed couple 'like some kind of giant insane lobster-man' (p. 45), his speechless rage can only find a typically Eisen-howerish epithet: '*You . . . You . . . You . . .* COMMUNIST!' (p. 46). This is sexual politics in an early version.

At the end of the novel Candy discovers an apocalyptic fulfilment not only for her need to be needed, but also for her own needs. In an extravagant mixture of religious and sexual symbolism, while Candy is meditating on the tip of Buddha's nose in the great temple at Lhasa, there is a tremendous flash of lightning that topples the statue of Buddha and half buries the temple in rubble. She is mysteriously thrown together with a dung and ash covered holy man, and as she struggles to free herself she only agitates 'her precious and open honeypot against the holy man's secret parts—which were now awakening after so many years and slowly breaking through the rotten old loincloth that swaddled them' (p. 222). Meanwhile, the nose of the broken statue of Buddha 'was slipping into Candy's marvelous derriere' (p. 223). Thus doubly penetrated, Candy realizes 'with the same lightning force of miracle which had split the roof, that wonder of wonders, *the Buddha, too, needed her!*' (p. 223). The miracle is completed when the rain washes clean the holy man in front and Candy perceives what she must have always known would be the apotheosis of her sexual odyssey: ' "GOOD GRIEF—IT'S DADDY!" ' (p. 224). Thus Buddha and Daddy working in consort achieve the ultimate sexual climax.

Portnoy's Complaint, Fear of Flying, Lolita, and *Candy* are, of course, only a sampling of the sexual writing in America in the past twenty-five years, yet, as a group, they represent a striking originality. There is no tradition of erotic writing in America as there is in France, so that originality and creativity seem to be involved in each writer's attempt to begin over again without relying on acknowledged models. Humour seems to be a dominant characteristic of American sexual fiction, as if the writers assumed that one cannot talk about sexual experience directly. Among more recent books, Gael Greene's *Blue Skies, No Candy* (1976) uses the sexual narrative as a vehicle for a wide-ranging satire on the fashionable mores of the American consumerist society. Her narrator is the enormously successful and chic screenwriter, Kate Alexander, who indulges her many expensive tastes including a passion for strenuous intercourse, especially of a theatrical, sadomasochistic turn. There is a wonderful mélange of sex, make-up, and designer clothes as Kate fantasizes a movie-set Armageddon:

> I suppose this is how I will function if they ever announce the world is about to end. A quick trip to M. Marc for a comb-out. A few minutes of indecision at the closet. Shall I be tailored and elegant or soft, monochromatic or subtly sexy, irrepressibly earthy? How will we meet Armageddon, barefoot with toes painted Teddy Bear rose or in our Chelsea Cobbler boots, kicking to the end? (pp. 343–44)

It is natural in *Blue Skies, No Candy* that the end of the world should be conceived as a media event. Greene generalizes desire beyond physical sex to all the longings of an upper-middle-class, leisured society in which the struggle for existence has been refined into a determined effort to stave off boredom.

William Kotzwinkle's *Nightbook* (1974) is also a notable attempt to use pornographic materials for a satirical purpose. The most brilliant device in *Nightbook* is the juxtaposition of tales from the Greek Anthology and from Greek legend with sordid and lurid fictions of contemporary sexual life. Thus literature and journalism are cleverly interwoven without any space left for transitions. Sometimes ancient and modern lusts are made to mirror each other, as in Chapter 4:

> One day, the goat began to sing as Cyno approached, rough guttural music breaking from his lips when he saw her. He stopped directly in front of her on the path. She smiled at this strange song, but she dared not laugh for his eyes were fierce and he was clearly not joking. And when she attempted to pass him, he blocked her path with lowered horns.
> 'How soon you think you have a book for me, kid?'
> 'A week,' said the young writer as he left the Pant Publishing house, his briefcase loaded with sample books which had fuck suck cock cunt on every page. (pp. 33–4)

This doesn't do justice to the author's subtlety in manipulating his ancient and modern narratives, but I think the point is clear that the sexual subject matter is displaced by the ubiquitous feeling of fabulation. In *Nightbook* sexuality is a form of fictionmaking, so that we are not surprised to find the narrator in one tale imitating the story she has just told:

> The ladies of Athens applauded the fine story and the teller of the tale raised her gown above her hips, so that her lovely distinguished cheeks were visible. And bending over she rotated her naked buttocks round and round, so that her little beard hung down between her gorgeous thighs, demonstrating exactly how the poor daughter of Megacles had been humped. (pp. 24–5)

This recalls the *Arabian Nights'* context of Sade's *120 Days of Sodom*, where the storytellers provide models that the spectators can then imitate. This is sexual mimesis at its most literal level, in which art and life are directly related to each other. Without the stories there can be no demonstrations.

One exception to these sexual displacements by art is Scott Spencer's recent novel, *Endless Love* (1979). This is a haunting story of sexual obsession that leads to crime, madness, and a profound alienation from all other values of American life. The very literalness of the sexual scenes is a release from the purely mental anguish of the earlier parts of the book. Although they are physical in all the details of fatigue, menstruation, the cheap hotel room, the plumbing in the toilet, and what happens to the sheets, the accumulated details take on a phantasmagoric and nightmarish quality. There is, of course, no relief for the reader either through humour or some non-sexual description, so that the narrative develops an intense eroticism that functions as a form of transcendence. The reader is caught up in a style that is hypnotically compelling and yet also surprisingly poetic:

> When her climax came—and it appeared suddenly, like an accident—Jade trembled and made a high whinny, as if in distress. Then she was absolutely still, like a startled animal etched in the brightening beam of speeding headlights. Her mouth was open; it seemed as if she might drool but she closed her lips and lifted her chin, breathing out so heavily that her belly swelled and made her look pregnant for a moment.
>
> Of course when you love someone it is a tireless passion to experience their pleasure, especially sexual pleasure. (p. 291)

'Tireless passion', 'endless love'—these are the sexual paradoxes that Scott Spencer manages to make credible, and he succeeds in a romantic and direct narrative that is impossibly difficult to do. Lawrence's *Lady Chatterley's Lover*, for all of its passion, founders in an artfully erotic rhetoric, but Spencer doesn't distract us with brilliant effects. His style is completely appropriate to his materials, and the only disappointment is an inherent one: there is no satisfying way of ending *Endless Love*.

Susan Sontag has done us a great service in recognizing the force of the 'pornographic imagination'. It has nothing, of course, to do with dirty words, despite George Steiner's fulminations, but rather with a fundamental translating of sexual experience into literature. Thus Sontag speaks of the effects of disorientation and psychic dislocation in both science fiction and sexual fiction: 'The physical sensations involuntarily produced in the reader carry with them something that touches upon the reader's whole experience of his humanity—and his limits as a personality and as a body' (p. 191). The physical absolutism and imperiousness of sexual writing cannot be ignored, but there is as wide a range of excellence and creativity in sexual novels as in any other genre of fiction. Most of our writers have approached sexual writing obliquely, especially through satire and extravagant humour, although it is also possible to have a sexual narrative like *Endless Love* that is both powerful and direct. We have only just begun to exploit the rich materials that the weakening of censorship has freed for us. Once the prurient interest has diminished, we can write sexual fictions of soaring intensity and imagination. In many important senses, we are discovering a new subject matter.

BIBLIOGRAPHY

Roland Barthes, *Sade Fourier Loyola*, trans. Richard Miller (New York: Hill and Wang, 1976).

Leo Bersani, *A Future for Astyanax: Character and Desire in Literature* (Boston: Little, Brown, 1976).

Maurice Charney, *Sexual Fiction* (London: Methuen, 1981). In New Accents series, ed. Terence Hawkes.

John Cleland, *Memoirs of a Woman of Pleasure* (1749; New York: Putnam, 1963). Also called *Fanny Hill*.

Michel Foucault, *The History of Sexuality, Vol. I: An Introduction*, trans. Robert Hurley (New York: Pantheon, 1978).

Sigmund Freud, 'The Most Prevalent Form of Degradation in Erotic Life' (1912), trans. Joan Rivière, in Benjamin Nelson (ed.), *On Creativity and the Unconscious* (New York: Harper & Row, 1958).

René Girard, *Deceit, Desire and the Novel: Self and Other in Literary Structure*, trans. Yvonne Freccero (Baltimore: Johns Hopkins University Press, 1965).

Gael Greene, *Blue Skies, No Candy* (New York: Warner, 1976).

Erica Jong, *Fear of Flying* (New York: New American Library, 1974).

————, *How to Save Your Own Life* (New York: New American Library, 1978).

William Kotzwinkle, *Nightbook* (New York: Avon, 1974).

D. H. Lawrence, *Lady Chatterley's Lover* (1928; New York: New American Library, 1959).

Norman Mailer, *An American Dream* (New York: Dial, 1965).

————, 'The Time of Her Time', in *Advertisements for Myself* (New York: Putnam, 1959).

Henry Miller, *The Air-Conditioned Nightmare* (New York: New Directions, 1945).

————, *Tropic of Cancer* (1934; New York: Grove Press, 1961).

Vladimir Nabokov, *Lolita* (1955; New York: Putnam, n.d.).

Philip Roth, *Portnoy's Complaint* (New York: Random House, 1969).

Marquis de Sade, *The 120 Days of Sodom and Other Writings*, trans. Austryn Wainhouse and Richard Seaver (New York: Grove Press, 1967).

Susan Sontag, 'The Pornographic Imagination', *Partisan Review*, 34 (1967), 181–212. Reprinted in *Styles of Radical Will* (New York: Farrar, Straus & Giroux, 1969).

Terry Southern and Mason Hoffenberg, *Candy* (1958; New York: Putnam, 1964).

Scott Spencer, *Endless Love* (New York: Avon, 1980).

George Steiner, 'Night Words: High Pornography and Human Privacy', *Encounter*, 25 (1965), 14–19. Reprinted in *Language and Silence* (New York: Atheneum, 1967).

Nathaniel West, *The Day of the Locust* (1939), in *The Complete Works of Nathaniel West* (New York: Farrar, Straus and Cudahy, 1957).

Part Two:
CONTEXTS

6

Phallic Worship: Some Personal Meditations on a Sacred Theme

by JAMES KIRKUP

I have always been interested in the phallus, partly, I suppose, because I am the proud possessor of one myself, and partly for aesthetic and religious reasons. The phallus is the only kind of god I have ever believed in, and the only kind of holy symbol I have ever worshipped. The phallus is my godhead, and priapic hill figures are my ancestral altars.

In an unusual and 'curious' little book, *Sex Mythology, Including an Account of the Masculine Cross*[1] Sha Rocco says, by way of introduction:

> The hallowed powers of one era become detritus of a later one; and in still later eons of time those decayed objects reappear as relics, and show, to our surprise, how much that is held to be original in our age is really the unconscious inheritance of a bygone ancestry. They also show early religious ideas were cast in a mold denoting a childlike apprehension, in conformity with things palpable and roundly pronounced, with the child's direct bluntness of expression.

He goes on to mention, and illustrate, the phallic and yonijic remains found in California, 'introduced to public attention as ancient relics belonging to the prehistoric stone age'. It is an

145

approach that reminds us of Werner Jaeger's *Early Christianity and Greek Paideia*,[2] the Orphic tracts and the symbolic letter Y of the Pythagoreans.

In *Sex Mythology*, the author ascribes the origin of the cross to the ancient symbol of generation and regeneration, the Nileometer, a horizontal piece of wood fastened to an upright beam to indicate the height of the river in flood, a symbol that is traced back to India, from which Egypt was colonized.

He goes on to explain the derivation of phallus and linga ('or Lingham'), the image of the male organ, and the yoni, or unit, for the female organ. The 'privy member' (*membrum virile*) signifies breaking through and passing into, surviving in the German *Pfahl* (and, I would add, in *der Pfeil*, arrow or bolt, which has particular significance in Japanese mythology, as we shall see), and in the English *pole*. The author also mentions possible Phoenician, Greek and Sanskrit origins of the word, and instances Phallu, the son of Reuben (Gen. xlvi, 9) as 'a distinguished one', 'he splits, divides', 'he is round and plump'—all pointing to a religion of sensual love.

Phallic emblems, he tells us, were common at Heliopolis in Syria, at Thebes on the temple walls, at Karnak and Danclesa, depicting the male genitals erect. In ancient oath-taking, the one who swore the oath placed his right hand upon the 'thigh' of the adjurer, that is, upon the most sacred part of a man's body, the genital member. The phallus as a symbol of generative power was so deeply revered in former times that if the organs were disfigured or lost the unfortunate man 'was unfitted to meet in the congregation of the Lord, and disqualified to minister in the holy temples. Excessive was the punishment inflicted upon the person who should have the temerity to injure the sacred structure.' A woman guilty of such an injury would have her hand cut off (Deut. xxv, 12).

The author proceeds, in his inimitable style:

> With people enslaved to such grovelling tenets, it was an easy and natural step from the actual to the symbolical; from the crude, and, perhaps, to some, offensive, to the improved, the pictured, the adorned, the less offensive; from the plain and self-evident, to the mixed, disguised and mystified; from the unclothed privy member to the letter T, or the cross; for these became the phallic analogues. The linga is the symbol of the

male organ and Creator in Hindostan. . . . Obelisks, pillars of
any shape, stumps, trees denuded of boughs, upright stones, are
some of the means by which the male element was symbolized.
Siva is represented as a stone standing alone.

The author has some interesting pages on temple virgins
and sacred prostitutes who had to submit themselves to the
visitations of the 'god' in the form of priests or male devotees;
Num. xxxi, 18 and 35 tells of this 'without a lisp or a twinge of
horror', in the story of the 'thirty-two thousand Midianitish
virgins . . . consecrated to this end. We need not go into details
about the manner in which the sacrifice was made.' However,
he compares the custom to the 'alleged spiritual form' of self-
offering in 'the nunneries of Christendom' and in 'Oriental
establishments where women consecrated their bodies and
themselves to fulfil the special duties of their sex'. For example,
that 'temple in Babylonia' where every female 'had to perform
once in her life a . . . strange act of religion: namely, prostitution with a stranger. The name of it was *Bit-Shagatha*, or, "The
Temple" the "Place of Union".' He quotes the ecstatic ejacu-
lations of Marie from Casgrain's *Vie de Marie de l'Incarnation*, in
some ways similar to St. Theresa of Avila's, as a proof of this.
The parallels, often very marked, between the life of Jesus and
that of Christna and other deities are also mentioned, and
related to sun worship, which is fundamentally the worship of
regenerative power, of the phallus.

Let me now say something about an unusual form of phallic
worship from my own experience in North-East England. This
region—Tyneside, County Durham and Northumbria—is a
sort of ghetto of Great Britain, a dead end to be escaped from
as soon as possible. But like other geographical regions 'apart'
from normal national life, it has some unusual customs and
relics of ancient religious rites.

The most remarkable feature of Geordie life is the mysterious
cult of the giant leek. This reminds me in some ways of the
curious cults of the onion worshippers in remote areas of
southern France and the Pyrenees, some of whose ecstatic
secret gatherings I have been privileged to attend.

In North-East England, as far as I know, there are no religious or ritual ceremonies connected with the growing of prize leeks, though these garden products enjoy pride of place at the harvest festivals of Christian churches and chapels, where they display their luxurious ithyphallic forms, often accompanied by the testicular shapes of prize beet or turnips, like symbols of the earliest religions, and of pagan ceremonies, tributes to the generative gods of creation. The cultivation of monster leeks is possibly part of an age-old phallic ritual or cult.

The art and craft of raising ithyphallic leeks is accompanied by intense passions: male rivalry (most growers are male), penis-envy and the youthful contests of penis-comparison, hatred of anyone growing a bigger one than your own, angry defensiveness. Some dedicated growers sit up all night as contest time draws near, to defend jealous marauders or slashers with their fists or even with shotguns and sledge-hammers.

Long before it became a fad for leisured matrons to talk fondly to their rubber plants, Geordie miners would sit up all night talking to their prize leeks, encouraging them to grow and swell to giant stature, in a kind of self-induced erection, a narcissistic mirror-image of fruitful masturbation. How zeal-ously they would rush out into the road with a shovel to collect the steaming balls of fertile dung dropped by passing horses! Now, artificial fertilizers are more common, though really dedicated growers have their own recipes for enriching the carefully-sifted soil round their leeks, some of which are said to contain the grower's semen.

Then, on the great day, the judgement day of the great show, an event like a vegetable wedding service, the monster member is chosen by his bridegroom grower for the nuptial bed of the Parks Committee display stall. It is carefully eased and lifted from the well-prepared earth in the back garden or council allotment. Reverently it is carried to the scullery, where it is gently washed, groomed, trimmed and polished. The long, fine roots, like a young giant's pubic hair, are shampooed in Lux, and tenderly curried, cossetted and combed into a downy, creamy nest from which the superb, hard, well-knit, glistening trunk rises in proud, impervious erectility, the slightly-swollen base taking the place of testicles, the beautifully-plaited terminal leaves like a luxurious dark green foreskin, carefully wiped with damp chamois leather, virginally new.

Comes the judgement by the Lady Mayoress, the Chief Constable and a Justice of the Peace. The most magnificent specimen is selected for first prize, the less magnificent for second and third places. It is always a delightful moment when we see the Lady Mayoress pick up, in virginal white-gloved hands, and weigh and closely inspect the gorgeous and engorged product of one of her pitman's back gardens, then pronounce it to be the champion. With what lingering regret she lays its gleaming, hairy weight back on the exhibition stand! With what troubling erotic confusion she garlands it with beribboned trophies and patriotic red, white and blue rosettes! Is even the thickest Lady Mayoress totally uncon-scious of the phallic and yonijic symbolism involved when she presents the blushing victor with the wide-hipped, profoundly pelvic silver cup, filled to the brim with foaming local beer? I think she must be, or she would be afraid of performing what is in effect a most ancient pagan rite.

In any case, such occasions are marked by an appropriate solemnity, suited to the mythomaniac fanaticism of the giant leek grower. A self-important seriousness and lack of humour pervade such provincial rites, and the absence of laughter (though not of absurdity) defuses their primitive potency. What is required at such events is the presence of some divine fool of sacred silliness, like my favourite saint, St. Philippe Neri, with his heavenly quirks of idosyncratic humour and disconcerting anti-gloom playfulness, as described so vividly by Marcel Jouhandeau in *St. Philippe Neri*[3]—for a true phallic ceremony leaves its mind-blown participants either doubled over with uncontrollable laughter or bending over backwards to flaunt and exhibit their pride and joy to the approving heavens.

That awful anti-joy monger, Sigmund Freud, has a lot to answer for, not the least being a certain obsessive eagerness in non-initiates of phallic worship to see phallic symbols every-where they look—surely an expression of quite unbridled and unhealthy sexual mania, totally unrelated to the hyperaesthesia

149

of well-ordered erotomaniac vision.

However, an obsessive enthusiasm for 'anything in trousers' is preferable to castrating indifference or merely lukewarm interest, as Jouhandeau so rightly says about St. Philippe Neri:

> ... il tenait pour assuré qu'il y a moins loin de certaines passions ou de certains vices à l'amour de Dieu que d'une tiédeur universelle. ...

So when some indignant nitwit calls you 'a fucking prick' you should accept it as a tribute to your manhood, an unconscious compliment and a sign of grace.

Some over-eager researchers into priapic symbolism tend to see the divine phallus in antique Victorian free-standing letter-boxes, painted a stimulating crimson. Many brave men join the Royal Navy because they are secretly devoured by a passion for the shapes and forms, not always of their bunk mates, but of conning-tower and periscope, and of the blunt thrust of the argument presented by a plunging submarine. As we drive south through France, who has not felt a shadow of delicious apprehension as those enormous grain storage towers and bristling T.V. and radar posts raise their ugly heads over the horizon? Those big-city tourist towers with their express elevators and revolving restaurants perpetually exciting their poured-concrete glans penis! O, Tour Eiffel, in the bold, straddling posture of a drunken Rimbaud pissing at the adoring heavens! O, Tokyo Tower, feeble and unsexy imitation of the great-girdered Parisian prick! Kyoto Station Tower, poor thing—so much like a limp white noodle, one wonders how it manages to keep its end up! And all those public arches—Marble Arch, Washington Square Arch, the Arc de Triomphe, the Arch of Constantine—enormous stone trousers, though without any reassuring bumps in the right places, at the beflagged and sculptured crotch!

In Paris, I often travel on Ligne 12 (Mairie d'Issy–Porte de la Chapelle) from St. Lazare to my studio near the Métro station of rue du Bac. All underground trains and tunnels are undeniably phallic, and have a haunting oneirism. Ligne 12's carriages are delightfully old-fashioned, with Belle Epoque woodwork and stencils that rarely invite the attentions of the many black felt-tipped pen graffiti artists in the Métro. Nor do they ever seem to be vandalized, as other lines are, the ripped seats exuding a brownish stuffing like dried menstrual blood. In the supermodern, faceless cars on the other Métro lines, with their *caca d'oie* plastic seats and strapontins slyly endowed with dead lumps of chewed bubble-gum, anarchy is rife, and not just in the capital A within any circle of print that presents itself. Now, many of the seats are covered with enormous drawings of highly-idealized *phalloi*, complete with perfectly-spherical and hairy balls, in the style beloved of darling *Charlie Hebdo* and *Hara Kiri*, and inscribed with descriptive captions like *le bite des voyous* or *pine d'un poète*. These crude phallic tributes often engender hilarious giggles and so perform a healthy function in an atmosphere of almost unbearable tedium and tension. It is a joy to see them, and they convey an unmistakable feeling of warmth and humanity, and the sense of relief one feels when entering a urinal adorned with such symbols—so different from the uneasiness and depression resulting from blank tiled walls!

Behold, a prim, uptight, disapproving Paris matron in a disgusting fur coat enters at Strasbourg–St. Denis, loud with jungle drummings, and through her harlequin specs (para-doxical attribute!) gazes swiftly about her, all hostility, defens-iveness and suspicion, and is so occupied with weighing up the criminal potentialities of the other occupants with her basilisk-blue tired eyelids on tired eyes that she fails to see the enor-mous *membrum virile* vigorously sketched on the seat, and lingeringly deposits her capacious bottom on the throbbing engine, to the suppressed smiles of the guitar-players hovering over her and hoping, in vain, for a small coin of appreciation.

The shape of the pricks drawn in the Métro are exactly the same as Man Ray's 'Priapic Paperweight'—surely the earliest form of 'executive desk toy'. In February 1980, I visited the great Man Ray exhibition of objects, paintings, sculptures and photographs (that wet Virginia Woolf, that god James Joyce) in the Kunsthalle in Basel. It was a display full of humour, strangeness and sexy mischief. A very large version of the 'Priapic Paperweight' in green marble was on show, a truly phallic sculpture of a powerful diagrammatic phallus consist-ing of a plain upright cylinder topped with a perfect sphere, the glans, and accompanied at its base by two identical spheres, the balanced balls—an image of vigorous and exhil-arating potency. Nearby was Man Ray's famous bust, like a visage from Angkor Wat, of de Sade, the divine marquis, placed next to a painting which represents a phallus amid forests of pubic scribbles, in authentic primitive surrealist style. I managed to dodge the attendants and take several pictures of these artifacts, despite the disapproving Swiss stares, as if I were committing an antisocial crime worse than walking on their barbered public lawns.

At this point, I must refer to a beautiful and unusual book, *Fleurs du Japon*[4]—an excellent selection of erotic Japanese woodcuts, wildly and brutally expressive, with their enormous fantasy-phalloi, voluptuous vulvae and upkicked heels amid swirling folds of kimono and loosened sashes. These are *shunga* or 'spring pictures' of great originality, variety and vigour, brilliantly composed, exquisitely coloured, stupendously ex-citing. In the Introduction (unsigned) the writer deplores the lack of frank sexual imagery in modern painting and sculpture, which he terms 'a-sexual'. He goes on:

> One cannot qualify as 'sexed' an art which is content to diminish full-bodied human attributes or to atrophy them by castrations of all kinds—physical, moral and aesthetic—beginning with the elimination of pubic hair, that uncrowned glory.
>
> Though man is not just a sexual object, it is nonetheless true that he is the product of eternal sexual energy, and that his full status as a male is merited only through the practice of sex in whatsoever form it may take. Western civilization limits such observations to the clinic, the laboratory and the psychiatrist's couch, through prudishness, Christian conventions, and, above all, fear. Our rational technical universe is afraid of sex, because it is to obverse of rational, *la folle du logis*.

Yet it was not always so, and indeed, in lands that are—thank Buddha—so very different from our own dear Thing-land, the phallus is accepted without ignorant, literal-minded censoriousness, and often displayed with pride and joy in mystical and religious-theatrical settings.

The origin of the complex *bunraku* puppet of Japan was the magical rod employed by Shinto priests to invoke the deities of the sun. In the far north of Japan, on the weird dormant volcano called Osorezan, the haunt of spirits, spirit-worshippers and sorceress-mediums, I have seen these possessed old women (called *miko*), on the occasion of the July festival of souls at Entsuji Temple, using this very magic wand. Jacques Pimpaneau, in a remarkable work,[5] describes how this simple stick gradually took on the appearance of a realistic phallus, similar to the giant phalloi still used by worshippers and priests in joyous and irreverent fertility rites all over the countryside in Japan.

On the island of Sado, once a place of exile for emperors and 'heretical' dissident priests, this crude basic form of puppet is still preserved in all its primitive expressiveness. At Awaiseda on the island of Shikoku, one of the great homes of hand-made paper and puppets, phallic dolls are used to accompany incantations for the presence of the gods at New Year. At the little port of Muki, in the southern part of Shikoku, fishermen during the summer festival of ghosts carry a gigantic bamboo phallus to a little island where it is placed on the altar of a temple dedicated to a love-lorn princess. On the island of Sado, a phallic doll is thrown into the vast crowd of worshippers, who fight furiously for possession of it. Four puppets then perform a short play in which Kinosuke, with erect sex, pisses on the public. Perhaps this explains the sad popularity of the bourgeois Belgian *mannekin pis* in Japan: there is one of these vulgar objects in the campus of my university, and even in the back garden of Yogen-in Temple in Kyoto!

Yet today we prefer the sexual substitutes of coy, smirking 'pin-ups' and the plastic banalities, like those inflatable lifesize dolls, of newspaper and magazine 'nudies' and 'cuties' which are about as sexually appetizing as slabs of whalemeat in a butchershop. No wonder they are called 'cheesecake', that bland, sticky, insipid goo (containing no cheese). Anyhow, why are there no male pin-ups on the deplorable Page Three of *The Sun* (ludicrous name and a desecration of the sun-worship associated with the phallus) and other 'saucy' publications masquerading as public news-sheets? Presumably 'cheesecake' is palatable, but 'beefcake' offends the eye of castrating female prudery and male penis-envy?

Well, as I have shown in the case of Man Ray, not all modern art is timid in this field. Some of Picasso's early cubist male nudes possess potent though diagrammatic sex organs

153

shaped like blunt explosive shells, half-erect. But on the whole, it is the female nude that prevails: she is less upsetting. In the vast Maillol exhibition at the Guggenheim Museum in New York a few years ago, there was only one rough sketch of a male nude. In Japan, all public statuary, lumpy pseudo-Maillols, is female, apart from the inevitable Rodin *Penseur* crouching in costive pose, as if straining at stool. Japanese museums and galleries contain only female nudes, and the Japanese flock to exhibitions of Renoir to gloat on the luxuriant flesh, rubicond with sex life, of the capacious female nudes, so different from the usual Japanese female. If it's male, the nude is rude.

Why is contemporary art so timid in this area? True art is a reconciliation of reason and passion, of seriousness and wit. But the British are notoriously 'cold fish', devoid of passionate intensity in either life or art. I remember E. M. Forster expressing frustration and disappointment with the tiny members of Greek art. He obviously hadn't visited the Museo Nazionale in Naples, where gigantic statues have correspondingly gigantic members, black with the sweat from a million groping hands. It seems as if today's artists accept the prevalent idea that sex is taboo, that sex is sin. In an age that prides itself on its 'liberation' it seems strange that there are no public collections of erotic art, no open displays of sexual sculpture such as one finds all over the East—my own favourites being at immortal Khajuraho's exotic temple complex, a convenient stopover on the flight from New Delhi to Calcutta. It is wrong that erotic art, and the cult of the phallus in particular, should be limited to the uninhibited enjoyment of the happy few who are initiates and amateurs of this genre so heavily-suppressed and ball-breakingly censored in the West.

Some of the best examples of modern phallic art are to be found in those glories of French civilization, the satirical magazines *Charlie Hebdo* and *Hara Kiri*, beside which our own dear *Private Eye* looks like a kids' comic. They are always being attacked by incensed ladies for being 'phallocrate' and 'sexiste', to the obvious delight of the editors. In the April 1980 issue, a genius of a comedian, Coluche, appears on the cover, jerking himself off into groaning demijohns of sperm. Included in the issue is a transparent plastic sachet containing a dubious-looking greyish liquid labelled 'Sperme de Coluche'. Instructions says that it is comestible, but that to be really effective it should be inserted in the vagina, guaranteeing horrible little Coluche brats, impersonated by Coluche himself in an ingenious photo-montage. Merci, *Charlie Hebdo*! Et vive *Hara Kiri*! On one famous cover, banned by the police and the French government, Madame Valéry Giscard d'Estaing was depicted nude in the arms of an 'oil-rich' sheik. In the subsequent issue, she was replaced by a life-size inflatable doll. Incidentally, once when I was carrying a bouquet of tea roses to the Aupick tomb where Baudelaire is buried, in the Montparnasse cemetery, I was startled and then overjoyed to see one of the sextons, slightly tipsy, emerging from a gardener's hut brandishing a fully-inflated rubber doll and exhibiting a solid erection. Even more stimulating than the idea of love-in-death is the experience of sex-in-death. Come on, Francis Bacon, David Hockney, show your mettle!

How I wish they sold supplies of fresh mothers' milk in supermarkets, instead of that disgusting cow's milk, fit only for calves! There must be abundant supplies of mothers' milk simply going to waste. Come on, *Hara Kiri*!

The frank attitudes towards sex and sexual symbols in the East is a whole new ballgame to the hagridden Westerner. The respect shown by the Chinese and the Japanese for the sexual parts can be seen in the poetic names they give to them. The penis in China is the 'jade stalk' while in Japan the testicles are called *kintama* or 'eggs of gold'. In Dr. R. H. van Gulik's inspired treatises on the erotic art of the Far East, particularly in his very rare *Erotic Colour Prints of the Ming Period* and the more accessible *Sexual Life in Ancient China*,[6] he gives several examples of this very sensitive poetic nomenclature, so different from our own blunt Anglo-Saxon terminology. In the latter, he informs us that the clitoris, that miniature, delectable, vestigial phallus, is called 'Jewel Terrace', while 'Jade Veins' (*yü-li*) indicate the place where the labia meet below the vulva. The 'Golden Gully' is the upper part of the vulva, and the right and left sides of the female organ are *pi-yung* or 'Examination Hall'. Sexual climax is 'Firing-time'. Curiously, a large clitoris was considered repulsive by the ancient Chinese. Well, it takes all sorts to make a world.

In another scarce book, the *Curiositates Eroticae Physiologiae, Or, Tabooed Subjects Freely Treated*[7] by John Davenport, there are extensive references to the importance of the prepuce in phallic symbolism, and in the giving of sexual satisfaction to woman. Male circumcision, considered barbaric by devout Hindus, but until recently widely practised as a fashionable non-extra (and an extra fee for surgeons) is now fortunately dying out, as it is to be hoped female mutilation will in the near future. Davenport quotes Bauer on the importance of the uncircumcized phallus: 'The pleasure of sexual union is greatly increased by the prepuce, for which reason women prefer co-habiting with those who retain it than with the Turks or the Jews.'

I have noticed that most Japanese males seem to be born circumcized, and Davenport enlightens us on this point:

> It must not, however, be supposed that this inconvenient length of the prepuce is common to all the Orientals, many individuals being met with among them having the prepuce naturally so short as scarcely to cover the glans penis, and native writers affirm that such is the case with those who are born during the wane of the moon.

In my own experience of the Far East, covering a quarter of a century, I have met with only two or three individuals possessing a proper prepuce, and only one case of phimosis. The Japanese males visiting European museums gaze in awe at classical statues of ephebes, always depicted with a capacious foreskin, now known in Japan as 'Greek style', and much prized by those who have foreign friends (usually German or Swiss) so constituted.

Probably the best book on phallic worship is that by George Riley Scott, *Phallic Worship: A History of Sex and Sex Rites in Relation to the Religions of all Races from Antiquity to the Present Day*, another fairly scarce book[8] but occasionally to be found in specialist book dealers' catalogues. It was privately printed for subscribers only, and I am fortunate to possess a signed copy of the numbered edition, with the highly symbolic number of 69.

As an epigraph, the author quotes Aldous Huxley's *Point Counter Point*:

> ... Why, the Christians themselves understood phallism a great deal better than this godless generation. What's that phrase in the marriage service? 'With my body I thee worship.' Worshipping with the body—that's the genuine phallism. And if you imagine it had anything to do with the unimpassioned civilized promiscuity of our advanced young people, you're very much mistaken indeed.

He also expresses his debt to a seminal work, Dr. Roger Goodland's monumental *Bibliography of Sex Rites and Customs*, a fascinating and learned compendium.[9] One of Riley Scott's best chapters is that on 'Phallicism in China and Japan', in which he relates phallicism to the Shinto religion, the source of the many rumbustious *hadaka matsuri* or 'naked festivals' I have so thoroughly enjoyed everywhere in Japan. The birth of the Japanese archipelago in legend is firmly phallic, as we learn from the book of ancient records called the *Kojiki*; here the first gods of Japan, the male god Izanagi and the female goddess Izanami come together and discuss their private parts:

> Descending from the heavens to this island (Onogoro, which Izanagi had formed by stirring the brine of the ocean with his jewelled spear), they erected a heavenly pillar and a spacious palace.
>
> At this time Izanagi-no-mikoto asked his spouse Izanami-no-mikoto, saying: 'How is your body formed?'
>
> She replied, saying: 'My body, though it be formed, has one place which is formed insufficiently.'
>
> Then Izanagi-no-mikoto said: 'My body, formed though it be formed, has one place which is formed to excess. Therefore, I would like to take that place in my body which is formed to excess and insert it into that place in your body which is formed insufficiently, and thus give birth to the land. How would this be?'
>
> Izanami-no-mikoto replied, saying: 'That will be good.'[10]

So they walk in a circle round the heavenly pillar, in opposite directions, and when they meet they 'commence procreation'.

This beautiful legend, so curiously potent in its reticent and delicate sexual imagery, is obviously phallic, and is the basis of all phallic worship in Japan.

An extremely good work on this theme is *Gods of Myth and Stone: Phallicism in Japanese Folk Religion*[11] by Professor Michael Czaja of the University of California at Berkeley, which is beautifully and profusely illustrated. He is particularly good on the origins and significance of animist and agricultural ceremonies as found today in the 'naked festivals' like that at Kohnomiya Shrine, near Nagoya, which I participated in many times when I lived there.

In my book, *Japan Behind the Fan*,[12] I give a very full description of two celebrated phallic festivals, at Saidaiji and at the great centre of phallicism in Japan, Tagata Shrine, near Nagoya, one of my favourite haunts. Here the worshippers

> crowd in adoration round a huge gilded penis (testicles are rarely represented in Japanese phalloi) which is carried under a sacred canopy by dedicated young priests. However, there is the same fairground atmosphere as at Buddhist rites. The stalls sell souvenirs, phallus-shaped candy and 'accessories' for both men and women containing miniature phalloi; or one can buy a brass phallus in a beautiful little wooden box lined with black velvet on which the sacred memento (called *ohmamori*) lies discreetly enveloped in white shrine paper. It is only about an inch long, but every one is different. It is beautifully made.

I saw the same attention to details of the phallus in the Philippines, in the wooden figures sold to tourists: lift the loincloth and you will see that each member is unique, as I have described in my *Filipinescas*.[13]

In another of my books about Japan, *Heaven, Hell and Hara-Kiri*,[14] there is one affectionate chapter on the phallic worship festival held at my favourite bar in Sendai, Robata, whose splendid master, Tomiya Amae, has always been one of my best friends. (A branch of this folkloric bar can be found, complete with a magnificent collection of primitive phalloi, just behind the police station at Sonezaki in Osaka.) This is what I have to say about the very potent and fertile-looking phallic object in its freshly-decorated shrine:

> ... this is a real god for real people, not some imaginary deity in the sky presiding blandly over flocks of sheep. I love the god

for his frankness, realism and strange beauty. Though earthy in an almost comically candid way, his symbol is also pure, sane, refreshingly innocent, because it is straightforward in its male dignity. I love and respect such honesty and cleanliness of spirit.

The spectacle of the phallic procession at Tagata Shrine is vividly reminiscent of the exquisite seals depicting similar celebrations in ancient Greece which adorn the thoroughly documented and finely and curiously illustrated *Sexual Symbolism: A History of Phallic Worship*[15] by one of the first and best authorities on the subject, Richard Payne Knight, introduced in this new edition by Ashley Montagu. It includes 'A Discourse on the Worship of Priapus' and 'The Worship of the Generative Powers during the Middle Ages of Western Europe' (the latter portion of the book by Thomas Wright). Payne Knight was a great collector of Greek and Roman antiquities, especially coins, medals and bronzes, and many of these are reproduced in his essential work, written in sedate eighteenth-century prose. The book also includes a short account of 'The Remains of the Worship of Priapus in the Kingdom of Naples' by Sir William Hamilton, K.B., His Majesty's Minister at the Court of Naples. For those who love Neapolitan ways, this is an illuminating essay in letter form, and reveals customs that can still occasionally be glimpsed, in various forms, in the Naples of today and its surrounding countryside.

A more modern work is Jacques Marcireau's *Le Culte du Phallus*[16] in the well-known series 'Connaissance de l'Etrange', and Jacqueline Khayat's absorbing *Rites et Mutilations Sexuels*[17] has important sections on circumcision and phallic rites.

Finally, though artists have not been very enterprising in using the phallic motif in modern times, few poets have done much better. Exceptions to this rule are very rare, but include Jean Genet and the marvellous Japanese phallic and homosexual poet, Takahashi Mutsuo, both of whom I have translated. Here is a stanza about worship of the phallus in the form of fellatio from Genet's *A Song of Love*:[18]

> Dare my tongue at the pouted lip of this petal only
> Half-shaken gather a falling drop? His milk

Thickens my throat like a long white flight of doves.
O, be always a rose, a pearl-dripping petal. . . .

This is strongly reminiscent of Takahashi's poem 'The Finger':

. . . Some day from that gloomy heaven blanketed in cloud
A single candid finger will emerge
And spurt forth
Discovering my rosy morn. . . .[19]

And in his 'Portrait of Myself at the Start':

A young man squats to fasten his shoelaces
How delicate the nape of his neck looks
The flesh on his shoulders that moves slowly and softly
And the two thighs projecting from his loins are young and
    proud
(The male nipple pressed hard between his thighs is still
    pale pink)
The clean straight eyes of a silent young beast
Are fastened to the fingers fastening the shoelaces
But the moving fingers are dreaming absorbedly
Of the region a little above them
Of the bottle to his belly that is lithe as a hungry wolf's
There where they would play with gentle Eros cased in his
    thin skin
And who now dozes in his lustrous tender grasses. . . .

Many of my own poems are phallic in content. Some are
understandable only to the initiate into phallic worship, but
most of them are direct and honest, like those about the male
and female organs of generation in my sequence *The Body
Servant*[20] inspired by the very frank anatomical notebooks of
Leonardo da Vinci, which were introduced to me by my dear
dead friend Marcel Jouhandeau, in a volume of his saintly
Journaliers.

What are the prospects for phallic worship in the future of
our doomed and benighted civilization? Very poor. The orgy
rooms and baths of Tokyo, Amsterdam, New York and San
Francisco, the extraordinary Gents with its voyeurs and
mutual masturbators at the Gare du Nord in Paris, the discreet 'houses of rendezvous' in Tokyo and Osaka, the 'gay

video' cinemas with their darkened recesses in Paris, Lyons and Nice, are no substitute for the real thing, the reverent and holy worship of the male member in all its forms and in all its glory.

Nothing exemplifies more the degeneracy of our times than these dreary and joyless establishments, offensive to the aesthetic, if not to the moral point of view. Nor are the 'Sex Shops' of Beata Ufise and the S.M. backrooms of Greenwich Village jockstrap joints, so vividly portrayed in the movie *Cruising*, an answer to the profound longing for an experience that is mystical, sexual, religious and ecstatic.

What we require is the establishment of a new kind of place for worship of the phallus, a church of the Masculine Cross where devotees can go to commune with others of the same soul-force, to offer themselves upon the sacred altars of prostitution with frank bodies and fearless hearts, in the service of the godhead, in ceremonies of incense, poetry, art and music devised by the high priests of a solemn but exquisitely comical cult.

This is the only solution, and it will never be found now in this world, in which for most people the headiest phallic symbol is the sex shop's crudely-moulded red or black candles, from whose tip, like a dejected, withered foreskin, a wisp of cheap and broken candle-wick forlornly hangs, sexless and dead, in the coming rain of atomic ash—the result of our wrong worship of the regenerating power of the sun and its heavenly sign, the noble, proud, erect pillar of the phallus, the root of all things.

NOTES

1. *Sex Mythology, Including an Account of the Masculine Cross* (Paris, privately printed, 1898; edition of 200 copies only). Introduction by Sha Roco, 1 January 1874.
2. W. Jaeger, *Early Christianity and Greek Paideia* (Belknap Press of Harvard University Press, Cambridge, Mass. 1965).
3. M. Jouhandeau, St. Philippe Neri (Librairie Plon, 'Hommes de Dieu', Paris, 1957).
4. *Fleurs du Japon* (Les Editions Nagel, Geneva, for *L'Or du Temps*, Paris, 1969).

5. J. Pimpaneau, *Fantômes Manipulés, le Théâtre de Poupées au Japon* (Université Paris-VII, Centre de Publications d'Asie orientale).
6. R. H. van Gulik, *Sexual Life in Ancient China* (E. J. Brill, Leiden, 1961).
7. J. Davenport, *Curiositates Eroticae Physiologiae, Or, Tabooed Subjects Freely Treated* (London, privately printed, 1875).
8. G. R. Scott, Phallic Worship (T. Werner Lourie, London, 1941).
9. R. Goodland, *Bibliography of Sex Rites and Customs* (Routledge & Kegan Paul, London, 1931).
10. *Kojiki*, trans. by D. L. Philippi (University of Tokyo Press, Tokyo, 1968).
11. M. Czaja, *Gods of Myth and Stone* (Weatherhill, Tokyo and New York, 1974), with a first-rate, exhaustive bibliography of the entire subject.
12. J. Kirkup, *Japan Behind the Fan* (Dent, London, 1970).
13. J. Kirkup, *Filipinescas* (Dent, London, 1968).
14. J. Kirkup, *Heaven, Hell and Hara-Kiri* (Angus & Robertson, London and Sydney, 1974).
15. R. P. Knight, *Sexual Symbolism: A History of Phallic Worship* (Julian Press, New York, 1962).
16. J. Marcireau, *Le Culte du Phallus* (Editions Alain Lefeuvre, Paris, 1979).
17. J. Khayat, *Rites et Mutilations Sexuels* (Guy Authier, Paris, 1977).
18. J. Kirkup, *Refusal to Conform* (O.U.P., 1963).
19. J. Kirkup, *Modern Japanese Poetry* (University of Queensland Press, St. Lucia, Qld., 1978).
20. J. Kirkup, *The Body Servant: Poems of Exile* (Dent, London, 1971).

7

Homosexuality and Literature

by WALTER PERRIE

The great complex of problems involved in the relations between homosexuality and literature can be resolved into at least three specific questions: are there any unusual conditions affecting how criticism ought to treat of literature on homosexual themes or written by homosexuals? Is there any specially intimate relation between a homosexual *eros* and literary ability as has been suggested by, for example, Marcuse and, on different grounds, the 'Men of the 'Nineties'? And what are the effects, if any, of the presentation of homosexual themes in literature on the perception of homosexuality by society at large and by homosexuals? For present purposes we will consider literature only in terms of what is broadly agreed to constitute the canon of European and American literature, that is, the serious novel, poetry and drama. No such agreement can be looked for on the subject of homosexuality which, in the course of this century, has been variously regarded as a criminal offence, an aesthetic ideal, a psychopathological condition, an hereditary affliction, and simple, outright wickedness. Our first imperative must therefore be to seek some clarification of the concept of homosexuality, and this may be made easier by a brief historical excursion.

Throughout the Middle Ages, Church and State were inextricably interwoven. The Church insisted that sodomy was a mortal sin. It was, therefore, also a crime and one for which the prescribed punishment was burning at the stake. A homosexual condition, that is, the experience of homosexual desires, has never been a criminal offence since criminality has traditionally resided in actions. The great majority of prosecutions appear, however, to have been associated with witchcraft and heresy trials, accusations of sodomy being a sort of regular chorus to a more general indictment of 'unnatural practices' as, for example, in the indictments framed against the Waldensians and Knights Templar.[1] Homosexual acts, sodomitical or otherwise, not associated with other offences, and therefore not perceived as threatening the established order, appear to have been tolerated by the authorities as private, if scandalous, peccadilloes, and this view is supported by the literary sources. Dante, for example, refers to Andrea dei Mozzi, Bishop of Florence, who had to be removed to another see on account of the scandal to which flagrant indulgence of his sexual tastes had given rise and gives the clear impression that the sodomites were as numerous, successful and respected as any other section of the Florentine community.[2]

Until the beginning of the modern period, which we can conveniently date from 1789, social and judicial attitudes to homosexuality remained basically unchanged: homosexual behaviour was chiefly associated with sodomy and with male-to-female transvestism. With the exception of a few notorious courts at which homosexuality had to be tacitly accepted, notably those of James I in England and Henri III in France, the social visibility of homosexuality was minimal and pre-reformation penalties remained largely in force until at least the Napoleonic period. The only substantial change, apart from a novel stress on marriage and the family as emotional as well as social relationships, seems to have been in the willingness of the reformers to isolate sexual from other misconduct and to prosecute and punish accordingly, but this was true of the whole range of sexual behaviour and not just of homosexual acts. The last man to be sentenced to death in England for sodomy was a Captain Robert James in 1772.[3] The pillory was the more usual penalty, but that was often a *de facto* if not a *de jure* death sentence and continued in use until at least 1811. In France burning at the stake continued to be the enforced penalty for sodomy until shortly before the Revolution.

In such circumstances the fact that European literature should be taciturn with regard to homosexual themes can hardly come as a surprise. Aside from numerous Puritan pamphlets inveighing against moral depravity, what references there are are derogatory or comic. The medium most obviously vulnerable to Puritan proscription, because the most public, was the Drama, which, until very recently, was never able to establish itself as a literary form in Scotland in the face of the unyielding opposition of the Kirk which regarded theatres as, if the pun be tolerable, hotbeds of depravity. Philip Stubbes, writing in England in 1583, alleged that 'Players and play-haunters in their secret conclaves play the Sodomites',[4] an accusation which has retained its currency if not its charm. Women, of course, were forbidden the Elizabethan stage and female parts were played by boys. At the Restoration the atmosphere of repression lightened a little but mainly in aristocratic and court circles. John Wilmot, Earl of Rochester, is usually credited with authorship of the pornographic farce *Sodom*,[5] and Vanburgh's *The Relapse* also deals with themes sodomitical, but between then and 1789 British literature has few references to the subject. Brian Merriman refers in *The Midnight Court* to 'nancy boys',[6] Charles Churchill wrote two anti-homosexual satires, *The Times* and *The Rosciad*, and Smollett in *Roderick Random* uses a homosexual seduction theme, but any writers who were themselves homosexual, such as Francis Bacon, were well-advised to discretion in an environment universally hostile. So far as literature and homosexuality were thought to have any relation whatsoever, it was the general view that sodomites would produce only a weak and effeminate art. As Brian Reade observes, though one might plead the qualified exceptions of Byron and Shelley, 'What is never felt in English literature since the seventeenth century up to about 1850 is that homosexual emotions were taken seriously, with the support of some aesthetic or moral principle . . . which provided . . . an orientation affecting the whole tone (let alone the substance) of a literary production.'[7] It is a very different situation today and Michel Foucault has highlighted the difference: 'Homosexuality appeared as one of the forms of sexuality when it was transposed from the practice of sodomy onto a kind of interior androgyny, a hermaphroditism of the soul. The sodomite had been a temporary aberration; the homosexual was now a species.'[8] There is a distinct sense in which the modern 'homosexual' is a nineteenth-century invention. Between 1789 and the present the articulation of that interior androgyny went on apace until homosexual behaviour has become an attribute of homosexual persons, with 'homosexual' connoting a whole system of social and psychological characteristics.

Before going on to consider something of the history of that development, it would be well to consider the earlier ideology, elements of which lingered on into the present, and to arrive at some general stance from which to consider the 'homosexual condition'. The rationale which underpinned the sodomy = witchcraft/heresy equation was that each was unnatural because each wilfully defied the laws not merely of man but of that God Who Ordained the Natural Order. Even where theological support for such a view has been undermined, either by revised interpretations of scripture or simply by the decay of the churches, the general view that homosexuality is somehow unnatural has lingered on in legal codes and social mores as well as in quasi-scientific theories of homosexuality. Of the many recent sociological investigations into the subject, two of the most methodologically rigorous are by Schofield in Britain[9] and Bell and Weinberg in the U.S.A.[10] Considering the difference in their scopes, objectives and milieux, they draw remarkably similar conclusions. Schofield interviewed homosexuals in prison, in receipt of psychiatric treatment and in socially well-integrated contexts with, in each case, non-homosexual control groups. Of the patients—and the same was true of the prisoners—he writes, 'The homosexual condition is irrelevant except in those cases where indirectly it had been the cause of the social pressures which in turn caused the breakdown';[11] and 'Although this research was designed to investigate differences between the homosexual and non-homosexual groups, in fact there were more differences between the three homosexual groups than there were between the pairs of homosexual groups and their corresponding control groups.'[12] Similarly, the Institute for Sex Research report observes, '. . . at the very least it will become increasingly clear to the reader that there is no such thing as *the* homosexual (or *the* heterosexual for that matter) and that statements of any kind which are made about human beings on the basis of their sexual orientation must always be highly qualified';[13] and 'They' (people in general) 'have believed that homosexuals are pretty much alike, but that this similarity necessarily involves irresponsible sexual conduct, a contribution to social decay, and, of course, psychological pain and maladjustment. . . . The present investigation, however, amply demonstrates that relatively few homosexual men and women conform to the hideous stereotype most people have of them. . . . Most are indistinguishable from the heterosexual majority with respect to most of the non-sexual aspects of their lives';[14] and, finally, 'Perhaps the least ambiguous finding of our investigation is that homosexuality is not necessarily related to pathology.'[15]

With all that in mind, an appropriate conclusion, if one needed drawing, would be that persons whose sexual inclinations are primarily homosexual do not belong to a different species from the rest of humankind and certainly do not, as some Victorians believed, constitute a third sex. Nevertheless, it remains a widely held and even institutionalized view, in literature as much as in society at large, that homosexuals are, if not of another species, at least abnormal or unnatural in some respect. Moreover, such views continue to form a powerful element in the anti-homosexual rationale and thereby to promote continued gross discrimination against homosexuals. In England, as in most States of the Union, homosexuals are still discriminated against in one aspect or another of the criminal code and the Scottish justiciary has only this year (1981) reaffirmed the rectitude of anti-homosexual discrimination in employment.[16]

So long as we are careful not to conflate a statistical average with an ethical norm, we might say that homosexual behaviour was abnormal inasmuch as it occurred less frequently than heterosexual behaviour, but we should then have to consider the social pressures militating against recognition of or accession to homosexual desires and it would be a peculiarly restricted usage of 'abnormal'. The notion that homosexual behaviour is in a non-statistical sense inherently abnormal finds its non-theological justification in variants of the following argument:

167

(a) Sexual behaviour not conforming to the purpose of sexual behaviour in general is abnormal.
(b) The purpose of sexual behaviour in general is the propagation of the species.
(c) Homosexual acts do not propagate the species.
(d) Therefore, homosexual acts are abnormal.

It would be tedious to detail in full all the confusions and errors of the above argument. Suffice it here to observe that the attribution of purpose to the sum of sexual acts confuses purpose with result and relies on a selection of *one* effect from a sum of consequences, rather than on the effect intended either in general or in any individual case. Additionally, premiss (b) is simply untrue if purpose must subsume intention and, finally, 'abnormal' is here a barely disguised normative expression smuggled into an argument the premisses of which are allegedly descriptive.

It is in any case clear that the intended effect of sexual behaviour from the individual's point of view is, in general, gratification of the sexual impulse and not procreation, and that, indeed, some trouble may be taken to avoid precisely that consequence. In most mammals sexual activity is restricted to periodic phases of adult life. After puberty, human sexuality is more or less continuous. Again, in most mammals other than man, the range of stimuli which can trigger a sexual response is relatively narrow. The opportunity for homosexual responses is thereby also curtailed though they do occur. Since human responses are not so bound to specific stimuli, virtually all human sexual behaviour is informed by empirical circumstance rather than by biologically preordained conditions and is, in that broad sense, learned or, at least, acquired behaviour. Because sexual arousal in man is open to the play of cultural factors, the range of potential stimuli is virtually unbounded as even the most brief survey of fetishism will confirm, and it is that very flexibility of learned response over instinctual determination which makes of man the exception to the mammalian rule and, incidentally, affords the ground for whatever limited freedoms man has acquired. This general human attribute of flexibility with regard to sexual stimuli makes a nonsense of the claim that homosexually stimulated arousal is in any sense abnormal or unnatural, and these observations should also clarify why no simple genetic base has been or is likely to be found for homosexuality since homosexual arousal lies well within the biological limits to learning capacity of any sexually functional member of the species. *Why* homosexual strategies are pursued by some persons and not by others is a matter for continuing research and controversy, and need not detain us here beyond the observation that a search for a single cause for so complex a phenomenon is unlikely to be rewarded.

The conclusions which, for the moment, we must draw from the above arguments and observations are that unless one is prepared to adduce reasons to the contrary, homosexually stimulated arousal has to be regarded as morally and empirically neutral; that the proper attitude for the critic is therefore one of detachment and that the contents of homosexual behaviour have to be judged on precisely the same grounds as those on which we would assess any other sexual activity. It is a correlate of these conclusions that where an author or critic diverges from such detachment, we are entitled to look for either a reason or a cause for that divergence.

By the end of the uproar which convulsed Europe between 1789 and 1815 a number of important shifts in sensibility can be detected. Such changes had been long prepared not merely by the increasingly swift transformation of economic relations but by all that went with them; rapid industrialization, increasing demand for female labour, the creation of an urban proletariat and, on the ideological plane, the growth of a literature of nostalgia for a vanished Golden Age: a prelapsarianism on which the whole Romantic movement fed and whose first fruits were the writings of Rousseau and Winckelmann. Both Hegel and Goethe testified to Winckelmann's influence on their development and in his *Lectures on the Philosophy of Art* Hegel claimed no less than that: 'Winckelmann by contemplation of the ideal works of the ancients received a sort of inspiration through which he opened a new sense for the study of art.'[17] In retrospect it seems far from accidental that Winckelmann should have been homosexual and a convert to Rome or that Pater should have devoted an essay to him in the enormously influential *Studies in the History of the Renaissance*. Hölderlin was likewise dazzled by Winckelmann's image of a classical paradise which modern scholarship finds altogether too aetherial: a paradise in which homosexual emotions were the paradigm of spiritual love. Winckelmann was, indeed, the proto-aesthete and to his influence may be attributed at least some of the credit (or blame) for the revolutionary claims advanced on behalf of art first by Kant and then by Hegel and his followers.

In Britain the new sensibility found its first full expression in the Wordsworth-Coleridge *Lyrical Ballads* in the *Preface* to which Wordsworth claimed that the poet was: '. . . endowed with more lively sensibility, more enthusiasm and tenderness, who has a greater knowledge of human nature, and a more comprehensive soul, than are supposed to be common among mankind—a man pleased with his own passions and volitions, and who rejoices more than other men in the spirit of life that is in him.'[18] The significance of an ideology which relates art to a psychology of sensibility and which sees that sensibility as making of the artist 'a man apart' should need no underscoring here. Shelley went a good deal further than Wordsworth in articulating the new sensibility and there is a nice irony in the observation that Shelley, who translated *The Symposium* and whose idealization of male-male friendships has distinctly erotic undertones, should have had as one of his mothers-in-law the formidable Mary Wollstonecraft, the founder of modern feminism whose *Vindication of the Rights of Women* had appeared in 1792.[19] If, in 1789, new hopes of liberty for some had raised in other eyes a spectre of anarchy and sexual libertinism, by the close of the Napoleonic period Europe was everywhere firmly in the grip of reaction and the period from 1815 to, roughly, 1845 was, by comparison, one of consolidation of the new sensibility.

By 1848, the Year of Revolutions, industrial capitalism had developed sufficiently to bring about major changes in the social roles of women at least in France and England and a new disquiet was evident in literature with regard to male perceptions of femininity. Women were presented as, on the one hand, creatures incapable of lust and, on the other, as the demonic destroyers of hapless males; a type of which Keats's 'Belle Dame' is an early intimation.[20] It is difficult not to see such schizophrenia as symptomatic of the increasingly stark contrast between economic developments and the ideology of bourgeois wish-fulfilment. Those same economic developments had by 1848 wrought havoc with the traditional role of the artist in relation to the body-politic, for the collapse of the *Ancien Regime* was also the collapse of secure patronage and of the close links which had obtained since the Renaissance between the aristocratic classes and the arts. It was in France that these changes, which had been working, to some extent, underground, broke spectacularly to the surface in the person of Baudelaire, and if England and Germany had dominated European letters from 1770, it was to France that that distinction now passed for the subsequent half century.

Baudelaire is a seminal figure for modern literature. His living out of the role of the newly urbanized, impoverished artist is reflected in both his style and choice of subject. His writings are peopled by society's rejects; the ragpickers, thieves, whores and, in the form of the lesbian, homosexuals. France was at that time the only country in Europe in which homosexual relations were, in certain circumstances, legal, having been made so under the *Code Napoleon*. In 1846 Baudelaire's publisher announced a volume to be entitled *Les Lesbiennes* though it did not in fact appear, but his concern for the exotic, the marginal and the scandalous did run through the whole of French literature for the rest of the century: a literature which, since then, has resembled nothing so much, if we may adapt Voltaire, as a silken robe smeared with filth. Baudelaire is a moralist: a judgement which Cocteau made of Genet[21] and which was certainly true of Gide.

It was, however, Baudelaire's friend Gautier who wrote what was to become the most influential single text for nineteenth-century English letters in *Mademoiselle de Maupin*: a character who blends male and female sex characteristics into one fascinating, androgynous figure. Paul Verlaine gave full expression to his homosexual emotions, and his affair with Rimbaud scandalized bourgeois Paris though his pornographic poems on homosexual themes, *Hombres*, were not published as a collection until well after his death and then privately.[22] Verlaine also wrote on lesbian themes and his pamphlet *Les Amies* appeared in 1867. Among the realists, the same concern for the socially and sexually heterodox is evident in Zola and

Maupassant, both of whom presented lesbian themes, and in Balzac, who, in the *Comédie Humaine*, presented a male homosexual relationship. For English writers the chief gain from symbolism was not, at least until Eliot and Pound, a technical one, though the innovations by Verlaine and others in the use of language as an associative and connotative instrument for the expression of feelings were inseparable from their concern with subjectivity, but was, rather, a new willingness to explore areas of feeling previously prohibited to serious literature. By the 1870s homosexual feelings and relationships had become something of an established feature of French literature.

If the sentiments to which Shelley gave expression in *Adonais* might have seemed to an eighteenth-century reader a trifle indulgent or unmanly, the sentiments which Tennyson expressed in *In Memoriam*, first published in 1850, would have seemed, not to put too fine a point on the matter, distinctly 'poofy'. Tennyson's elegy for his friend Hallam became one of the most widely read English poems of the century and while its homoerotic components are perhaps subdued, they are distinctly present in such lines as Tennyson's description of Hallam as: 'The human-hearted man I loved',[23] in his description of his grief at Hallam's death:

> Ah yet, ev'n yet, if this might be,
> I, falling on his faithful heart,
> Would breathing thro' his lips impart
> The life that almost dies in me;[24]

and in his reaction to their friendship:

> And all the secret of the Spring
> moved in the chambers of the blood.[25]

Tennyson's ambiguous blend of high-seriousness and homoeroticism was very soon overtaken by much more explicitly erotic writings; a development made possible not merely by French writers but by others such as Whitman whose *Leaves of Grass* first appeared in 1855 and in which male-male friendships described in strongly erotic terms are viewed as virtually co-extensive with democracy and the independent spirit. The idealization of male-male friendships with romantic and religious overtones was most fully expressed by the poets of the

172

Oxford Movement (Froude, Faber, Cory, Dolben and others): converts to Rome, popularly known on that account as The Perverts. Most of the adherents to that movement have been long forgotten but it was influential at the time. The key figure seems to have been William Cory who exercised considerable influence on figures as diverse as Bridges, Symonds and Hopkins, who was probably the most accomplished writer to have been influenced by the Oxford Movement.[26] Perhaps the most striking feature of their writings was the development of the idea of chivalric love between men and in this we can quite clearly trace the emergence of that 'interior androgyny' of which Foucault wrote; sentiment openly declared and readily provoked and sensibility elevated to a principle of moral or religious stature. These were attributes which the Victorians reserved for women, at least in their idealized aspect. A remark of Johann Huizinga's is revealing in this context *à propos* pornography: 'Erotic thought never acquires literary value save by some process of transfiguration of complex and painful reality into illusionary forms. The whole *genre* . . . with its indulgence toward the lies and egotism of the sexual life, and its vision of never-ending lust, implies no less than the screwed-up system of courtly love, an attempt to substitute for reality the dream of a happier life.'[27] One need not share Professor Huizinga's jaundiced view of the sexual life to find in the notion of chivalric love between men, as expressed in the writings of the mid-Victorians, something deeply distressed as well as a large measure of what must seem to modern readers naïve wish-fulfilment fantasies. But, in its time, such an idea was quite adventurous, and misery and the dream of a happier life can seem naïve only to an age so steeped in disappointment that it has given up wishing for anything and one hopes that, in time, some of these excessively neglected writers will be treated with more sympathy than seems likely at present.

No lack of sexual fulfilment seems to have troubled the redoubtable Swinburne who was strongly influenced by Gautier and who published in 1866 the first poem in English to treat overtly of homosexual themes since the sixteenth century.[28] Swinburne, Pater, Symonds and, a little later, Wilde shifted the accent away from religiosity and toward aestheticism as the rationale justifying their use of homosexual themes which

173

was by the 1880s becoming quite overt. As Brian Reade observes: '. . . the pace established in the 1860s was beginning to alter its momentum. This was due mainly to the arrival of younger generations of literary men accepting homosexual sentiment as part of the whole range of feeling which waited to be explored. The next stage was when the admission of such sentiments, albeit only among a few people who were haunted by them, grew into a belief that the more acute sensibility of the "artistic temperament" was often allied to the frustrated senses of the homosexual. To be homosexually inclined thus became one of the secondary qualifications for declaring one-self an "artist" ',[29] and indeed 'musical' became the 'in-word' of the '90s as a synonym for 'homosexual'.

The theorists for the aesthetes were Pater in his *Studies* and *Marius the Epicurean* and Symonds in *A Problem in Modern Ethics*,[30] which deals entirely with the question of homosexuality, but it was Wilde who most fully caught the public imagination in his playing out of the role of aesthete and Wilde who published the first piece of serious fiction in English to deal overtly with homosexual themes in the modern sense.[31] From then until 1895, when Wilde's trial wrote a sudden full-stop to the whole movement, was the heyday of aestheticism in English letters. The main propaganda vehicle for the movement was a magazine called *The Artist* and round it gathered a great many curious figures including, in social circles, the young Yeats, but it was Wilde again who sounded the first notes of modernism.

The reaction of the aesthetes to the increasingly apparent marginality of the writer in relation to society at large, and to the increasingly extravagant claims advanced for the arts by a whole series of philosophers from Hegel through the miso-gynistic Schopenhauer, incidentally, the most perceptive aesthetician of the nineteenth century, to the megalomaniac visions of Nietzsche of the artist-as-redeemer, was a dual one. On the one hand it showed itself in an insistence on the non-utilitarian character of art. If art and the artist could serve no obvious function, then let them be decorative and to hell with utility! But, at the same time, some obeissance had to be made toward rationality and to the claims registered for art as the product of a more acute sensibility. The aesthetes' resolution of this dilemma was to locate their claims in the personality of the artist; a personality which had, therefore, to live out this indulgent, aristocratic decorativeness so that homosexuality became for Wilde and his companions a defiance as well as a claim to greater sensibility. It was this dilemma which Yeats must have had in mind when, much later, he posed it as 'perfection of the life/ or of the work?' Wilde's life and work display an extraordinary blend of poise, grace and insecurity—like Nietzsche's tightrope walker. It was an impossible ethos to sustain, as became quickly apparent when the pressure was on during Wilde's trial. The remark, doubtless apocryphal, attributed to Wilde at his trial—that he did not care for the opinions of the court because all London was behind him, to a boy—perfectly catches the fragility and wit of an episode which could only end in catastrophe given the inherent conservativeness of public opinion. George Steiner suggests that: 'Wilde's bilingualism may be an expressive enactment of sexual duality, a speech-symbol for the new rights of experiment and instability he claimed for the life of the artist. Here, as at other important points, Wilde is one of the true sources of the modern tone.'[32] One of the other important points is certainly Wilde's use of irony, but his sexual and linguistic uprootedness seem much more a response to the cultural and social trends we have been at pains to outline than any rationalization Wilde may have offered in terms of 'new rights'. Wilde was a key figure not just for modern literature but for those ideas about homosexuality which have filtered through to the popular imagination from serious literature; his foppishness, irresponsibility, unhappiness and 'feminine' wit have become established features of the homosexual stereotype.

Although the Wilde trial effectively ended the experiments of the aesthetes, their literary influence was very considerable and, as Paul Fussell has shown in his excellent *The Great War and Modern Memory*, resurfaced in the homoerotic components of much of the English poetry of the Great War, not only in terms of an already established sensibility in respect of male-male eroticism but also in choice of image and metaphor.[33]

When Foucault wrote of 'interior androgyny' he was being quite precise. From about 1860 competing 'scientific' theories of homosexuality had begun to be aired. Earlier in the century homosexuality had been generally held to be a form of 'moral insanity'. The expression 'homosexual' was coined in 1869 by a Hungarian doctor (Benkert) but did not gain widespread currency until the present century. Like many phenomena, it did not really have a complete identity until named and once named tended to fit that Procrustean bed. Through the 1870s and '80s the idea promoted by Ulrichs[34] that homosexuals were female brains in male bodies—proved by the fact that homosexuals found difficulty in whistling—gained ground, and by the close of the century, thanks to the popularity of the works of Krafft-Ebbing and Havelock Ellis, it was well-nigh universally agreed that homosexual behaviour resulted from the imperfect evolution of the foetus from its primary, andro-gynous form. Homosexuals were biological mistakes and herculean efforts were made to fit every conceivable pattern of homosexual behaviour into that schema. The only advantage for the homosexual was that it did begin to shift the accent away from his criminality, though the advantages of that shift remain debatable. Arno Karlen, in a passage rich in ironies, describes the general concensus: 'The congenital urning' (homosexual) 'had no heterosexual feelings, was physically feminized and showed an interest in cooking, sewing, *belles-lettres* and other feminine occupations, "even to the extent of giving himself entirely to the cultivation of the beautiful".'[35] The parallel with aestheticism is obvious.

It was against this background and in the year of Wilde's trial that the torch of homosexual characterization passed out of the hands of the literati and into the hands of Freud and all who came after him, for in that year Freud published the first major document of psychoanalysis, *On the Interpretation of Dreams*. It was some time before Freud's ideas gained any currency but in the meantime Havelock Ellis, who prescribed chastity belts to stop boys masturbating and with whom Symonds had co-operated in *Studies in the Psychology of Sex*, held the field. It would be tedious to examine in detail the development at the hands of the psychoanalysts of the notion of interior androgyny, and in any case psychoanalysis only now seems to be filtering through to the popular imagination, though a crude Freudianism can be found in the mouths of even the most ill-informed of literary critics. Freud's basic advance was to shift the notion of androgyny away from a physical to a psychic basis. Working in the milieu of late-nineteenth century bourgeois Vienna, Freud took it for granted that homosexual behaviour was pathological because it did not conform to the prejudices of his received culture. Homosexual behaviour was presumed to be necessarily maladaptive on the basis that it was in fact maladaptive in that particular culture. Until very recently indeed that premiss went without serious question, with often barbarous consequences for the individuals whom analysts tried to 'cure'. Since the psychoanalytic definition of health was basically that of conformity, its definition of pathology was similarly limited and necessarily constituted a reinforcement of existing social and cultural relations and it was against the background of those relations that the last major shift in the use of homosexual themes in literature came to be developed.

In France Gide, Proust and Cocteau continued a tradition which, essentially, looked back to the '90s for its ideas and metaphors, though Gide and Cocteau were rather less discreet than they could possibly have been in England where the post-'90s reaction did not really begin to evaporate until the middle '50s. Auden and Isherwood both spent much of their time out of England, and both they and Spender were very cautious indeed in their use of homosexual themes. Auden's marvellous 'Lay your sleeping head my love' is quite indeterminate as to gender. Forster prohibited publication of *Maurice* until after his death and, as John Lahr says in his biography of Joe Orton: 'On stage, the treatment of the homosexual was as violent and narrow-minded as the laws. In 1965 Terence Rattigan, explaining why he had transformed a homosexual incident to a heterosexual one as the basis for *Separate Tables*, said "The Lord Chamberlain, our stage censor, forbids any mention of that subject",'[36] and Forster in his afterword to *Maurice* was provoked to observe that: 'We had not realized that what the public really loathes in homosexuality is not the thing itself but having to think about it.'[37] One is tempted to add that the same is true of just about everything.

It fell to France again and in particular to Jean Genet, picking up in a sense where Baudelaire had left off, to make a more lively use of homosexual themes. Genet is, in my view, essentially a moralist; a view particularly supported by the plays. Genet has taken to its logical conclusion the marginality

177

of the writer and fabricated out of that a world in which all the conventional negatives become positive—theft, murder, rape, homosexuality are the themes around which Genet spins his fantastic web. The flies he catches are the imbecile critics who see in him, as Huxley saw in Baudelaire, merely the wilful perversity of the Satanist. At the heart of Genet's monstrous vision is love and the power of the human imagination, even in circumstances of the utmost alienation from everything bourgeois society values. Genet's genius may be flawed but genius it undoubtedly is, and his use of homosexual themes as both a defiance and an expression of alienation were quickly taken up by James Baldwin, Joe Orton and many others. Since then there has been the whole gay-lib movement; a case of *Après Genet, le deluge*, and a great deal of nonsense in the name of the 'sexual revolution', none of which we can investigate here beyond remarking that the hopes so fervently expressed in the '60s could not but be disappointed, however much they may have deserved to be fulfilled.

It will be observed by the perceptive reader that I have not advanced any positive theory of homosexuality. Theories of homosexuality can safely be left to those who believe that human behaviour is simple enough to be explained by such theories. I do not. In fine, I do not believe that it is in any way helpful or informative to classify persons—even authors—on the basis of their sexual tastes. That said, are we any nearer to an answer to the three questions posed at the beginning of this essay? So far as criticism is concerned, the only special burden which homosexual themes place upon the critic arises from the fact that homosexuality has been the subject of so much prejudice, and still is. The good critic should in any case attend to context, and so it should be unnecessary to plead for special attention to be paid to the author's perception of social attitudes toward homosexuality: should be, but probably is not. Beyond that, works dealing with homosexual themes call for no special duties over and above those demanded by works dealing with heterosexual themes. It is bad critical practice to praise or condemn a work on the basis of its relation to any particular cause, as some gay-libbers are inclined to do, and however admirable the cause. The very difficult question of assessing the relation between a work and its own ideological premisses can only be resolved on a text-by-text basis. Similarly, if it is absurd to castigate Dante for his attitude to sodomy, it is equally absurd to castigate a contemporary writer for the same attitude *on an aesthetic basis*. We are certainly entitled to condemn writers for what we regard as moral failures, if we feel so inclined, and may even feel that such are but the reflections of deeper, imaginative failures, but we are not entitled to condemn literary works for non-literary reasons unless we clearly state that we are so doing. I deplore the politics of T. S. Eliot. Nevertheless, since my political views did not comprise a feature of Eliot's artistic prospectus, they can have no part in my judgement as to the artistic success, or otherwise, of Eliot's efforts to carry out that prospectus. I am, of course, entitled to dislike the whole enterprise. The same holds true for sexual as for political themes. However strongly one may suspect an author of moral or imaginative failures, unless there are grounds for locating such failures in a text, one's suspicions have no place in honest criticism. To give but one example: much of the poetry of the Great War in English draws on homoerotic themes. Its purpose in so doing is to contrast the legalized, public murder of the battlefield with the illicit eroticism of private experience. Freud suggested that homosexuality was an infantile form of sexuality. Were a Freudian interpretation to be applied to the use of homosexual themes in the poetry of the Great War, and the eroticism of those poems to be found immature as a consequence, a critical blunder of stupendous insensitivity would result. Desire does not arise with a label attached saying 'pathological'. As with every other form of literature, unless the critic can make the requisite willing suspension of disbelief, then he has no business to be writing criticism.

As to a special connection between a homosexual *eros* and literature, we have seen that there are good and adequate historical explanations for such claims and I have found no shred of evidence to suggest that such claims are anything more than ideological. In a famous passage from *Eros and Civilization*, after remarking that his classical source is Ovid, Marcuse claimed that: 'The classical tradition associates Orpheus with the introduction of homosexuality. Like Narcissus, he rejects the normal Eros, not for an ascetic ideal, but for a fuller Eros. Like Narcissus, he protests against the repressive order of

179

procreative sexuality. The Orphic and Narcissistic Eros is to the end the negation of this order—the Great Refusal. In the world symbolized by the culture-hero Prometheus, it is the negation of *all* order; but in this negation Orpheus and Narcissus reveal a new reality, with an order of its own, governed by different principles. The Orphic Eros transforms being; he masters cruelty and death through liberation. His language is *song* and his work is *play*. Narcissus's life is that of *beauty* and his existence is *contemplation*. These images refer to the *aesthetic dimension* as the one in which their reality principle must be sought and validated.'[38] The last sentence quoted makes it clear that Marcuse's claim is consciously ideological. If we interpret it in any other way, then it becomes nonsensical and wholly dependent on his very Freudian view of sexuality as the key to liberation, bearing in mind that Freud in *Civilization and Its Discontents* had argued that all culture arose out of the sublimation of sexual instincts. Even at the ideological level, there is much to take issue with in Marcuse's assertions though his ideas are valuable in relation to the most recent period in literature and, in particular, with regard to such writers as Genet, Baldwin, Burroughs. However, Marcuse adduces no evidence whatsoever to lead us to believe that he is making an empirical claim and there, for this essay, the matter must rest.

As to the final question of the trilogy, the historical evidence strongly suggests that literature does play some part in shaping perceptions of homosexuality and, indeed, it would be extraordinary if it did not. I suspect it further shows that, by and large, literature—most of the time—only serves to confirm and elaborate stereotypes or to shift the tone of a stereotype from one aspect to another. The question of the degree to which literature affects such perceptions seems to me to be answerable only in relation to specific works, if at all. In conclusion, Brigid Brophy may have the last word, writing about Genet: 'The most astonishing metamorphosis of all is the one which transforms the images that activate Genet's personal erotic tastes . . . into poetry, poetry being, precisely, a universal imagery of eroticism, which provokes the imagination to an intangible but all the same completely sexual erection—a universal love-language which is, however, in fact understood by fewer readers than French and practised by fewer devotees than the most esoteric sexual perversion.'[39]

NOTES

1. N. Cohn, *Europe's Inner Demons* (St. Albans, 1976). See especially Chapters 2 and 3.
2. D. L. Sayers (ed. & trans.), *Dante: The Divine Comedy* (Middlesex, 1949). Dante put the sodomites in the seventh circle of Hell and on the seventh cornice of Purgatory. Miss Sayers provides excellent notes on the theology of Dante's decisions.
3. L. Stone, *The Family, Sex and Marriage in England 1500–1800* (London, 1977), pp. 541–42.
4. A. Karlen, *Sexuality and Homosexuality* (London, 1971). Quoted on p. 116.
5. D. Loth, *The Erotic in Literature* (London, 1962), pp. 85–8.
6. At least in Frank O'Connor's translation in the *Penguin Book of Irish Verse* (Middlesex, 1970).
7. B. Reade (ed.), *Sexual Heretics* (London, 1970), p. 7.
8. M. Foucault, *The History of Sexuality, Vol. I* (London, 1979), p. 43.
9. M. Schofield, *Sociological Aspects of Homosexuality: A Comparative Study of Three Types of Homosexuals* (London, 1965).
10. A. P. Bell & M. S. Weinberg, *Homosexualities: A Study of Diversity Among Men and Women* (London, 1980). This publication of the Institute for Sex Research is the most ambitious sociological survey on the subject to date.
11. M. Schofield, op. cit., p. 161.
12. Ibid., p. 209.
13. Bell & Weinberg, op. cit. p. 23.
14. Ibid., pp. 229–30.
15. Ibid., p. 231.
16. Court of Session, Edinburgh, *Regina v. Saunders*. For an account of the degree of anti-homosexual discrimination in the U.K. useful documents are the reports of the Commission on Discrimination of the Campaign for Homosexual Equality. London, 1979 and 1980.
17. Quoted by Pater in his *Studies in the History of the Renaissance*, in the essay on Winckelmann (London, 1873).
18. R. L. Brett & A. R. Jones (eds.), *Wordsworth and Coleridge—Lyrical Ballads* (London, 1965), pp. 255–56.
19. Mary Wollstonecraft was the mother of a love-child to Godwin, later Mrs. Mary Shelley. Shelley's translation of the work now usually known as *The Symposium* was entitled *The Banquet of Plato* which, though translated in 1818, was not published until 1840 and even then with the provocative passages deleted by Mrs. Shelley.
20. A. Karlen, op. cit. See Chapter II for a much fuller account of the relations between feminism and the Romantic movement.

21. J. Cocteau, *Professional Secrets* (New York, 1972), p. 309.
22. Privately printed in Paris in 1903 and now available in several editions.
23. A. Tennyson, *In Memoriam*, section XIII.
24. Ibid., section XVIII.
25. Ibid., section XXIII.
26. B. Reade, op. cit. Gives a very full documentation of the homosexual literature of the period 1850–1900.
27. J. Huizinga, *The Waning of the Middle Ages*. Quoted in A. Karlen, op. cit., p. 107.
28. A. Swinburne, *Poems and Ballads* (London, 1866), 'Hermaphroditus'.
29. B. Reade, op. cit. p. 31.
30. W. Pater, *Marius the Epicurean* (London, 1885). Symonds published the *Problem* anonymously in 1891.
31. In *Blackwood's Magazine* (Edinburgh, 1889).
32. G. Steiner, *Extraterritorial* (Middlesex, 1975), p. 16.
33. P. Fussell, *The Great War and Modern Memory* (London, 1975).
34. K. H. Ulrichs, a German lawyer, was the first to suggest that homosexuals were the product of an arrested embryonic development. See A. Karlen, op. cit. Chapter 10.
35. A. Karlen, op. cit., p. 192.
36. J. Lahr, *Prick Up Your Ears* (Middlesex, 1980), p. 188.
37. Ibid. Quoted on p. 188.
38. H. Marcuse, *Eros and Civilization* (London, 1969), p. 125.
39. B. Brophy, *Genet* (New York, 1979), p. 75.

8

Erotic Poetry in English

by DEREK PARKER

Landscape and love are the two chief themes of English poetry, and considering the fact that there is a sexual element in almost every man-woman relationship, it is astonishing that there is not a stronger erotic element in love poetry as a whole. Of course there are various reasons for this, one of which is the puritan attitude which resulted in a great deal of censorship—preventing for instance the publication of several of Donne's poems during his lifetime, and for well over two centuries after his death. Another reason is the shyness of poets themselves: Donne, after the shifting of his poetic drive away from this world and women to the other world and Christ, was extremely reluctant to have his love poetry published; and other poets, like some artists, did their best to conceal any erotic poems they wrote. Sometimes their friends continued to conceal them, as Watts-Dunton concealed Swinburne's flagellatory poems, long after the death of the poets themselves.

But there is perhaps another reason why erotic poetry is not as common as one might expect, and that is the difficulty of writing it, which is of a somewhat different nature to the difficulty of writing poetry on any other theme, of finding the right words and images to convey one's meaning, of persuading or forcing them into the right form. In writing of sexual love the poet was for many centuries inhibited by the fact that the society to which the poetry was to be offered, or before which it might be placed, or at least within which it was written, had many inhibitions about the public expression of sexuality, and certainly about the language which might be used to discuss it. The inhibitions continue: there are some journals which in the 1980s would hesitate to print a poem containing such words as *fuck* or *cunt*, and would be chary of publishing a poem dealing with, say, cunnilingus or fellatio. The fuss about a poem, by James Kirkup, printed in *Gay News* which concerned a homosexual's necrophiliac lovemaking with the body of Christ outraged public opinion rather more, it can be asserted, on sexual than on religious grounds; some aspects of sexuality still cannot be discussed in public without giving serious offence. (I had better make the point that I see no distinction between the erotic and the pornographic in literature, and make no distinction between them here. Nor do I believe that sexual activity is an area of human life necessarily improper to be explored by the writer or artist.)

Much English erotic poetry has therefore been produced for private circulation, or even (as seems clearly to be the case with Swinburne's 'The Flogging Block') for private masturbatory purposes. This does not necessarily mean that it is bad, though in many cases it is. The Earl of Rochester, capable of such moving verses as the 'Song of a Young Lady to her Ancient Lover', in his 'A Ramble in St. James's Park' was intent solely to titillate and perhaps even to shock, though his intimates seem to have been eminently unshockable. In any event, such lines as

> Poor pensive lover in this place
> Would frig upon his mother's face
> Where rows of mandrakes tall did rise
> Whose lewd tops fucked the very skies

are neither witty nor ingenious, nor do they have much of a sensual charge. Other poets rose to the occasion with greater pith and ambition, and the result was better verse.

The real reason why the sexual experience does not seem to have evoked, or provoked, much good poetry is almost as mysterious as the full sensual and psychological effect of orgasm itself. At its most basic, in a quick act of masturbation for instance, sex provides for the man a process of simple evacuation which, like defecation, may be 'necessary' or 'satisfying', but is scarcely a matter for much exploration as to its philosophical meaning, or even its psychological nature. And after all the best poetry, *pace* Housman, is 'intelligent', does concern itself with the exploration of an act, an emotion, even a landscape. Perhaps the fact too that orgasm brings an evacuation of semen in the male, and of tension, perhaps (not always) emotion, certainly of energy in both man and woman, has something to do with the poet's reluctance to write really intensely and seriously about it. Many sportsmen still lead a celibate life before an important event, and not necessarily in order to conserve their physical energy; there is some magic about it, the mystique of the virtue of semen which has always been important to sportsmen and warriors. (It would be interesting to discover whether sportswomen have the same impulse.) Apart from the physical energy used in sexual activity, there is also the instinct that one is losing—'spending' is of course the traditional term—something else, some other kind of energy, which had better be preserved, if one is to be at one's best in some other activity. Bernard Shaw was only one of a number of writers who believed that a conservation of sexual energy meant an increased reservoir of emotional and mental energy. Does the poet, consciously or unconsciously, shrink from even the attempt to describe the sexual act with real vigour and intensity, for some such 'magical' reason? It is not a theory that would probably have occurred to the Rochesters or the Sedleys, though the former, writing of his temporary and unfamiliar impotence, noticed that his phallus, not incapable of rising to the beautiful woman to whom he wanted to pay tribute, was in general

> Through all the town a common fucking post
> On whom each whore relieves her tingling cunt
> As hogs on gates do rub themselves and grunt.

The writing of such verses as 'A Ramble in St. James's Park' may certainly be equated with that kind of rubbing and grunting. The talent, the instinct, the true sensuality needed to produce Rochester's 'Song of a Young Lady to her Ancient Lover' is entirely another matter. Did the semi-masturbatory effort of producing his scabrous verses inhibit Rochester as a 'real' poet? Even prevent him from writing good erotic poetry, or even good pornography?

But verse is in any event a poor medium for the pornographic instinct. An air of reality is vital if one is to be moved by pornography. Rowlandson's many erotic drawings are magnificent *as* drawings—beautifully sketched, funny, amusing; but hardly ever erotic, for after all they remain caricatures, and the sight of a caricatured copulation rarely moves us to sexual excitement. Occasionally, of course, it can happen; there is a drawing of a handsome young sailor busily rogering a blowsy woman in an upstairs window of an inn, while she waves goodbye to her husband, off and away in the street below. Rowlandson there catches the mood of the moment, and restrains his impulse to caricature his subjects, sufficiently for there to be a strong sexual element conveyed not only by the imagined situation but by his depiction of it. But it is an exception. The case is much the same with modern, carefully posed photographs of copulation, in which only the juxtaposition of the bodies, rather than any indication through facial expression, much less any more overt sign, suggests that real passion is involved. Similarly with the film in which the angle of photography is carefully contrived to disguise the fact that the phallus of the male participant is not erect. The successful pornographic film is almost always careful not only to show erection but ejaculation, which after all cannot be easily disguised; occasionally the producer even goes, we are told, to the lengths of splicing in a few feet showing the ejaculation of some other penis than that of the actor concerned, knowing that the customer needs evidence of the actor's pleasure before he can counterfeit it in himself. Perhaps one reason why women are allegedly less moved by pornographic films is that the ecstasy of the female actors can so easily be faked?

The missing element is, of course, love, whatever one means by that word. Very occasionally a flash of what appears to be real tenderness may illuminate the screen or the page; but it is, one imagines, difficult to find lovers prepared to take part in the making of pornographic movies or the taking of explicit photographs; the act of love when it takes place between a loving couple is indeed too private for display—the one tenable argument against pornography. Pleasure in the physical act itself, between mere friends or acquaintances, or strangers, need not be counterfeited, but must in the end lack psychological conviction. Literature, poetry or prose, should in theory be able to convey the full experience of loving to shocking and memorable effect.

What it can do, pornography does best in prose. The reasonably literate reader should have no problem in identifying with any character in a pornographic novel, and in the best pornography (Cleland's *Fanny Hill*, to use the most quoted example) there are certainly few barriers between the reader and the experiences of the heroine. There is also a true tenderness; who can read, un-moved, the description of Fanny's loving examination of her lover's body on the morning after her seduction? In poetry, the problem of identification is almost insurmountable because of the problem of form. A film made of Rochester's 'Ramble', exclusively making use of his images, would certainly succeed in arousing lust; but in reading the poem, the very elements which *make* it a poem— prosody and rhyme—get in the way of the *reader's* imagination, and thus choke Rochester's erotic expression at source. To that extent, his poem fails as pornography, displaying his arousal but failing to arouse the reader. Here is perhaps the primary reason why the successful erotic poem is very rare indeed.

When an erotic poem is successful, it is because the poet contrives to find a universally acceptable, a uniformly effective, image. Of course this is true of poetry of every type, to a great extent; but because we respond to sexual stimuli in such a very personal manner, because our reactions are so thoroughly tied in with our own psyches, are so much more complex and personal than our reactions to, say, a flower or a cat, a landscape or even a political attitude, it is far more difficult to make a common coinage.

To turn to particular examples, it seems to me that the earliest truly effective erotic poem in the English language is Sir Thomas Wyatt's 'The Forsaken Lover', from the first quarter of the sixteenth century, with its electric opening lines:

> They flee from me that sometime did me seek
> With naked foot stalking in my chamber. . . .

187

The poem has almost every element of the successful erotic poem: universality, immediate and sharp visual elements, vivid language, memorable imagery; we all have memories of such moments as Wyatt describes:

> In thin array after a pleasant guise
> When her loose gown from her shoulders did fall
> And she me caught in her arms long and small
> Therewithal sweetly did me kiss,
> And softly said, 'Dear heart, how like you this?'

The poem has the individual as well as the general touch, and happily (by good luck of course rather than good judgement) none of the language used has dated or changed meaning. For the general reader, changing fashions in language and imagery do present a problem. For two hundred years or so, for instance, the intensity of the orgasm was compared to death, and this gave poets an image which could be freely and ingeniously used. Sir Robert Aytoun, for instance, translating Guarini, was able to start a poem:

> The shepherd Thirsis longed to die
> Gazing on the gracious eye
> Of her whom he adored and loved . . .

and while the lines had the romantic ring of the old tradition of courtly love, every reader grasped too the carnal meaning; the shepherdess was certainly aware of it, for she was quick to protest

> O die not yet, I pray.
> I'll die with thee, if thou will stay.

However, language presents few problems that a footnote or two will not solve, if sometimes the continual use of classical allusion bogs a poem down to such an extent that it becomes genuinely difficult for any modern reader, lacking a classical education, to enjoy it. Chapman's 'Ovid's Banquet of Sense', for instance, is a good and well-sustained long poem with obvious beauties—

> Now as she lay attired in nakedness
> His eye did carve him on that feast of feasts . . .

—but the reader will meet, within a few stanzas, anachronisms such as fot (for fetched), tire (for attire), meed (for excellence), sulphure (for sulphurous), Pelopian (for ivory), prorected (for reflected), while there are references to 'a burning vapour' (a comet), the 'sweet fields of life' (the fields of paradise), Auriga (a constellation) and 'the heavenly goat' (Capella). The reader who comes to this poem because of a general interest in and enjoyment of poetry will not hesitate to take the difficulties in his stride; but a lack of immediate enjoyment stands much in the way of an appreciation of the sensual qualities of Chapman's work. Of course this is a general problem in reading verse of previous centuries; it is however heightened where erotic poetry is concerned, and not least because poets have been driven to extremes of imagery, of literary contortion and distortion, in their attempts to convey their emotions.

The nature of the sexual impulse has not much detained poets, and where it has, the result has not really been erotic verse. Rubens's wedding portrait of himself and his wife, or Van Eyck's 'Arnolfini and his wife' say more about the *nature* of sexual love than, say, Picasso's spirited drawings of nymphs and satyrs enjoying convoluted copulations. Similarly, in poetry, it is probably true that Donne's 'The Awakening' says more about the condition of being *in love* than his celebrated nineteenth Elegy. Donne knew all there was to know about the lover's longing for complete absorption in the loved one, about the changing of eyes, about the abstract longings. But he also knew about the purely sensual aspects of love—'Unless I labour, I in labour lie.' In order to arouse lust in their readers (and one definition of erotic poetry must surely be the old definition of pornography in general, as that which makes us as randy as possible as quickly as possible) poets, like painters, must be explicit.

And here the problem of language arises again. Obscenities whispered in the bed have their emotional charge when we are making love; in cold print, on the page, they lose that charge and become *merely* obscenities. It is the objection many otherwise liberal people have to visual obscenity: that the act of love is so essentially private that a depiction of it is always a gratuitous intrusion. Well, one could apply that argument to many other areas of life—a mother's suckling her baby, for instance? The main problems are still problems, it seems to me, of interpretation; and without doubt they are difficult problems, and rarely approach successful resolution.

Which is not to say that a great deal of erotic poetry is not worth reading, for a variety of reasons, not least of which is that it is often very amusing. The limerick, for instance, which has become almost exclusively a vehicle for sexual innuendo or scatology, is at its best a very entertaining form of light verse. It is not a form which is easy to use, and there are relatively few first-rate limericks; take up any collection of them, and it will be found that the majority are wanting in scansion or rhyme or both. A few take hold of elderly jokes and make a good thing of them. One of the most popular and best of the modern limericks goes:

> A persistent young plumber called Lee
> Was plumbing his girl by the sea.
>> Said she, 'Stop your plumbing,
>> There's somebody coming.'
> 'I know,' said the plumber, 'it's me.'

Look at the 'Ballad of Oyster Nan', first published in about 1700, and we find a vintner seducing his doxy:

> But being called by company
>> As he was taking pains to please her,
> 'I'm coming, coming sir,' says he,
>> 'My dear, and so am I,' says she, sir.

A few limericks pack allusion and *double-entendre* engagingly into their ingenious form, and come up with verses which merit their tenacious hold on popularity. Thus:

> There was a young man of St. John's
> Who attempted to bugger the swans.
>> He was stopped by the porter
>> Who said, 'Take my daughter—
> The swans are reserved for the dons.'

or

> A roving young sailor called Quegg
> Had a body as bald as an egg,
>> His girl-friend one night
>> In a throe of delight
> Fell off him, and fractured a leg.

190

Though scarcely erotic in the full sense of the word, humour has always been a major preoccupation of poetry on sexual themes, sometimes very successfully. Flagellation may not, on the face of it, seem a very likely subject for sophisticated humour; but taste, for instance, Sir John Davies's short poem:

> When Francus comes to solace with his whore,
> He sends for rod and strips himself stark naked:
> For his lust sleeps, and will not rise before,
> By whipping of the wench, it be awaked.
>   I envy him not, but wish I had the power
>   To make myself his wench but one half hour.

That is a poem successful on every ground; and on a theme which has given rise to the most dreadful verse—as in Swinburne's flagellatory poems. Charm and wit do occasionally rise triumphantly, and those for whom humour is an essential part of love will have no difficulty in identifying with poets such as the anonymous author of 'The Bathing Lady' (c. 1700), watching the admired beauty taking a skinny dip, and paying her a graceful compliment:

> Each fish did wish himself a man—
>   About her all was drawn—
> And at the sight of her began
>   To spread about his spawn. . . .

Or there is the enchanting sonnet of Bartholomew Griffin, in which Cytherea watches Adonis dive into a brook to cool himself, and in frustrated ecstasy cries: 'O Jove! Why was I not a flood?' Much coarser poems than this work very well on the level of the simple joke, often with a satirical gloss—as in the anonymous 1720s poem collected by Burns:

> Yestreen I wed a lady fair,
>   And ye wad believe me,
> On her cunt there grows nae hair,
>   That's the thing that grieves me.
>
> It vexed me sair, it plagued me sair,
>   It put me in a passion
> To think I had wed a wife
>   Whase cunt was out o'fashion.

But humour is, after all, anaphrodisiac. *The Wit's Cabinet* or *Merry Drollery Complete* were, like some of Rochester's poems, meant for reading aloud in company during a drinking bout, as a sort of knowing cabaret, to amuse rather than arouse. No doubt there were whores to serve that purpose, like the strippers in today's drinking clubs. It might appear at first glance that erotic poetry, mostly written until this century by men (with a very few honourable exceptions such as Aphra Behn) is chauvinist. And in some cases, of course, it is. On the other hand in many cases, and much more often than in pornographic prose, there is a concern for the woman's sexual satisfaction, shown as Dryden shows it in 'Marriage-à-la-Mode', when Alexis

> . . . found the fierce pleasure too hasty to stay,
> And his soul in the tempest just flying away.

Whereupon his Celia rebukes him ('I am robbed of my bliss'), and engages him in a second bout, when he

> though in haste,
> And breathing his last,
> In pity died slowly, while she died more fast;
> Till at length she cried, 'Now, my dear, now let us go,
> Now die, my Alexis, and I will die too.'

The poets were in the main intelligent and sophisticated men, and in many cases practised amorists—in others, they were so in theory if not in fact—for whom their mistress's satisfaction was a matter of honour. So a concern with premature ejaculation and impotence appears in a great many erotic poems, not only because it gives the poet an excuse for further lubricity, but apparently because he sees it genuinely as a case for concern that the mistress should be left unsatisfied while the lover goes happily off about his business. The male poet takes much the same view of the matter as Aphra Behn, in 'The Disappointment', which is a poem explicitly about impotence. Lysander, making love to Cloris, is 'o'er-ravished' by his emotions, and cannot perform. Cloris somewhat insensitively takes this as an insult; when she found a flaccid penis beneath her hand

The blood forsook the hinder place
And strewed with blushes all her face,
Which both disdain and shame expressed.

Rochester, in 'The Imperfect Enjoyment', paints the same
picture; when he ejaculates before penetrating his mistress,
she takes this, naïvely perhaps, as a compliment; but swiftly
becomes disappointed when he cannot immediately gather his
powers together for a second attempt. The more she demands
it (a familiar psychological problem) the more his body refuses
to comply, his penis 'Shrunk up and sapless like a withered
flower'.

The penis is, unsurprisingly, featured overtly in a great
many erotic poems, sometimes hectored for its lack of stamina
in such episodes as that described by Rochester, sometimes for
its hyperactivity (as in Robert Graves's 'Down, wanton,
down'). Rochester celebrated his own extremely active tool in
the very poem in which he records its shortcomings, 'The
Imperfect Enjoyment':

When vice, disease, and scandal lead the way
With what officious haste dost thou obey!
Like a rude, roaring hector in the streets
Who scuffles, cuffs and jostles all he meets . . .

lines which irresistibly remind one of Philip Roth's *Portnoy's
Complaint*.

Few poems in celebration of the phallus work as successfully
as Vincent McHugh's 'Suite from Catullus', a loving cele-
bratory poem as explicit as it is inoffensive:

When he wakes for love again
he is like a boy waking on Saturday
At first he does not know what day it is;
he hunches and rolls over
If I call him he will not answer
You call him
See him spring up as he remembers all the happy things he
meant to do with you

There is, of course, an element of male chauvinism in erotic
poetry; all things considered, it would be surprising if there
were not. As with pornography in general, it mostly takes the

form of wishful thinking—of the invention of women as randy and insatiable and willing as any man could desire. This is married to the theme (*pace* Rochester) of the miraculously potent lover—and to the proposition that man is naturally polygamous. Herrick, the parson with a predilection for women's footwear, puts it quite unequivocally in 'The poet loves a mistress, but not to marry':

> The man is poor
> Who hath but one of many;
> But crowned is he with store
> That single may have any.

The continual inference is that a 'proper man' will have no difficulty in seducing (if not raping) any woman he fancies; as Robert Gould put it,

> Take not a woman's anger ill,
> But let this be your comfort still,
> That if one won't, the other will. . . .

And most poets rush to confirm Gould's proposition that 'All women love it.' The country lad meeting a lass had only to express the wish, and the skirts swirled up; down she would lie; and he had only to 'push it in', when she would exclaim, 'Oh what a fool was I/ So long to live a maid, ere I/ Did this same sport begin. . . .' And after a number of encounters would still encourage him:

> I pleasure feel in every vein,
> My joys do now begin;
> O dearest, quickly to't again,
> And stoutly thrust it in. . . .

It is only comparatively recently that a genuine note of understanding of woman's psychological needs has found its place, not only in male poetry—such as Ronald McCuaig's splendid 'The Commerical Traveller's Wife', where a frustrated woman is callously rejected by an unthinking man:

> 'Jack, don't you want me?' 'Oh, don't be an ass,'
> I said; 'Look at yourself in the glass.'

—but in women's poetry too, perhaps for the first time in Edna St. Vincent Millay's splendidly cool and acerbic sonnet in which a woman, having allowed herself to be seduced once, and facing the man's inevitable assumption that she is to be continually available, comes back with the ultimate in put-downs:

> 'let me make it plain:
> I find this frenzy insufficient reason
> For conversation when we meet again.'

That tone is rare. More often than not, the writer of the overtly erotic poem is out to record the simple operation of lust, and since this depends on individual taste as well as on the pendulum of fashion, it would be stupid to assume that such poetry will be universally appealing (except, of course, that human nature has not noticeably changed in the past 4,000 years or so; look at Grecian erotic vase paintings). We are conditioned to view child molestation with horror; no doubt properly. But Nabokov was not the first writer to imagine a man enslaved by a nymphet. Thomas Carew, whose 'A Rapture' is almost as well known as Donne's nineteenth Elegy, wrote in 'The Second Rapture' of his longing for 'a wench about thirteen'

> Whose kisses, fastened to the mouth
> Of threescore years and longer slouth,
> Renew the age . . .

and there are of course respectable, indeed Biblical precedents for elderly men taking very young mistresses. Dryden wrote of a girl of 14 longing for a lover ('Take me, take me, some of you . . .'), while Sir Charles Sedley remarked on the increasingly early coming of puberty in girls, and made an 11-year-old remark that

> She stays at least seven years too long
> That's wedded at eighteen.

The admiration of the elderly, or not so elderly, man for even pre-pubescent girls may be a dirty joke, but it is also a commonplace, and has been for longer than the literature which records it. At the other end of the scale, lust in age is, in poetry at least, celebrated rather than rebuked. Certain difficulties present themselves, but under the right conditions they

195

may be triumphantly overcome, as Rochester suggested:

> Thy nobler part, which but to name
> In our sex would be counted shame,
> By age's frozen grasp possessed
> From their ice shall be released
> And soothed by my reviving hand
> In former warmth and vigour stand.

The disgust which plagues the unwary after the gratuitous act of lust is occasionally recorded by the more sensitive among the poems: Shakespeare, of course, and Jonson:

> Doing, a filthy pleasure is, and short—
> And done, we straight repent us of the sport.

Masturbation is less often mentioned, though poets' attitudes to it are as easy as Dr. Alex Comfort himself would advise: in John Hopkins's 'To Amasia, Tickling a Gentleman', for instance, and certainly in Fleur Adcock's 'Against Coupling':

> Five minutes of solitude are
> Enough—in the bath, or to fill
> That gap between the Sunday papers and lunch.

Guiltless sex is, happily, celebrated much more often than the traumatic or windward side of love, the poet taking licence to pretend that no unwonted ill consequences can follow (references to unwanted pregnancy, or the pox, are either entirely absent or used to comic purpose). Sir Charles Sedley takes up the theme at its most basic:

> None but a muse in love can tell
> The sweet tumultuous joys I feel
> When on Celia's breast I lie,
> When I tremble, faint and die,
> Mingling kisses with embraces,
> Darting tongue and joining faces,
> Panting, stretching, sweating, cooing,
> All in the ecstasy of doing.

Though contemporary 'girlie' magazines rely on photographs of naked women exhibiting their genitalia, pornographic art in general has always relied chiefly on a portrayal of man and woman (or man and man, or woman and woman, or whatever) actually making love, or perhaps more accurately 'having sex'. English erotic poetry has yet to find its Aretine, and as far as the pornographic is concerned—that is, poetry which actually arouses—perhaps it is in the area of description that it is most successful, notably in the celebration of a woman's, and more rarely a man's, body. Clothes are incidental; very occasionally there is a striptease, as when George Moore in a sonnet clandestinely watches his mistress rising in the morning, and dressing:

> Drawing along her legs, as white as milk,
> Her long stockings of finely-knitted silk. . . .

More often the attitude is that of Donne:

> To teach thee, I am naked first, why then
> What needst thou have more covering than a man. . . .

or of Herrick:

> Away with silks, away with lawn,
> I'll have no scenes or curtains drawn;
> Give me my mistress as she is,
> Dressed in her naked simplicities. . . .

Many voyeuristic poems involve bathing beauties, or sunbathing damsels. The male body is less often celebrated, chiefly of course because most of the poets have been male, and the majority heterosexual. Not all, however; among the exceptions is Marlowe, who in 'Hero and Leander' pleases his audience by describing the mistress, but also pleases himself by describing the lover:

> I could tell ye
> How smooth his breast was, and how white his belly,
> And whose immortal fingers did imprint
> That heavenly path with many a curious dint
> That runs along his back . . .

and later is able to describe the seduction of Leander by King Neptune himself, as the waters of the sea run between the swimmer's arms and legs, embracing him, caressing 'his breast, his thighs, and every limb', until Leander is forced to protest: 'You are deceived, I am no woman, I.'

Homosexual erotic poetry is comparatively rare, and frequently bad. There was a mild blossoming in the '80s and '90s of the last century, in the sub-Wildean vein (and it is difficult to write much less well than Wilde in in the poetry written before his imprisonment). Theodore Wratislaw's 'To a Sicilian Boy' is a fair example, with its slack opening:

> Love, I adore the contours of thy shape,
> Thine exquisite breasts and arms adorable. . . .

John Addington Symonds is almost as bad. Gerard Manley Hopkins, had he been able or felt the impulse to write overtly sexual poetry, might have been spectacularly successful, for there is a real erotic charge in his 'Harry Ploughman':

> Hard as hurdle arms, with a broth of goldish flue
> Breathed round; the rack of ribs; the scooped flank; lank
> Rope-over thigh; knee-nave; and barrelled shank. . . .

More successful, I think, than Whitman. There is a certain honesty of emotion in 'Don Leon', which George Colman wrote in imitation of Byron:

> How oft at morn, when troubled by the heat,
> The covering fell disordered at his feet,
> I've gazed unsated at his naked charms
> And clasped him waking to my longing arms. . . .

But Colman becomes as tedious as Swinburne in 'The Rodiad'— all those white bottoms and red weals. However keenly the sadist or masochist feels the pleasures of flagellation, it is not an activity which seems to be capable of celebration in verse. The activity of writing the flagellatory poem seems, somehow, too self-conscious: the original *ms* of Swinburne's 'The Flogging Block' ('by Rufus Rodworthy, annotated by Barebum Birchingley') shows such nervous haste, such tremblingly hasty calligraphy, that its masturbatory nature is clear.

To produce a poem, even a set of verses, which is to be memorable for any reason connected with literature, something other than the simple sexual impulse is of course necessary. Sometimes the miracle seems to occur spontaneously, as is often the case with anonymous poetry (though of course one does not know how much polishing such poetry received in passing from tongue to tongue). 'The Lonely Maid', written in about 1600, is so simple and forthright in its presentation of the theme of awakening adolescent sensuality that it succeeds almost despite itself; the young girl who 'can, nor will, no longer lie alone' is treated sympathetically as well as humorously:

> If dreams be true, then ride I can—
> I lack nothing but a man,
> For only he can ease my moan . . .

and the anonymous poet feels the restlessness, the ague of pubescence:

> When day is come, I wish for night;
> When night is come, I wish for light;
> Thus all my time I sit and moan. . . .

Honesty is the necessary ingredient so often lacking in the self-consciously clever or self-consciously lusty erotic poems of well-known authors. How much more successful is that last poem than those of the Georgians; indeed, how much more successful than such a poem as 'The Tenement', written later in the same century, which invented a tenement called Cunny Hall:

> It stands by Cunny Alley
> At foot of Belly Hill,
> This house is freely to be let
>   To whomsoever will.

This is the equivalent of the most carelessly produced pornographic prose, and indeed many such scabrous rhymes appeared in *The Pearl* and other Victorian pornographic magazines. A poem such as 'The Dream', a decade later, has from its opening the quick sense of reality:

> She lay all naked in her bed
>   And I myself lay by;
> No veil nor curtain there was spread,
>   No covering but I.

So has 'Arithmetic of the Lips' (1641), with its marvellous central quatrain:

199

Were the bright day no more to visit us,
Oh, then for ever would I hold thee thus,
Naked, enchained, empty of idle fear,
As the first lovers in the garden were.

Despite these rare glories, it is indisputably true that if one takes the whole corpus of erotic poems—that is, openly and explicitly sexual poems as opposed to 'love poems' which for whatever reason avoid taking a sexual tone—the success rate is much lower than with poems of similar ambition on any other theme. One might have expected the present generation of poets to have overcome the difficulty, with the new freedoms of language, social behaviour, psychological flux. That has not happened. There is, of course, the usual acceptable crop of humorous verse, some of it thoroughly bad (like the widely-circulated set of verses by W. H. Auden), some middling, and some in its vein extremely good (Gavin Ewart is surely as good a light versifier about sex as, say, e. e. cummings). But the good serious poem about sex is rare indeed. What is needed, of course, is a poet whose capacity for thought is matched by a capacity for conveying a sturdy sexual drive. Donne provides the pattern in the nineteenth Elegy, which opens with an image as explicit as that on any Soho screen: that of an erect penis—but engagingly describes it in terms of warriors 'tired with standing though they never fight'. Then comes the invitation to disrobe, the description of the mistress undressing, and the final glories of her body which are compared to those of a spirit—good or ill? Good, for 'those set our hairs, but these our flesh upright'. The constant juggling of the metaphysical with the carnal was obviously a titillating pleasure for Donne, and is no less so for the reader.

Again, the explicit:

Licence my roving hands, and let them go
Before, behind, between, above, below . . .

then the evocation of what was a very strange and modern geographical discovery—'O my America, my new found land'; on quickly to a political image: 'My kingdom, safeliest when with one man manned'—also of course a sexual image; the duality managed even in a reference to the bonds of love, where again we get a *double entendre*: 'Then where my hand is set, my seal shall be.'

Then comes the paen of praise to nakedness: 'Full nakedness, all joys are due to thee'—followed again by metaphysical speculation, then by one of the most daringly sexual images of the poem, the desire that the mistress should show herself to her lover 'As liberally as to a midwife', with the implications of widely spread legs; and finally the thrusting aside of the sheets, and the splendid last couplet

> To teach thee, I am naked first, why then
> What needst thou have more covering than a man.

The combination of elegance of language and thought, wit, nicety of allusion, with the courtly compliment but also with the earthy, is irresistible. In four hundred years few other poets, if any, have equalled it. Why not?

9

Literature and Pornography

by COLIN WILSON

Let me begin this analysis by quoting two passages: one of literature, one of pornography:

> With a queer obedience, she lay down on the blanket. Then she felt the soft, groping, helplessly desirous hand touching her body, feeling for her face. The hand stroked her face softly, softly, with infinite soothing and assurance, and at last there was the soft touch of a kiss on her cheek.
>
> She lay quite still, in a sort of sleep, in a sort of dream. Then she quivered as she felt his hand groping softly, yet with queer thwarted clumsiness among her clothing. Yet the hand knew, too, how to unclothe her where it wanted. He drew down the thin silk sheathe, slowly, carefully, right down and over her feet. Then with a quiver of exquisite pleasure he touched the warm soft body, and touched her navel for a moment in a kiss. And then he had to come in to her at once, to enter the peace on earth of her soft, quiescent body. It was the moment of pure peace for him, the entry into the body of the woman.

Here is the second:

> Suddenly he pushed the bedclothes away and raised my night gown. My heart began to pound with fear and desire even though there was still, at the back of my mind, a vague suspicion that he was testing me. Sitting up beside me, he carefully moved my feet so as to open my legs. I offered no resistance but,

when he began to stroke my vulva, I could not suppress the tremors that seized me and, at the first sigh of response on my part, he stopped moving his hand.

To reassure him, I began to snore a little. Then he placed himself between my outspread legs, supporting his weight on his arms so that he touched me with only the very tip of his organ. Quite overcome by desire I began to move myself gently against him as he prodded me, all the while snoring quietly. He seemed content simply to lodge the head of his instrument inside me, but he moved it about so effectively that I became intensely aroused. At any moment, I hoped, he would spear me to the hilt. I was half out of my mind awaiting this moment when, quite unexpectedly, he flooded me with his discharge. At once he pulled away from me, taking great care not to disturb my sleep.

If you read these two passages in isolation, would you know which came from a work of literature, and which was from a pornographic novel? The first passage is, admittedly, more 'poetic'; the second has the precision of a police report. But the second is certainly not badly written; it has no embarrassing phrases like 'a quiver of exquisite pleasure', which sounds as if it came straight out of a dirty book.

In fact, the first passage is from *Lady Chatterley's Lover*, the second from the famous German pornographic novel *Josephine Mutzenbacher*, written around the turn of the century and published anonymously. (It is, in fact, written so well that it has been attributed to Arthur Schnitzler and to Johannes Spyri, the author of *Heidi*.) The second passage, you observe, contains no 'dirty words'; and the writer is obviously envisaging the events very clearly, and trying hard to convey the actual physical progression of events. The same is true of Lawrence, with the description of fumbling at her clothes, then removing her knickers.

You might point out that the second passage is slightly less credible than the first. Is it really likely that a girl would pretend to be asleep while a man (in fact her father) climbed between her legs? Is it likely that the man would honestly believe he could satisfy himself without waking her? But the passage in *Lady Chatterley* is, in its way, just as unlikely. Lawrence wants to convince us that his aristocratic lady would give herself to her gamekeeper, but he is not sure how to obtain the desired result. So Lady Chatterley is made to sit holding a new born chicken in her hand; its helplessness makes her burst into tears. Lawrence was not happy with the passage; in fact, he was not happy with the whole book; he rewrote it three times. In *The First Lady Chatterley*, he makes no attempt to describe why she submits; he only describes the gamekeeper's 'boundless desire', and how he lifts her in his arms. 'And she, lifted up, for one moment saw the brilliant, unseeing dilation of his eyes. Then he was clasping her body against his. And she was thinking to herself: "Yes, I will yield to him! Yes, I will yield to him." '

And in the next sentence it is already over.

Lawrence could see that this was unsatisfactory. In the second version, *John Thomas and Lady Jane*, he expands for another half page; this time, the gamekeeper is unable to prevent himself from caressing her back as she crouches with the chicken, crying, and when he has replaced it, 'his hand slid slowly round her body, touching her breasts that hung inside her dress'. They embrace for a moment, then he invites her into the hut. In this second version, Lawrence omits the fumbling with her clothes and the removal of her knickers. In the third version, he obviously still feels that the scene is unreal, so he underlines her heartbroken sobbing—he 'felt that really her heart was broken and that nothing mattered any more'. He also experiences a surge of violent desire for her, and 'instinctively' strokes her crouching loins. The phrase about 'nothing mattered any more' is clearly intended to over-come the reader's lingering objection. So they go into the hut and she accepts his invitation to lie down on a blanket.

Looking at it in the various versions, we can see that Lawrence is struggling with the problem of making the scene credible, and that the solution he plumps for—making her break down and sob broken-heartedly—is basically uncon-vincing. Why is she sobbing? We can believe she might shed a few tender tears at the sight of the frail chicken, but this broken-hearted sobbing seems unmotivated. Moreover, the detailed description of their move into the hut increases the reader's incredulity. A girl about to give herself to a stranger will almost certainly begin to feel awkward and self-conscious as he invites her into a gardening shed and spreads a blanket for her to lie on. (In the second version, he only invites her to put her head on it, so the mating takes place on the bare floor; Lawrence obviously felt that a full-length blanket would relieve the reader's vicarious anxiety about splinters in the behind.)

In short, the scene of intercourse between the gamekeeper and Lady Chatterley is unbelievable in all three versions, and Lawrence only makes it worse by adding precise details; we feel he is trying to make us forget the question: 'Why is she doing this?'

These objections may seem trivial; but they point to a serious problem in this matter of drawing the line between literature and pornography. You might say, as a rough-and-ready distinction, that literature has a certain depth and reality, while pornography aims only at producing an erection. But the scene from *Mutzenbacher* has as much precision and reality as the scene from *Lady Chatterley*; moreover, we can see that Lawrence himself felt that his excuse for making them lovers was too thin, which implies that he *started* with the intention of making them lovers, and tried to work out a convincing way of doing it. This sounds more like the procedure of pornography than literature.

Let me complicate—or, hopefully, simplify—the issue by quoting a third passage: this time neither literature nor pornography, but unembroidered fact:

> Suddenly a light dawned upon me from some remark she made. 'It's her brother who fucked you first.'—She broke out into laughter, and denied it.—But I insisted, and at last she admitted it.
>
> Carry had to fetch pails of water upstairs, and the lad used kindly to do it for her—one morning her mother had gone out to work at six o'clock, when the lad knocked at the door, and asked if he should fetch her a pail full. She accepted and he fetched it. She instead of getting up when her mother left she went to bed again, and was in her chemise. He wanted to bring the water in.—'No, put it down outside.' He said he'd throw the water away. So she let him in, he put down the pail and began kissing her, she'd already seen his prick, and his spunk, he'd seen her cunt, and a few minutes afterwards, that lucky lad's prick was in her virgin niche, her hymen was but a bleeding

split, his sperm was sticking his balls to her buttocks.—She was in for fucking after that.—When once a female's tasted the sugar stick, it's not long before she gets another taste.

This is from the anonymous work called *My Secret Life*, printed privately in the 1880s. 'Walter', the narrator, is describing a conversation with a girl he has picked up and taken to a brothel. Clearly, it is not pornography in the usual sense of the word—literature designed to be 'read with one hand'. Yet the tone here is the tone of pornography; he is gloating, trying to conjure up the scene 'that lucky lad's prick was in her virgin niche, her hymen was but a bleeding split, his sperm was sticking his balls to her buttocks.' It is obvious that Carry has not *told* Walter these details; he has added them, purely for the pleasure of trying to re-create the scene.

And here, I think, we are coming close to the essence of pornography. *My Secret Life* is a vast—2,500-page—account of the author's sexual experiences. He is obviously obsessed by sex. He feels that it is deliciously lewd, and we get the feeling that half the pleasure comes from the thought of what respectable Victorian matrons would say if they could see him seducing a 13-year-old girl in a cab. . . . This is not the open, realistic attitude of Boccaccio or Rabelais or Shakespeare. It is the kind of sex that schoolboys like to talk about as they share a cigarette behind the lavatories.

The essence of the scene I have quoted from *Mutzenbacher* is that it is her father who is trying to seduce her. In fact, there is nothing in the least far-fetched about the episode; from the point of view of realism, it is far more convincing than Lawrence. Josephine's mother is dead. Her schoolmaster has recently been sentenced to prison for seducing his female pupils, including Josephine, so her father knows she is no longer a virgin. Nothing is more likely than that a man living alone with an adolescent daughter should become morbidly obsessed by the thought of her seduction by the schoolmaster, then (when drunk), should attempt to possess her too. (Half a page later, he does precisely this.) In fact, there is very little in *Mutzenbacher* that is not believable—particularly when applied to slum conditions in a slum suburb of Vienna at the turn of the century. The fact remains that *Mutzenbacher* is quite clearly pornography because it has no other intention than to detail one sexual experience after another, and to break every possible taboo. There are sexual scenes between brothers and sisters, mother and son, father and daughter, priest and penitent, schoolmaster and pupils, and so on. That is to say, the author's basic desire is to exploit the *forbidden*. So even though parallels to every situation could probably be found in the Vienna police files, there can be no possible doubt about the intention: to aid masturbation. Lawrence's book remained banned for thirty years because the guardians of public morals felt that the majority of people who bought it *would* use it as an aid to masturbation, and because the sexual scenes are detailed enough to be used for this purpose. (By comparison, the first version is reticent: ' "Yes, I will yield to him." Afterwards, he was gloomy and did not speak a word.') The intention is obviously not to arouse sexual excitement, but to say something about human relations and social relations.

This conclusion seems so convenient—and obvious—that there hardly seems to be need to say any more. Pornography is intended simply to excite lust; literature *may* excite lust, but this is only a secondary intention. . . . But the passage from *My Secret Life* raises a complication. Is this written purely to excite lust? Obviously not. The author writes out of the same motive that makes a traveller describe his experiences: to enable the reader to share them. He may gloat a little—rather as a traveller might linger over the description of a sunset—but his main intention is to state the facts. Is it, then, written as 'literature'? Clearly, the answer is again no. So it would seem that although *My Secret Life* is a 'banned' book, it cannot be classified as either literature *or* pornography. Which complicates what looked like a charmingly simple conclusion.

The problem, I would suggest, is that we are being too simple-minded and wholesale about pornography. It is as if some grey-haired, pink-cheeked headmistress were to say: 'This is not a question that should confuse any right-thinking person. Our sexual organs have been given to us by God to reproduce the species. And when a man and woman are in love, they accept sex as something simple and natural that leads to the pleasures of parenthood. That is the right attitude. But alas, the world is full of irresponsible and selfish individuals who develop a warped attitude to sex, and who think of it as something wicked and thrilling. They have corrupted God's gift—or allowed it to corrupt them—and pornography, like adultery and prostitution, is a direct consequence of their sinful attitude.'

Oddly enough, this is almost exactly what Tolstoy said in his story *The Kreutzer Sonata*. Sex is intended for reproduction, not for pleasure. And mankind's tendency to treat it as pleasure has led to most of our sexual problems. . . .

This attitude would be worth careful consideration if it corresponded with the facts. But it seems to start off with a false assumption: that 'sex' means very much the same thing to a man and a woman. What Tolstoy—and our hypothetical headmistress—seem to be describing is a *woman's* attitude to sex. Where sex is concerned, women seem to be more realistic than men. They are seldom interested in sex in the abstract. For them it means sex with a specific male, as part of a definite relationship, preferably one involving love and protection. The male is much more abstract about it. A character in a Kingsley Amis novel remarks that even the words 'Girl, twenty' in an advertisement are enough to give him an erection.

Feminists may wish to argue that this is a specious simplification. Of course women need to be more 'personal' about sex than men because they are the ones to bear children, and who therefore need a 'protector'. But this is a result of our male chauvinist society. If the burdens were equally distributed, and women were allowed fuller self-expression, they might take an altogether less personal attitude towards sex. . . .

With the greatest sympathy for their argument about the subjection of women, I cannot swallow this. I have just finished reading a recent novel by the feminist Fay Weldon, *Praxis*. There is a great deal of sex in it; the heroine loses her virginity to two college students, climbs in and out of many beds, often with other people's husbands, and even becomes a prostitute for a time, simply to make money. One of her clients is her own father, whom she hasn't seen since childhood. Yet what struck me most about this novel is that at no point did the sex cause the slightest stirring of physical excitement. This is because she somehow makes it sound like having a tooth out.

Philip bore her down upon the ground. The grass was damp and chilly, but his body was warm and welcome. His belt and buttons scratched her. As if in the interests of her comfort, he removed his belt and undid his trousers, scarcely rising from his prone position; unaware that his shirt buttons were making severe indentations on her right breast. As fast as he assuaged one wound, it seemed he created another. His knee came between hers, forcing them apart. . . .

And at this point, we are given a slice of her stream of consciousness as she loses her virginity. A page later: 'Praxis, her body impaled, found her mind agreeably free to wander.' And you feel that this is what always happens in bed with her; her mind wanders while the man impales her, reaches orgasm, and rolls off her. Her disinterest amounts to schizophrenia.

And in fact, if you find a letter in a girly magazine that purports to have been written by a woman describing her sexual experiences, you can always recognize that the real author is a man. 'More kisses—then I felt his hand lift my pleated skirt, and those bloody knickers were off. . . . Then I felt his dick penetrating my open cunt. . . .' 'His cock's big, glistening glans stabbed between my flesh cut [*sic*], then I screamed out as he shoved it right up me.' 'He decides to take me like an animal, so I kneel down, my pointed breasts brushing the leaves, and he gets behind me and sticks his cock inside my cunt. It feels very good and I move up and down with all my schoolgirlish enthusiasm. And then he shoots the whole lovely lot inside my cunt. I put my knickers and school uniform back on. . . .' This is the male, gloating on such details as removing her knickers, separating her legs, entering her body (sometimes several sentences are devoted to this alone).

Lawrence remarks in the second version of *Lady Chatterley*: 'But she was not aware of the infinite peace of the entry of his body into hers. That was for the man: the infinite peace of the entry into the woman of his desire.' As far as I can see, Lawrence is right. Walter (of *My Secret Life*) liked to get women to describe it to him as he did it. 'What am I doing?' 'Putting it up me.' 'Putting what up you?' 'Your prick.' 'Where . . .' etc. It is as if he wants to see the situation in a mirror, to increase his sense of its reality. Lawrence himself decided to cut out the two sentences quoted above, presumably because he felt they gave too much away. What he is really saying is that the gamekeeper is thinking: 'My god, she's really lying under- neath me with her legs open, and I'm penetrating the most intimate part of her body. . . .' And he might have added: 'And she's a lady and I'm a gamekeeper. . . .' And this, in turn, is only one step away from a Don Juan who keeps a drawer full of pairs of bloodstained panties to show off to his male friends.

What I am suggesting here is that this element—which could be called gloating—is a *basic* part of a male's sexual response, even if he is making love to someone he adores and feels protective about. I am reminded of a story told me by Calder Willingham, the author of a novel called *Eternal Fire*. *Eternal Fire* has a disagreeable character called Harry Diadem, who takes great pride in his powers of seduction. There is a scene in the novel where Harry ingratiates himself with a girl on a long distance bus—a sweet, timid girl of religious inclina- tions—and, having convinced her that he wants to marry her, gets her into a bedroom at some roadside restaurant, and takes her virginity. Then, as the girl sobs with pain, he makes her get fully undressed, and does it again. (This chapter was printed separately in *Playboy*.) Willingham told me how, at a party in his house, one of the male guests got drunk, and began proclaiming: 'I am Harry Diadem, all men are Harry Diadem.'

And he had, I would suggest, a definite point. Of course not all men are accomplished seducers; not all men have a touch of sadism; not all men take an empty-headed pride in their sexual prowess. The fact remains that as a man enters a woman, he experiences a feeling that could be verbally trans- lated 'I made her.' Lawrence's comments about the 'infinite peace' experienced by the male as he enters 'the woman of his desire' virtually admits as much.

Now this, I submit, is highly disturbing. For Lawrence is, so to speak, our chief witness for the essential distinction between literature and pornography. 'What many women cannot give, one woman can', he insists. The relationships between lovers in Lawrence's novels are always deeply personal; each is as fascinated by the other's individuality as by his (or her) sexuality. Lawrence's central message is that sex should be 'personal' for both parties, not just the woman, and that Don Juanism is stupid, disgusting and superficial. So, he argues, literature deals with real relationships between men and women, while pornography deals with cardboard figures of lust.

Now I find that what Lawrence has to say 'rings a bell' in my own experience. Young men are often in such a generalized state of sexual excitement that anything in a skirt represents a challenge, and causes a kind of harsh flow of desire. Yet this desire has a self-defeating element in it. Even if you were an absolute despot, who could snap his fingers and order any girl to his bedroom, this element of unfulfilment would probably remain. For, in fact, sex is best when there *is* a strong personal relationship as well as a sexual attraction.

Now there is, I would suggest, a sound psychological reason for this. Sex can too easily get 'out of focus', and become a mere physical act. In *Go To the Widow Maker*, James Jones has the sentence: 'He rolled over on to her, stuck it in her, and pumped away until he came.' Clearly, his hero is not experiencing any triumph at entering the body of the woman; it might as well be a hole in the ground. Sex can too easily be reduced to this mere physical activity, even between people who love one another. And this is not because it 'loses the magic'. It is simply because it has got 'out of focus', like an unfocused telescope or camera. If I tried to read a book only two inches from my eyes, and the print looked blurred, I would not blame the print, or suppose that it was deteriorating; I would know it was my own fault. Human beings habitually lose focus because they see things too close-up. Our jobs, our relationships, our lives, can all be taken for granted until they bore us—although if they are threatened, appreciation returns quickly enough. Sexual conquest is also subject to this rule. But the personal relationship with someone we love has strong subconscious underpinning—like a mother's feeling for her baby. *This* is why 'What many women cannot give, one woman can.'

Having said which, it is necessary to return to that basic fact that, for the male, there is always an element of 'conquest' in sexual fulfilment. There is probably an element of conquest in a woman's attitude to the male, but it is of a different kind. If

211

she feels, of the man who is making love to her, 'He's mine', it is because she feels that he now belongs to *her*. Before that, he was fair game for all the females in the world; now she has pinned him down. He has become her property—hopefully. This attitude—although it certainly *can* exist in a man ('I'd love to have a paper doll to call my own/ A doll that other fellows cannot steal')—is certainly less typical of the male. *He* feels that the world is full of beddable girls who are inaccessible to him for various reasons, but at least he's got *this* one undressed. . . .

One logical—if brutal—response to this situation is rape. Somewhere in my files, I have an account of an American murder case. The killer had been in prison several times for rape, and one day he decided that, in future, he would kill his victims after rape, so they could not identify him. He and another man approached a girl who was about to get into her car, on her way to the office, forced her into their own car, and took her to an empty house, where both raped her several times. Then she was taken to a culvert in a lonely spot and shot through the head—a disposable sex-object, like a disposable cup or handkerchief. Both were caught and sentenced to life imprisonment—a disadvantage that the man had left out of account. The article contains a photograph of the girl as she was found, her dress around her waist, her legs open and bent at the knees, like a discarded doll.

Pornography is a more civilized version of rape. That is to say, it is an appeal to this masculine desire to conquer and penetrate, without personal involvement. In the last chapter of Apollinaire's pornographic novel *Les Exploits d'un jeune Don Juan*, the young Don Juan contemplates with satisfaction a parade of women he has impregnated, including his sister and aunt (the aunt, of course, is young and beautiful), and we catch that essential flavour of the male congratulating himself on his prowess, like a prize bull. Rape has been transposed into the world of imagination. Apollinaire's book is undoubtedly pornography, not literature. Yet it expresses as essential an element of the male's response to woman as *Carmen* or *Manon Lescaut* or *Adolphe*.

Which brings us to the interesting question: *should* pornography be banned? If, in fact, it expresses an aspect of

212

masculine sexuality that is usually ignored, would it not be more honest to grant its right to exist? Most civilized countries in the world have sex shops where it is possible to buy vibrators, dildoes, life-size rubber dolls, erection cream and blue movies. That is to say, we acknowledge that sex is not something that should be confined to the marriage bed. Then why not accept pornography as an aid to masturbation, and cease to treat it as wicked and degrading? Is our attitude to pornography not a hangover from the days of puritan morality?

The argument is plausible; yet I find it unacceptable. For while it is true that pornography faces an aspect of the truth that tends to get ignored by 'literature', it can also be accused of its own kind of untruthfulness. If, for example, a novelist wrote a series of works glorifying the pursuit of money and success-at-all-costs, and implying that the man who achieves these will live happily ever after, critics would lose no time in accusing him of propagating false values. And yet this—with the substitution of sex for success—is precisely what pornography does. There is an implication that sex is an ultimate pleasure that will never fade. 'Wave after wave of blissful excitement was coursing through me. . . .' 'Groaning out as Alan fucked me at a furious speed, I knew I was free.' (The author of this tale has the grace to add: 'For that moment of supreme pleasure anyway.') 'His masculine strength seemed to erupt inside me, ripples of heavenly pleasure passing through my body.'

This, you might say, is harmless enough; sex *can* be 'blissful' and 'heavenly'. But pornography goes beyond this. De Sade, as usual, crystallizes that basic assumption in *Philosophy in the Boudoir*: 'In whatever circumstances, a woman, my dear, whether unwedded, wife or widow, must never have for objective, occupation or desire, anything save to have herself fucked from morning till night; for this unique end Nature created her.' Which is, quite simply, a lie. This is sex from the masculine point of view. If all women believed this, then every girl in the world would be instantly available to all vigorous young males, and there would be no more frustration. . . . But a man or woman who fucked from morning to night would soon find it abysmally boring. The fact is that although sex is important, human beings have other—and more important—

213

appetites. Nature clearly did *not* create us merely for this end. And these other appetites—for beauty, for ideas, for knowledge—are, in the last analysis more interesting than our sexual functions. If literature is supposed to tell the truth, then it has to be reluctantly concluded that pornography is 90 per cent lies.

The same objection applies to a work like *Josephine Mutzenbacher*. If it was what it pretends to be—the memoirs of a nymphomaniac who become a prostitute—it might have some claim to be considered as literature. But the underlying philosophy is that of Sade's *Philosophy in the Boudoir*. From the first page, all the characters are simply concerned with sexual pleasure, as if it were an end in itself, and as if it could never pall. There is, for example, an episode in which a teenage boy describes how he has become the lover of both his sisters, then his mother. The implication is that this family, who have cast off all taboos, are getting far more pleasure out of life than the average family. The elder sister is represented as being far more restrained and virtuous than the younger one, while the mother only gives way to her desire with the utmost reluctance. But anyone can see that, in real life, the younger sister—who is a nymphomaniac—would end as a prostitute, while the other two would soon find sex with an adolescent boring, and would seek out more suitable lovers. But then the elder sister would probably not invite her brother to take her virginity anyway. She sounds like the kind of girl who knows that her virginity is a useful bargaining counter in the marriage lottery, and who would save it for some respectable bank-clerk. Again, we feel that the writer is trying to pull the wool over our eyes, to convince us that black is white or that one and one makes three. Pornography is based on an *unreal* assumption, like Batman or Superman. But unlike Batman and Superman—which make no attempt to disguise their unreality—pornography pretends to be telling the unpalatable truth, which the rest of us dare not face: that human beings are really animals, and that sexual intercourse is their highest happiness. De Sade actually dares to state all the hidden presuppositions of pornography in the form of philosophical propositions. ' "Yes," Madame Delbène [the mother superior of a nunnery] replied, "why yes. I am anxious to take her education in hand. Just as I have told you, I should like to cleanse her of all those infamous religious follies which spoil the whole of life's felicity. I should like to guide her back to Nature's fold and doctrine and cause her to see that all the fables whereby they have sought to bewitch her mind and clog her energies are in actuality worthy of nought but derision" ' (*Juliette*). But it is soon clear, even in this first chapter, that she is actually saying that her lesbian relationship with two novices is capable of bringing all three of them continuous ecstasy. In fact, mere sensual pleasure is not capable of sustaining the full weight of our interest for any length of time. We can see that Sade is simply pitching his claims too high, like one of those advertisements that implies that a certain product is capable of solving all personal problems and bringing domestic bliss to the whole family.

In the twentieth century, this Sadeian philosophy has found a more respectable form of expression in the works of the Freudian psychologist Wilhelm Reich. The claims Reich makes for sexual fulfilment are in some degrees closer to the philosophy of D. H. Lawrence; yet where he resembles Sade is in implying that this is a be-all and end-all. Freud regarded sex as an immensely powerful instinct whose suppression can cause mental illness. Reich took the logical next step, insisting that sexual release is the answer to true happiness and mental and physical health. All the problems of our civilization, he said, are due to sexual repression. The repressed sexual energies turn sour, and cause all kinds of miseries—including cancer. Much of what Reich says makes sense. His view of sex is close to that of the poet William Blake, who argued that sexual desire is as 'holy' as our religious impulses. But Blake would have been shocked by Reich's insistence that our religious impulses are merely sublimated forms of sex. Reich feels, quite simply, that if human beings could make love as naturally as they eat and drink, all human problems would vanish, and our lives would become as happy and natural as those of the South Sea islanders. But the history of the past few decades has shown that sexually permissive societies have just as much neurosis as sexually repressed societies. Reich's mistake, as we can now see, lay in supposing that man can experience no higher fulfilment than in lovemaking. He is giving expression

215

to the unstated philosophy behind pornography.

The real objection to pornography can be seen if we transpose it into another field. Let us suppose that some writer of extreme political views—say, a hatred of all immigrants—wrote a series of books in which the hero walked around the streets, continually losing his temper with the objects of his dislike and inflicting various forms of punishment on them. 'His hand shot out and grabbed the old woman by the throat. Her scowl changed to an expression of terror. Slowly, inexorably, his steely fingers closed, until her face became purple and her eyes stuck out like marbles. "I'll teach you to insult a good patriot", he murmured softly, and his knee crunched into her crotch. . . .' We would all agree that a book that contained dozens of episodes like this—whose whole aim was to give expression to rage and disgust—would be socially injurious. No one denies that it can also be injurious to bottle up anger and frustration. But to systematically allow it full expression would be negative. By encouraging people to indulge in this kind of daydream, it would damage their adjustment to reality; it would incubate paranoia.

Yet many works of literature are aimed at precisely these same negative emotions. Molière's *Tartuffe* encourages us to detest Tartuffe, then satisfies us by showing him exposed. Dante's *Inferno* is full of people he detests, burning in brimstone. Satirists have always enjoyed creating villains and hypocrites, and then making them writhe. But a few touches of satire are enough to satisfy our desire to see the hypocrite exposed, the biter bit. If a satirist goes on shaking his quarry for too long, finding new objects for his scorn and indignation, we begin to feel that he is undermining our appreciation of normality. Everything begins to look jaundiced.

Yet the answer is plain enough: that scorn and indignation do no harm when taken, as it were, in homeopathic quantities, and as a part of a *balanced diet* of other emotions and responses. There is a natural, instinctive principle of health inside most of us that rejects large doses of morbidity and triviality.

The same, I would suggest, applies to pornography. If it is, in fact, simply an expression of the natural male attitude to sex, then it certainly has its place in literature. In fact, it finds its way into literature, and always has, in legends of great lovers. (To call it male chauvinism, and suggest men ought to be ashamed of it, is a waste of breath, since it appears to be a part of the biology of the male sexual urge.) The novels of Maupassant, for example—especially *Bel Ami*—are expressions of this purely predatory attitude of the male towards the female. If we find ourselves slightly revolted by Maupassant's attitude (as Tolstoy was), then it is important to ask ourselves why, and get our instinctive objections out into the open. In fact, Tolstoy did even better than that; he wrote a novel— *Resurrection*—that was basically a counterblast against Maupassant. What he said there was that if a man treats a woman purely as a sexual object, the result is likely to be misery all round. And in doing so, Tolstoy had established a purely practical distinction between literature and 'pornography'. That is: literature *goes deeper*; it is an attempt to tell the truth about human existence.

But this definition makes us instantly aware that there is no clear dividing line between literature and—let us say—non-literature. We admire Shakespeare and Tolstoy because they seem to be able to create real human beings and show the real consequences of their actions. You could, in other words, take them as a rough guide to life. Open any cheap pulp magazine, and you will immediately see the difference: these people and their situations are not real, and any inexperienced teenager who took them as a guide to life would soon find himself in as much trouble as Don Quixote. But in that case, the romances that confused Don Quixote are as much non-literature as *Josephine Mutzenbacher*. Is it fair to ban *Mutzenbacher* and not *Amadis de Gaula*?

The answer has to be the purely practical one that, as a guide to life, *Mutzenbacher* would do a great deal more harm than *Amadis*. And for an obvious reason. The mediaeval romances of chivalry imply that women ought to be treated as goddesses, and that men ought to behave with exaggerated courtesy and concern for other people. *Mutzenbacher* implies that the chief aim of life is sexual pleasure, and that men and women ought to regard one another basically as instruments of pleasure. We have seen that this was, in fact, the attitude of the rapist who always killed his victims.

Does this imply that I am in favour of banning *Mutzenbacher*

217

and books like it? If so, I am placing myself in an absurd position, for I bought my own copy quite openly. The same applies to *My Secret Life* and the works of De Sade. If I really believe they should be banned, then I ought to burn my copies.

And here, I think, we go to the heart of the matter. While I do not see much good in pornography, I cannot take my stand with the book-burners. Because I cannot see where the line should be drawn. I could quite imagine a society that began by banning pornography, ending by banning all imaginative literature. Starting with pornography—'books one reads with one hand'—you could go on to works portraying violence, then to horror comics and tales of vampires and monsters, then to ghost stories, and probably end with fairy stories. All these could be condemned for having harmful effects, encouraging a retreat from reality.

Why do we not consider banning these types of 'literature'? Because we take the commonsense view that any harm they do will not be serious. Moreover, we recognize that different minds will have different responses. You might allow your 12-year-old to stay up to watch *Dracula* on television, but not his 6-year-old brother. Why? Because the 6-year-old is more likely to take it seriously and have nightmares. Magazines with pictures of nude women and pornographic stories usually carry an inscription saying they are not to be sold to anyone under the age of 18. I regard myself as adult enough to read *My Secret Life* (although it is so dreary and repetitive that I doubt whether anyone has ever read *all* of it), but I do not leave it where my children can get hold of it.

One of the basic aims of society is to educate its members, to allow them the opportunity to mature and expand. This is done by making available to them various kinds of experience—intellectual, emotional and physical—from which they can choose. But if you are offering a choice, then you take the risk that some things may do harm as well as good. An intelligent adolescent of today has a greater choice than at any period in history. Where literature is concerned, he can read revolutionary tracts, horror stories, tales of violence and explicit descriptions of all kinds of sexual acts—all of which he can probably borrow from his local library, without having to look in 'specialist' booksellers. Under the circumstances, it seems absurd to pass a law banning any kind of literature. If a bookseller chooses not to stock copies of magazines like *Silk* and *Stud*, and books like *Mutzenbacher*—or even *Lady Chatterley's Lover*—that is his business, and no one has a right to object; and if he chooses to stock them, he should be equally free to do so.

For what we really want, in the long run, is to produce an *intelligent* society, that will think for itself about the disadvantages of pornography. It is important to recognize that pornography is not questionable because it is about sex, but because it tells lies about sex. But then the libraries are full of books that tell lies, from romantic trash by lady novelists to books by Nobel Prize winners like Samuel Beckett. I would be delighted to live in a society that not only regarded pornography as childish rubbish, but that felt the same way about a dozen or so eminent authors and thinkers who seem to me to be liars or life-slanderers. But the only way in which such a society is likely to evolve is if everyone is free to make up his own mind. Literature is centrally about freedom; and the only certain way to increase freedom is to encourage people to think.

Notes on Contributors

ALAN BOLD was born in Edinburgh in 1943. He has published many books of poetry, including *To Find the New*, *The State of the Nation* and *This Fine Day* as well as a selection in *Penguin Modern Poets 15*. He has edited *The Penguin Book of Socialist Verse*, *The Martial Muse*, the *Cambridge Book of English Verse 1939–75*, *Making Love: The Picador Book of Erotic Verse*, *The Bawdy Beautiful: The Sphere Book of Improper Verse*, *Mounts of Venus: The Picador Book of Erotic Prose* and *Smollett: Author of the First Distinction*. He has also written critical books on *Thom Gunn and Ted Hughes*, *George Mackay Brown*, *The Ballad* and *Modern Scottish Literature*.

PAUL-GABRIEL BOUCÉ was born in 1936 in Versailles and belongs to a Cotentin family. He was educated in France, Britain and the U.S.A. After two years as a Naval Reserve officer he was, in 1963, appointed a lecturer in English literature at the Sorbonne where he took his D.Litt. in 1970. Since then he has always taught at the Sorbonne, and, in 1971, was appointed Professor of eighteenth-century English literature. He is currently editor-in-chief of *Études Anglaises* and editor of *Sexuality in Eighteenth-century Britain*.

MAURICE CHARNEY was born in New York in 1929 and was educated at Harvard and Princeton; he is Distinguished Professor of English at Rutgers University, New Brunswick, N.J. His most recent book is *Sexual Fiction*, published by Methuen in the New Accents series. Other publications are *Comedy High and Low*, *Shakespeare's Roman Plays*, *Style in Hamlet* and *How to Read Shakespeare*.

ANGELINE GOREAU was born in Wilmington, Delaware, in 1951. She received a double degree in French and English literature from Columbia University in 1973. Her study *Reconstructing Aphra: A Social Biography of Aphra Behn* was published in 1980; a documentary history of the 'feminine sphere', entitled *The Whole Duty of a Woman*, is in progress.

PETER GREEN was born in London in 1924 and educated at Charterhouse and Trinity College, Cambridge. He is Professor of Classics at the University of Texas at Austin. A writer and a translator, his publications include *The Sword of Pleasure* (Heinemann Foundation Award, 1957), *Kenneth Grahame; A Biography* (1959), *Essays in Antiquity* (1960), *The Laughter of Aphrodite* (1965), *The Year of Salamis 480–479 B.C.* (1970), *Armada from Athens* (1971), *Alexander of Macedon 356–323 B.C.*, and numerous translations, including two Penguin classics, *Juvenal: The Sixteen Satires* and *Ovid: The Erotic Poems*.

220

JAMES KIRKUP, born on Tyneside in 1928, has travelled the world collecting experiences and information related to phallic worship, and has recently been investigating shamanism 'in the field' in Siberia and Korea. Resident for the last twenty years in the Far East, he is now Professor of English literature at Kyoto University of Foreign Studies. 'An Outcast of the Islands', he has written many books of prose and poetry about the Far East, Europe, the U.S.A. and England, including *The Boy Servant: Poems of Exile* and *Heaven, Hell and Hara-Kiri*. Latest publications are *The Guardian of the Word*, *To the Unknown God*, *Cold Mountain Poems*, *Scenes from Sutcliffe*, *Zen Gardens*, *The Tao of Water* and *Dengonban Messages*. A Fellow of the Royal Society of Literature since 1964.

DEREK PARKER was born in Cornwall in 1932 and went straight from school into local journalism. He has worked as a drama critic and as a television reporter and presenter, and since 1959 as a freelance broadcaster and writer. Between 1965 and 1970 he edited *Poetry Review*, and his early poems occasionally reappear in anthologies. He reviews regularly for *The Times*. Among his books are biographies of Byron and Donne and of the eighteenth-century astrologer William Lilly. He co-edited *The Selected Letters of Edith Sitwell* and anthologies of erotic verse and prose.

WALTER PERRIE was born in 1949 in the Lanarkshire mining village of Quarter. Educated locally and at Hamilton Academy he worked in a steelworks and libraries before taking an M.A. in philosophy at the University of Edinburgh. A full-time poet and essayist, his last two volume-length poems have attracted attention and a good deal of abuse. The recipient of various literary prizes and awards, he lives in Edinburgh. His first collection of essays on the philosophy of literature, *Out of Conflict*, appeared in 1982.

PETER WEBB was born in Hove in 1941 and trained as an art historian at Cambridge University and the Courtauld Institute. He is Senior Lecturer in History of Art and Design at Middlesex Polytechnic. His publications include *The Erotic Arts* (1965) and *Marquis von Bayros* (1976). He was Art Editor of the *Visual Dictionary of Sex* (1978).

COLIN WILSON was born in Leicester in 1931, son of a boot and shoe worker. After a secondary school education he left school at 16, spent some time working in taxes and the R.A.F., then became a tramp and did various labouring jobs for several years while writing his first novel *Ritual in the Dark* and then his first book *The Outsider*. When this became a best-seller in 1966, he moved to Cornwall, where he has lived ever since.

221

Index